Running a Successful Live Service Game

This book unveils the secrets of extraordinarily successful games and hands you a smarter way to create exceptional engagement and convert it into revenue. It teaches you detailed LiveOps techniques that show you how to keep your game appealing through engaging events, personalized experiences, and smart monetization.

You'll discover the "3 LAPs of Operations" framework—a dynamic, question-driven process that you can implement to systematically boost retention and achieve your game's financial goals. This book delves into the intricate business of live service games, explaining how to enhance your operational efficiency with precise toolset implementations and analytics.

While some studio leaders merely talk about "riding the trend," this approach is far too passive. Embrace the shift toward people-driven game development, where your players evolve from mere consumers into active co-creators. This transformation allows you to construct your own trend, known as People's LiveOps, where you engage your most devoted fans and offer them opportunities to earn a living through their creations.

Essential for professionals in live service games, this book is also invaluable for aspiring talents and seasoned experts aiming to enter or excel in the gaming industry.

Running a Successful Live Service Game
Live Outside of Game Updates

Sergei Vasiuk with Vlad Dubrovskyi

CRC Press
Taylor & Francis Group
Boca Raton London New York

CRC Press is an imprint of the
Taylor & Francis Group, an **informa** business

Designed cover image: Siarhei Vasiuk

First edition published 2025
by CRC Press
2385 NW Executive Center Drive, Suite 320, Boca Raton FL 33431

and by CRC Press
4 Park Square, Milton Park, Abingdon, Oxon, OX14 4RN

CRC Press is an imprint of Taylor & Francis Group, LLC

© 2025 Siarhei Vasiuk

ISBN: 9781032731667 (hbk)
ISBN: 9781032718200 (pbk)
ISBN: 9781003427056 (ebk)

DOI: 10.1201/9781003427056

Typeset in Times
by codeMantra

Contents

Preface

In the year of my birth, the gaming landscape was forever changed by Atari Inc., which transformed the way we interacted with video games by bringing the arcade experience into our living rooms. With the release of *Space Invaders* on March 10, 1980, Atari accomplished the first official licensing of an arcade game for consoles, turning the Atari VCS (Atari 2600) into an unprecedented sensation. This pivotal move not only quadrupled the sales of the Atari VCS but also marked *Space Invaders* as the first "killer app" for video game consoles. Renowned as one of the most influential video games ever created, *Space Invaders* kick-started the golden age of arcade video games, inspiring countless games and designers across various genres.

This happy coincidence of my birth year and such a monumental event in gaming history is a quirky personal fact. Yet, it allowed me to witness firsthand the industry's significant transformations—from the early days of arcade gaming, which necessitated visits to gaming rooms, to the concept of games as products that I could purchase and bring home on CDs for my PC or cartridges for my console. With the advent of the internet, the game-as-a-service business model revolutionized how I played and communicated with friends, eliminating the need to leave home. Now, as we step into an era where games transform into platforms for creating other games and acting as a medium to connect with an anticipated 3.8 billion gamers by 2030, my journey through the evolution of gaming feels even more interconnected with the industry's own narrative.

My 1980s offered a gaming experience with a distinct twist, shaped by the unique circumstances of growing up in the USSR. Technological advancements often arrived with notable delays or were redesigned from their Western originals, leading to a blend of envy and yearning as I pored over rare articles from the Eastern bloc, dreaming of access to such technological marvels. Reflecting on those times, I can assert with full confidence that the true essence of video games—their ability to evoke deep emotions—transcends any technological limitations I faced.

During the early 1980s, the peak of arcade gaming, it was hardly surprising that my initial foray into the world of video games was through an arcade machine. However, the Soviet ideology of that era influenced the thematic direction of these games. They were designed to impart practical skills, such as driving, shooting, and aiming, in stark contrast to the Western focus on battling space invaders or rescuing princesses from fantastical adversaries.

My first encounter with a video game occurred in a pioneer camp, where I played on a famous Soviet arcade machine called Morskoi Boy (*Sea Battle*), essentially a localized rendition of the *Sea Devil* by Midway Inc. The primary manufacturers of these machines were military factories, utilizing surplus parts from actual weaponry, electronics, and industrial equipment due to their access to resources and technical expertise. The Soviet government viewed arcade machines as prohibitively expensive; consequently, the state refrained from establishing specialized companies for arcade game production, resulting in a lack of mass production for arcade machines within the Soviet Union. This backdrop of scarcity defined the unique texture of my early gaming experiences, highlighting how, despite the absence of a widespread gaming culture, the enchantment of video games could still flourish under the most unassuming conditions.

My initial foray into PC gaming was in the computer class at the college where my mom taught geography on an "Electronika 60." This machine holds a special place in the history of gaming as the platform for the original implementation of *Tetris* by Alexey Pajitnov in 1985. Experiencing *Tetris* on this device was nothing short of incredible and undoubtedly marked the beginning of my love for all types of computers. The anticipation of accompanying my mom to her workplace was immense, as it offered me the opportunity to dive into the captivating world of *Tetris* once again.

In 1989, a significant milestone in my gaming journey occurred when my parents gifted me my first handheld device, the ELEKTRONIKA-IM 02, which came with only one game, *Nu, Pogodi* (*Wolf & Eggs*). This game, an analog of Nintendo's *EG-26 Egg* from the Game & Watch series, introduced me to the world of handheld gaming. The simplicity and portability of the device made it an instant favorite, offering endless hours of entertainment.

The early 1990s brought another pivotal moment when a friend invited me over to showcase his birthday present—a Dendy console. My first game on this console was *Mortal Kombat*, an experience that was both thrilling and eye-opening. It was only later that I discovered the Dendy was a hardware clone of Nintendo's Famicom, marking my console gaming experience as beginning from the third generation of home video game consoles. The Dendy's lack of memory for saving games meant that titles requiring this feature, such as *Final Fantasy*, *The Legend of Zelda*, and *Metroid*, were beyond our reach at that time. This limitation, however, did not diminish the joy and excitement that my first encounters with console gaming brought into my life.

The year 1995 was definitively rooted as the one that would shape my future career. In recognition of my admission to an advanced math and physics class for my final 2 years at school, my parents gifted me a PC powered by an Intel Pentium processor. The introduction of Windows 95 opened up an entirely new world of video games for me. I remember playing *Doom* for the first time and being completely awestruck by the gameplay. It was my initial foray into the realm of first-person shooters (FPS), and I was instantly hooked. The thrill of taking on countless demons and striving to complete each map fully made the time fly by. This period kick-started my Games as a Product journey, transforming my PC into the nucleus of an ever-expanding collection of game CDs. Each disc was more than just a game; it was an entryway to new worlds. Regular trips to the local market to buy, rent, and swap CDs became my ritual, building a community of friends united by our love for gaming. This vibrant culture of exchanging physical games underscored the era's emphasis on the tangible connections between players and the immersive universes of video games.

My university years at the Faculty of Information Technologies were deeply influenced by a legacy of computer science in my family. In 1973, my father's groundbreaking PhD work on adapting university course difficulties using Artificial Intelligence laid the groundwork for my own career path. My student years were marked by my engagement with two types of games. I've always been a huge fan of sports, especially Formula 1, leading me to explore all possible sports games from EA, including *FIFA*, *NFL*, *NBA*, as well as every racing game I could get my hands on, like *The Need for Speed* and *Grand Prix Legends*. At home, I indulged in these games, immersing myself in the digital representations of my favorite sports. Meanwhile, the early 2000s at the university campus were all about LAN parties where we played *Counter-Strike*. Oh, those were the days! The camaraderie, the intense battles, and the shared love for gaming among my peers are memories I cherish deeply. These experiences not only fueled my passion for gaming but also played a significant role in my career path, intertwining my love for technology with the world of video games.

Although game development as a profession was a dream deferred by a decade, upon graduating from university in 2002, I found the gaming studio landscape in Belarus to be quite sparse. Consequently, I joined a software company as a Java developer, where I eventually ascended to the role of a software lead, taking charge of technology and architecture decisions. Despite this detour into software development, my passion for gaming as a player never waned but instead continued to evolve along two distinct paths. At work, I indulged in the camaraderie and competitive spirit of LAN parties with *Quake 4*. On the solo front, the advent of Steam heralded a new digital era in gaming for me, eliminating the need to visit a retailer by bringing titles like *Call of Duty: Modern Warfare 2*, *Fallout: New Vegas*, and *Dragon Age II* directly to my PC. This seamless access to a plethora of games kept my love for gaming alive and thriving, blending my professional growth in software with my enduring enthusiasm for gaming.

Craving a career adventure, I turned to my lifelong passion for games. The pivotal moment came when my friend and colleague since 2002, Fedor Belov, invited me to interview at one of my favorite companies, Wargaming, developer of my favorite game *World of Tanks*. I vividly recall dressing up in a suit, tie, and cufflinks for my December 2011 interview with Wargaming, only to hear nothing back—a silent hint that perhaps the cufflinks were a bit much. That initial rejection was a wake-up call, revealing I wasn't as prepared as I needed to be. Determined to succeed, I dedicated myself to becoming the ideal candidate. I immersed myself in project management, earning a PMP certification, deeply studied Wargaming's business model, and familiarized myself with their key metrics. This rigorous preparation led to a series of four to five interviews over 4 months starting in July 2012. By November 1, 2012, my perseverance paid off as I held my access card on my first day in the gaming industry, marking the end of my quest and the start of an exciting new chapter.

My career at Wargaming, starting as a technical project manager in the Web Team, was intrinsically linked to the games-as-a-service model from the very beginning. Initially tasked with everything beyond gameplay development, we essentially laid the groundwork for what would now be considered platform services, supporting the Wargaming trilogy of *World of Tanks*, *World of Warships*, and *World of Warplanes*. Our work spanned from authentication/authorization and digital distribution to creating real-time recommendation solutions to enhance player experiences. Throughout this journey, my roles evolved, offering me comprehensive insights into the games-as-a-service ecosystem. From leading data warehousing solutions that highlighted the importance of data in live service games to managing the integration for the mobile launch of *World of Tanks Blitz*, overseeing DevOps and Release Management for around-the-clock game support, and directing development to equip publishing and marketing teams, each experience was pivotal. Collectively, they honed my understanding of the intricacies of operating live service games, shaping my career's trajectory in the gaming industry.

Transitioning from my role as a development director, where I led the creation of a real-time recommendation engine to enhance the publishing and marketing teams' efforts, marked a pivotal shift in my career. This engine was designed to personalize the onboarding experience by analyzing players' acquisition channels, segmenting players for more targeted communication, and selecting the best offers in the game store based on their playing and payment behaviors. However, we soon realized that the tool, while powerful, was not user-friendly for those without an engineering background.

In 2017, this challenge caught the attention of Marianna Pantelidou, Chief of Staff at Wargaming. She recognized not only the toolset's potential but also its underutilization due to its complexity. Marianna reached out to me with a proposition: to join the Marketing team, establish a dedicated team, and develop processes to harness this technology effectively, thereby founding the LiveOps discipline at Wargaming. This moment marked a significant transformation in my career, moving away from 17 years in development to a new focus on publishing, marketing, and operations. It was also the year I first met Vlad Dubrovski, signaling the beginning of a new chapter in my professional journey, where my past development experiences would converge to shape the future of live services at Wargaming.

Vlad made his first video game when he was just 11 years old. It was a simple creation, coded in Turbo Pascal and run on MS-DOS, crafted during after-class hours in his school's computer science lab in Kharkiv, Ukraine. The game featured two players controlling and shooting geometric figures resembling tanks, all played on a single keyboard with WASD and arrow keys. As Vlad and his classmates played, bugs surfaced and new features were added, breathing life into the game for a brief period before they moved on to other pursuits.

Ironically, 14 years later, Vlad found himself working at Wargaming, a company known for developing *World of Tanks*, the largest tank video game in history. There, he was tasked with running Live Operations (aka LiveOps), where he engaged in the same cycle of observing player behavior, experimenting with new ideas, and measuring impact—all in the pursuit of enhancing player engagement across millions of passionate players worldwide.

For Vlad, and many others in the industry, making video games is more than just a job—it's a passion. It's about bringing the concept of player interaction with characters and imaginary worlds to life through pixels and software, akin to creating a film or writing a book. Vlad's experience in running games has been equally exhilarating. Like a rock band adjusting their performance to suit their audience, live game teams fine-tune, experiment, and react to their player base, treating it as the ultimate real-time strategy with elements of puzzle-solving and team management.

My initial year with the marketing team posed significant challenges, compelling me to bridge the gap between my technical background and the nuanced world of game marketing, publishing, and operations.

To facilitate this transition, I even requested the Chief Marketing Officer at Wargaming to enroll me in a week-long course on marketing strategy. This wasn't just about learning a new set of skills; it was about adapting to a new language. Traditionally a "binary person," accustomed to the straightforwardness of "0" and "1," I found that immersing myself in the business side, for which I had previously only written code, broadened my perspective immensely. It transformed me into a bridge between the realms of engineering and business, enabling me to translate complex technical concepts into strategic business advantages and also in the opposite direction.

During this period, I delved into the intricacies of monetization, player experience personalization, and the orchestration of in-game events. My development background became a crucial asset, helping to minimize the gap between the operations and tool development teams. This synergy eventually bore fruit in 2018 when Wargaming decided to establish an in-house audience management agency. This new venture was tasked with managing the player base across *World of Tanks*, *World of Warships*, and *World of Warplanes* for PC, Console, and Mobile platforms. Leading this agency was a significant milestone in my career, and having Vlad Dubrovski join the team as the Head of LiveOps was both an honor and a testament to the collaborative journey we were embarking on, leveraging our combined expertise to shape the future of player engagement at Wargaming.

This book encapsulates a comprehensive approach to creating value with live service games, focusing on players, employees, and shareholders alike. It draws on firsthand experiences to illustrate how to deliver, promote, and capture value through development frameworks; various marketing, publishing, and operational strategies; and analytics frameworks that underpin data-driven decision-making. The genesis of this book dates back to the summer of 2019, when I was invited to discuss the tools developed by the Wargaming platform team and our wish list for future tools. To my surprise, the meeting was attended by members from diverse departments such as legal, finance, HR, and BI. The range and depth of their inquiries highlighted a widespread interest in understanding the whys, whats, and hows of our studio's operations aimed at entertaining our players.

The advent of COVID-19 and the resultant lockdowns not only afforded me ample time to indulge in gaming but also prompted our team to ponder over collaborative educational initiatives. This period of introspection led to the creation of short presentations and videos elucidating our work processes and objectives. These resources proved invaluable, especially in streamlining the onboarding process for new team members, effectively reducing the time required to familiarize them with our team's operations and goals.

In December 2022, as my son faced the pivotal moment of selecting his subjects for The International General Certificate of Secondary Education (IGCSE), we delved deeply into discussions about his preferences, potential universities, and consultations with his school's career adviser. This process underscored the challenges young people encounter when navigating their educational and career paths. It led me to reflect on the disconnect many graduates experience when trying to enter the gaming industry, where there's a noticeable gap between the academic knowledge they possess and the practical expectations of hiring managers in gaming studios.

At Wargaming, we address this gap through an initiative called Wargaming Forge, offering training courses and future internship programs across all Wargaming titles. Recognizing the shift toward online education and leveraging the substantial amount of educational content we had produced in recent years, our team decided to develop a comprehensive online LiveOps course. This course not only provides in-depth training but also offers participants the chance to join our team as interns for the summer of 2023.

The preparation of this course, the quality of the applicants, and the motivations of the final interns surpassed all our expectations. However, during our graduation ceremony, a significant moment underscored the journey's impact: several students suggested the potential benefits of publishing a book on the subject. Inspired by this feedback, I was thrilled when, 3 months later, I received an email from Taylor & Francis expressing their interest in publishing our book.

I hope this book proves invaluable to its readers. Vlad and I have poured all our knowledge and experiences into it, marking an emotionally charged journey for us. I must extend my deepest gratitude to my wife and children, who saw me confined to our home office for 6 months leading up to the publication. Their patience and support were instrumental in bringing this project to fruition.

Acknowledgments

Throughout the journey of exploration, study, mentorship, and implementation that helped forge this book, I've been incredibly fortunate to draw on the wisdom and support of my colleagues, friends, and students. Your support and insights have been like rare power-ups on my quest to complete this epic adventure. While I can't list everyone who's joined me on this journey, a few MVPs definitely deserve a special mention.

I'd like to begin by thanking Vlad Dubrovski, whom I first met in 2017. Vlad was the pioneering force in Wargaming with "LiveOps" officially part of his job title. His contributions have been critical, from advocating for LiveOps as a key discipline within Wargaming to providing essential content for this book.

In a crucial moment of one of my projects, when our drive for speed led to an oversight and an unintentional flood of free in-game currency, I was introduced to Oksana Kot. She had always been an advocate for robust operations management processes, a voice of caution we needed. At that pivotal point, I approached her, simply stating, "Oksana, I need help." Without hesitation, her response was, "Sure, how can I help you?" Her guidance from that moment forward has been invaluable, helping us establish operations management in LiveOps. Moreover, Oksana has nurtured and mentored a galaxy of outstanding experts whose skills have been crucial in both our LiveOps courses and the content of this book. Kseniya Vasilyeva, Andrey Nichiperovich, Andrey Bushmakin and Georgiy Lesev have each played significant roles and their collective expertise has enriched our projects immeasurably.

Over many years, my friends Margaux Frank, Stefano Incollingo and Julien Alphonse have developed a profound mastery in running LiveOps events, which ultimately culminated in the creation of a cohesive LiveOps event canvas. Their expertise and innovative personalization techniques have greatly influenced this book. Their dedication and insight have not only enhanced our LiveOps practices but also enriched the content of this book, making their contributions invaluable.

I owe a tremendous thank you to Fedor Belov, who not only introduced me to Wargaming but also collaborated with me on launching a Data Warehouse for the entire organization. This crucial project significantly shaped my experience and drove me to make LiveOps as data-driven as possible. I am also deeply grateful to Kirill Gamazenkov and Aliaksandr Kokhna, who were instrumental in launching our real-time Player Relationship Management platform. This platform later became the foundation for the personalized experiences we have been able to create within LiveOps, enriching our engagement strategies immensely.

I am deeply appreciative of Sergey Smolsky, who brought me into his team back in 2012. At that time, it was primarily a web development team, yet under his guidance, we pioneered a toolset for live service game operations. This early innovation laid the groundwork for what would eventually expand into the comprehensive Wargaming platform, including the LiveOps toolset we rely on today.

As an engineer, I always viewed analytics as an exact science. However, upon joining the marketing team, I was surprised to discover its complex and nuanced nature. Alexey Azarov and Denis Yakutovich were instrumental in guiding me through the labyrinth of "statistically significant" details. Their expertise helped me grasp the subtleties of analytics in marketing and publishing, a journey for which I am profoundly grateful.

I must express my profound gratitude to Juuso Myllyrinne and Sergey Osipov, who saw potential in me and provided an incredible opportunity to expand my academic horizons at INSEAD Business School. The approach to education I experienced at INSEAD has significantly influenced how I structured this book. Their belief in my capabilities and their support in furthering my education have been instrumental in shaping the insights and methodologies shared within these pages. Additionally, my years spent with Wargaming's marketing and in-house agency teams have added more color to my professional life. I am immensely grateful to these teams for transforming my binary world into a creative realm where I can imagine and visualize my thoughts as images.

I am deeply thankful for the opportunity to apply my skills across an array of remarkable titles including *World of Tanks*, *World of Tanks Blitz*, *World of Tanks Modern Armor*, *World of Warships*, *Caliber*, *Total War Arena*, and *Pagan Online*. The experiences and challenges faced with each team have profoundly shaped my skills and expanded my perspectives. I am immensely grateful to all the teams involved for their impact on my professional journey and for the unique insights each project provided.

I am immensely thankful that Wargaming launched the WG Forge initiative, which includes training courses and future internship programs across all Wargaming titles. A special shoutout to Anton Pankov, who championed WG Forge at the executive level. The WG Forge team was instrumental in helping me develop the LiveOps course, which, after inspiring our first cohort of students in 2023, evolved into this book. Special thanks to Irina Oliva, whose insights were invaluable in refining the course content to enhance student understanding.

I extend my heartfelt thanks to Solomon Foshko and Sergiy Galyonkin, who provided invaluable feedback during the review of this book. Their insights and suggestions were crucial in refining the content and ensuring its quality. Their support throughout the editorial process has been greatly appreciated and has significantly contributed to the book's final form.

Why all the unicorns in this book? Well, the credit goes to my daughter, Masha. Back in August 2019, as I was gearing up for a streaming session, Masha laid one of her unicorn drawings in front of me and said, "Here's a unicorn for you, it will help." And it sure did! That's why you'll find unicorns throughout these pages—not only as a nod to Masha's encouragement but also thanks to the incredible talents of Zakhar Shlimakov, Kate Shmonina and Ira Levshinskaya, who turned my thoughts into these magical creatures.

The idea to write this book took root during lengthy discussions with my son about his subject choices for his General Certificate of Secondary Education (GCSE) exams and our explorations of his university options. It became clear to me that there was not just a shortage of educational programs but also a dearth of resources for young people aspiring to enter the gaming industry.

Therefore, I dedicate this book to my children, Roma and Masha, and to all young individuals like them, filled with goodwill and dreams. My hope is that this book contributes, even in a small way, to creating a world where players, game studios, and the creator community can thrive together in harmony.

I owe a huge thanks to my wife Yulia for her unwavering support throughout this project and her constant belief in my potential. Yulia, you are truly the love of my life.

Author Biographies

Sergei Vasiuk is an executive leader with over 25 years of experience. His career commenced as a full-stack developer and progressed into a software lead role, where he made critical technology and architecture decisions. Utilizing his technical expertise, he has played integral roles in the gaming industry, including establishing successful Live Services Games Operations at Wargaming, constructing a data-driven organization, and overseeing a diverse team comprised of over 17 nationalities. Sergei has significantly contributed to the company's success by enhancing operational efficiency, spearheading effective live services game development, and mentoring team members to reach their full potential.

Volodymyr Dubrovskyi is a seasoned Video Games Business leader, who boasts over a decade of Live environment and Live Service development expertise. Grounded in data and economics, Vlad combines a passion for gaming and player empathy to innovate LiveOps strategies for PC and Console games.

Introduction

All human beings like to play, and the video game industry has extended entertainment in recent decades. A player launches a game to have fun, meet friends, and joyfully spend his leisure time. Since the beginning of the Third Industrial Revolution, most visionaries on the gaming subject have merged technological change with progress, and eventually, it paid off. Digitization of the playing experience as the composite process of storing information in a digital format and almost endless distribution capabilities of that information over online networks finally has allowed gaming enthusiasts to make dreams come true.

Video games have entertained both kids and adults for decades and have come a long way since the early days of simple computer games and the first Nintendo and Atari consoles. The primitive graphics and basic sound of those early games are long gone, replaced by highly realistic visuals and audio. As technology advances, video games continue to improve.

Content-rich, engaging, and visually attractive gameplay is just the tip of the iceberg that a player sees on the screen. Developing video games has become a more complex and expensive process. The cost of producing a game has increased significantly due to this complexity. Whereas spending millions on game development was once unimaginable, today, it's common for games to cost tens or even hundreds of millions of dollars. This escalation in development costs was highlighted during the acquisition of Activision Blizzard, Inc. by Microsoft Corporation. Reports from this event revealed that some AAA game franchises, such as *Call of Duty*, now have development budgets that exceed $300 million, underscoring the massive financial commitments involved in creating cutting-edge video games.

Video games are typically categorized into two types: Premium, also known as "boxed" games, which are sold once and do not change, and Live Service Games, which include titles like *PUBG*, *CS:GO*, *League of Legends*, and *World of Tanks*. Live Service Games are continually updated with new content to keep players engaged (see Figure I.1). Premium games, such as *Spider Man*, *Kingdom Come Deliverance*, and *Just Cause 3*, often see a spike in popularity right after release, but this interest usually declines over

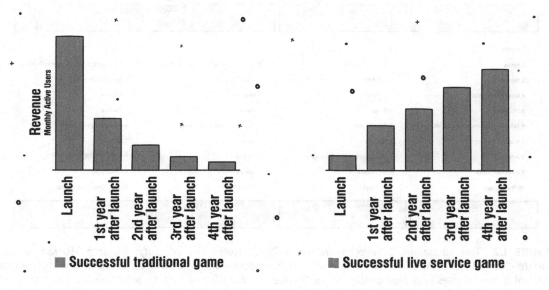

FIGURE I.1 Differences in revenue and Monthly Active Users' dynamics between traditional "box" games and live service games.

DOI: 10.1201/9781003427056-1

1

time. Additionally, there are annual franchises like NBA2K, EA Sports FC, and Madden, which release new versions each year with updated rosters and features. These franchises show trends similar to Live Service Games, with annual updates and roster changes.

Both business models, Premium and Live Service, continue to find success in the modern video game industry. However, with the rise of digital distribution, which has largely replaced physical sales and made content easily downloadable, Live Service models have become increasingly dominant among the top-grossing games.

Statistics from Newzoo in 2023 highlight this trend (see Figure I.2), showing that 60% of playtime was dedicated to games that were 6 years old or older. The top 10 games on each platform, ranked by their average number of monthly active users (MAU), predominantly feature well-established titles. Fortnite led the pack across various platforms including Switch and PC. Other familiar names populate the list, such as *Grand Theft Auto V, Counter-Strike 2, Roblox, Minecraft, Rocket League, Apex Legends, Fall Guys, Valorant,* and *Call of Duty*. Notably, across Xbox and PlayStation consoles, the only single-player game to make the top ten was *Starfield*, underscoring the predominance of multiplayer and live service games in maintaining player engagement over time.

The enthusiasm for live service games, driven by their promise of recurring revenue and sustained player engagement, has captured the imagination of many in the games industry. However, transitioning every game to a live service model is not necessarily the best strategy for all. The allure of these models must be balanced with a clear understanding of what's right for both the players and the developers.

For players, it's essential to consider whether the shift to live services aligns with the expectations and habits associated with a particular IP. If a game is traditionally known for its self-contained, single-player experience, asking players to commit to it as an ongoing hobby may not resonate well and could lead to disappointment. On the other hand, for IPs where players are already engaging long term without live features, introducing them could enhance their experience. Developers must critically assess whether adding live services will genuinely benefit the game and enrich the player's experience, rather than just serving as a tool to extract more revenue.

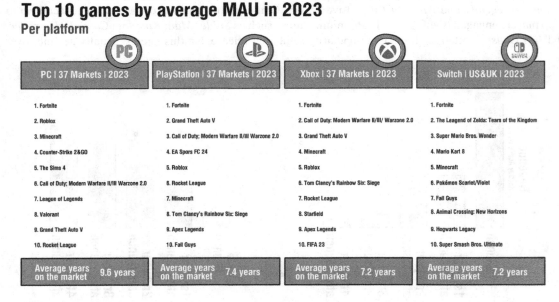

FIGURE I.2 Top 10 games by average MAU in 2023. Note: *Call of Duty: Modern Warfare III* and *Counter-Strike 2* share the same executable with their predecessors, and these rankings include the average MAU of those releases plus their predecessors. Source: Newzoo Game Performance Monitor | PC, Xbox, PS coverage for 37 Markets (excl. China & India) | Switch coverage for US & UK | 2023.

From the developers' perspective, transitioning to live services requires a profound shift in approach—from game design and development to post-launch support. This shift is not just about adding new content; it involves changing the operational and development culture, which can be a challenging adjustment. Developers need to be passionate and well-prepared for these changes, or the project may suffer. Furthermore, the additional workload and complexity of maintaining live services can significantly impact budgets and focus, potentially detracting from the core aspects of game development. It's crucial for studios to evaluate if they are ready to embrace these changes fully or if doing so might compromise the quality and integrity of the gaming experience they aim to provide.

Technological advancements have profoundly reshaped our ways of working and living, making live service games quintessential products of the 21st century. Despite these changes, the core principles of visionary product-based companies remain largely the same. The video gaming industry, though relatively young compared to established sectors like film, music, or media, offers significant opportunities for professionals skilled in marketing, sales, and operations to transfer their expertise and align their careers with the evolving landscape of video game operations.

This book is structured to guide you through the entire process of releasing and supporting a live service game, offering step-by-step guidance and instructions. Starting with the foundational principles of live service games, it provides a framework to evaluate whether your concept is ready to transition into a live service model. From there, the focus shifts to generating added value to the base game, enhancing both the player experience and the game's profitability.

As you delve deeper, the LiveOps techniques section offers detailed insights into the specific daily operational tasks, enabling you to understand the nuances of maintaining a live service game. The competition through operations chapter outlines the necessary organizational and process-level operations that need to be established, assisting in toolset selection and building robust analytics frameworks. Finally, the People's LiveOps section provides a forward-looking perspective, equipping you with strategies to sustain and grow your business in the gaming industry.

Creating a great game is not the same as operating a game greatly over several years; these are two distinct skill sets that few teams possess simultaneously. While the development of a game focuses on design, storytelling, and technical innovation, operating a game successfully as a live service requires ongoing engagement strategies, dynamic content updates, and meticulous community management. This book specifically addresses the latter, guiding you through the essential practices and strategies needed to maintain and enhance a game's value long after its initial launch. It is designed to help teams not just launch a game but sustain its success and relevance in the competitive landscape by continually creating value for players and stakeholders year after year.

BOOK STRUCTURE

PART 1—Before starting the fascinating journey around live service game, it's important to step back and tell the story of the gaming industry over the past decades. Part 1 pays tribute to the framework that makes up the game operations enabling added value creation. Video games have transitioned from a product-based model to a game-as-a-service model and now transformed into platforms. Chapter 1 sets the stage based on the last 50 years of game content transformation.

LiveOps as a discipline has become an integral part of any live service games and must be carefully planned throughout the game design phase. Chapter 2 starts the introduction to the main areas that must be considered while thinking about LiveOps.

Creating value is the ultimate goal for any long-running game to expand players' engagement and revenue. Chapter 3 explains the value creation chain and types of content that help capture value in the different phases of game operations.

PART 2—With that being said about fundamentals, any company producing great products utilizes a long-known marketing framework, starting from market analysis and strategy and finishing with communication and go-to-market plans. Gaming companies leverage their power of knowing players' behavior to shape the segments, assume their problems, and create and promote products best suited to them. Part 2 paves the player's own path and shows consistent steps of how games can gain a lot from data and as a result enhance and personalize player experience. Whether we're just getting started or are looking to improve game operations frameworks, there are three questions and principles that should be borne in mind when building player relationships:

What Are We Doing? Happy player is the ultimate goal of any game, that is why the most important metric is lifetime. Chapter 4 continues with the idea of value creation to sustain long-term relationships.

Why Are We Doing This? Games entertain players and give them emotions when, in return, players give their time, advocacy, and money. Chapter 5 paves the way that maintains a mutually beneficial exchange of this relationship.

How Are We Doing This? Gaming audience consists of large number of segments and the biggest challenge is to uncover differences among players. Chapter 6 establishes the framework that tailors the relationship to those differences.

PART 3—In this part, we unwrap how live service game performance is achieved. Using data and analytics, LiveOps teams define and optimize monetization techniques and methodologies. The cornerstone or "the North Star metric" of a live service game is the lifetime value (LTV) of its players—it defines how much the product can spend on user acquisition, how long the player journey lasts, and pretty much sets the upper limitation on what the game can achieve. The LTV can be impacted by a set of monetization, engagement, or referral techniques described in this chapter.

Addressing the challenge of user acquisition, Chapter 7 explains how platforms and business models shape user acquisition and explores strategies that harness media mix, influencer marketing, partnerships, and virality to effectively draw new players into live service games.

Tackling the broad and elusive challenge of player engagement, Chapter 8 breaks down essential components and enablers that boost long-term player involvement in live service games.

Facing the challenge of revenue generation in Free-to-Play models, Chapter 9 discusses the creation of in-game economies and various monetization strategies to maintain financial viability without compromising player satisfaction.

Confronting the need for dynamic player engagement, Chapter 10 offers insights into using the LiveOps Event Canvas to plan and execute events that captivate and retain players' interest.

Addressing the challenge of player engagement and monetization, Chapter 11 uses predictive modeling and the 3LAPs operations framework to deliver personalized gaming experiences that enhance player engagement and drive revenue.

PART 4—Zara and Amazon have operations management to outperform their competitors with the top-notch supply chain of fabric or engines; a gaming company has operations management to support content ordering, creation, mockup, and delivery with their own virtual warehouse in the cloud. Part 4 explains the core engine of any live service game and clarifies how to compete through operations with a focus on delivering value.

If issues are caught on the final business dashboard or, worse, if players start reporting them, you are already late. Do not launch a campaign or an event if you don't have a 24/7 team that can respond, even at 1 am on a Saturday night. Chapter 12 explains how to effectively manage live service games globally through operations management.

The "build or buy" dilemma always depends on a variety of conditions, as well as your game's current and future goals. Chapter 13 describes the toolset needed for a live service game, helping you better align them with internal processes, team expertise, and specific game objectives.

Raw data holds paramount importance, but like everything else in our lives, it requires clarification. Chapter 14 enables your data to tell the story by establishing a clear data language that everybody understands and, most importantly, embraces. A set of data definitions, metrics, processes, and business rules ensures that the data is consistent and trustworthy.

PART 5—Part 5 offers interaction with the players to take place outside the game client and is aimed at maximizing attention time, when the player comes into contact with the game, while not currently playing. Attention is what our businesses rely on, and without a deep understanding of the nuances of our audiences, capturing and maintaining players' attention become a daunting task. Chapter 15 shifts operations from increasing playtime to extending attention time.

Digital transformation fuels the pace of content consumption growth that eventually pushes gaming companies to find a way to create content in appropriate quantity and quality. Gone were the days when a game team could hire internal talents and fulfill players' demands. Chapter 16 shows how to engage your best fans and provide them with the ability to earn a living from it.

Facing the challenge of maintaining player engagement and content freshness, Chapter 17 explores how transforming games into adaptive ecosystems can facilitate this. It discusses the shift from "Game-as-a-Service" model to a "Game-as-a-Platform" approach, where collaboration with creators and brands extends content creation beyond the capabilities of first-party game developers alone.

PART I

Game as a Business

From ancient times to the present day, human beings have continuously sought various forms of entertainment, demonstrating an innate desire for social interaction and personal amusement. A good example of games transitioning into a business model is seen in the Victorian era, particularly through the popularity of parlor games. Games such as *Blind Man's Bluff* and *Twenty Questions* were not only played for entertainment but also commercialized, signaling the beginnings of game monetization.

In the Victorian era, entrepreneurs quickly recognized the potential for profit in these games. They began to professionalize the gaming experience by manufacturing and selling complete game sets and detailed rulebooks. This allowed the games to reach a broader audience, extending beyond the confines of those who could invent and remember complex rules.

Moreover, these games were strategically marketed in magazines and newspapers, often highlighted as ideal activities for family gatherings. This approach tapped into the family-centric values of the time, positioning these games as essential components of family life and social events. They were adaptable, catering to different social settings and preferences, which is reminiscent of how today's video games are continuously updated to maintain player interest and adapt to changing market demands.

Furthermore, the endorsement of games by cultural figures of the era helped embed them into the social fabric, enhancing their appeal and legitimacy. This practice can be likened to modern-day influencer endorsements, which are a significant marketing strategy in the gaming industry.

This part also sets the stage through the lens of the history of video games, which explores significant technological advancements and the introduction of creative new content. It outlines the evolution from games primarily focused on unit sales to a model centered around player engagement. This shift is exemplified by the emergence of live service games, which aim to keep players continuously engaged with new content and interactive experiences. Ultimately, the gaming industry has developed sophisticated methods to not only captivate players but also create substantial value for its employees and shareholders.

DOI: 10.1201/9781003427056-2

A Brief History of Video Games

1

Since it first appeared as a technological novelty at a science fair in the 1950s, gaming has grown into one of the world's most lucrative entertainment sectors. The story of video gaming is like a colorful adventure, made possible by clever inventions and ideas. The entire history of video gaming can be observed through the lens of three areas: It has experienced significant changes in technology, introduced creative new content, and explored different ways to distribute games to people. Here are a few examples of how each chapter in this story has been driven by significant breakthroughs that have directed the course of gaming.

Technology: Transistor-transistor logic (TTL) circuit is the muscle behind the blinking lights and bleeps of arcade classics, sparked an arcade revolution. Then came the microprocessor, embedded within the Atari 2600, which heralded the migration of gaming from public arcades to the intimacy of the living room.

Distribution: The introduction of CD-ROMs brought the ability to hold a lot more game data, which meant games could be bigger, look better, and tell richer stories. The internet tied everything together, making it easy for gamers, game makers, and storytellers from all over to connect and share in the game world.

Content: Smartphones came in and changed the game again. They turned our little phones into gateways to amazing game worlds, freeing gaming from the TV and making it possible anywhere. Live-streaming has become a pivotal extension of gaming culture. Platforms like Twitch and YouTube Gaming have turned game playthroughs and competitive matches into spectator sports, creating a new genre of entertainment content.

To grasp how video games have flourished so significantly, it's important to examine the four key eras of the industry: Game-as-a-Club (late 1960s to mid-1980s), Game-as-a-Product (mid-1980s to early 2000s), Game-as-a-Service (early 2000s to mid-2010s), and Game-as-a-Platform (from mid-2010s to the present). Every one of these stages transformed gaming in a big way, moving from the old-school arcade machines to today's games that we can access from the cloud, showing us how gaming is always creating new ways to play.

In the late 1960s, Sega and Taito sparked an interest with the release of *Periscope* and *Crown Special Soccer*, drawing crowds and sowing the seeds of Game-as-a-Club. By 1972, Atari transformed the initial sparks of interest into a blazing fire, not only creating games but also shaping an entire industry and setting a new standard for communal gaming spaces, turning arcades into the communal hubs of the modern era.

With the 1973 launch of *Pong*, they offered more than just a game; they created a central gathering spot for competition and social interaction. During the late 1970s, an interesting trend emerged across the United States, with chain restaurants installing video game machines to capitalize on the growing gaming craze. This initiative did more than just entertain; it ignited a competitive zeal among players, who battled to top the high-score charts. This early competitive drive in arcades laid the foundation for what we see in today's live service games, where leaderboards continue to fuel a competitive spirit among players globally.

DOI: 10.1201/9781003427056-3

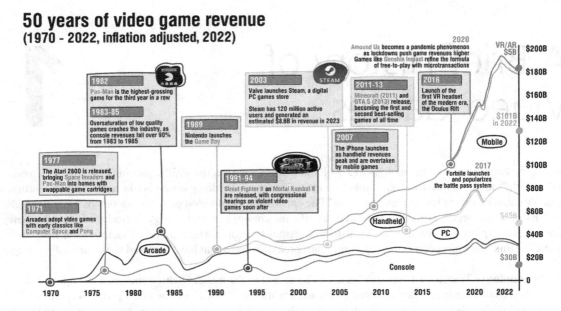

FIGURE 1.1   50 years of video game industry revenues. Source: Pelham Smithers.

Technological progress, highlighted by Intel's creation of the first microprocessor, enabled the development of *Gunfight* in 1975, the inaugural multiplayer combat game. *Gunfight*, notable for its innovative dual-joystick control system for movement and shooting, marked a significant moment in arcade gaming. The use of microprocessors made it possible to bring *Space Invaders* to the Atari 2600 in 1980, starting the trend of playing video games at home. This led to a boom in gaming, with many new companies and consoles entering the market. However, too many consoles and not enough good games caused the 1983 video game crash, resulting in big losses and lots of bad games being dumped in the desert (Figure 1.1).

The rise of home computers began to challenge the console's dominance. These machines boasted superior processing power, allowing for more complex and engaging gameplay. They also opened up new avenues for gaming, including the ability for developers to create new content. The Game-as-a-Product era marked a significant chapter in the history of video gaming, with product-based revenue dominating the industry. During this time, publishers and developers focused on selling physical media—discs and cartridges—through retail outlets to consumers who primarily engaged with content on consoles or PC.

The early 1990s witnessed the crystallization of this era, as box titles began filling shelves in major retail chains like GameStop and Walmart. Players paid a single, one-time fee in exchange for access to content, which laid the foundation for the premium business model for years. These sales were deeply intertwined with the hardware cycles of console manufacturers, emphasizing a symbiotic relationship between console launches and game releases.

This era saw the first steps toward connecting players through networks, a concept that would eventually become a cornerstone of modern live service gaming. Iconic games like *Doom* in 1993 and the advent of LAN parties started a multiplayer revolution, further accelerated by the introduction of affordable networking solutions and the public release of the World Wide Web software by CERN in 1993.

Though the mid-1990s attempts by Sega, Nintendo, and Atari to introduce online gaming through cable providers stumbled due to technical and logistical hurdles, the dream of a connected gaming world persisted. It wasn't until the launch of the Sega Dreamcast, the first console designed with internet connectivity in mind, that online gaming began to truly take shape. The Game-as-a-Product era, therefore, was not just a time of physical media and retail dominance but also a period of technological innovation and networked experimentation. It set the stage for the digital distribution and online communities that would define the future of live service gaming (Figure 1.2).

FIGURE 1.2 The Game-as-a-Product era, with revenue primarily derived from traditional "box" games with physical media and dominance in retail.

The technological advancements in internet capabilities and computer processing power since the early 2000s have been nothing short of revolutionary. With the cost of technology and internet access plummeting, high-speed online experiences have become the norm, paving the way for the game-as-a-service model. The advent of digital distribution platforms has fundamentally altered the gaming landscape, marking a pivotal shift in how games are accessed, enjoyed, and shared. In 2003, Valve Corporation launched Steam, a trailblazer in video game digital distribution and storefront services, setting a precedent for the industry. Not long after, in the mid-2000s, giants like Xbox with its Live Marketplace and Sony with PSN followed suit, embracing the digital shift. These platforms have revolutionized the gaming experience, transforming the way games are bought, updated, and how the gaming community interacts.

The mid-2000s saw the gaming industry's traditional publishers grappling with the challenges of digital distribution, which, at the time, represented a minor portion of their revenue. Meanwhile, a new wave of developers seized this opportunity to redefine gaming with innovative gameplay, distribution methods, and by tapping into a global audience. By the end of the 2000s, the digitalization of entertainment and the ubiquity of online connectivity had firmly established the game-as-a-service model. This approach differed significantly from its predecessor; it was built on direct downloads of interactive content to devices. Gamers adapted to a new norm where games could be free or inexpensive upfront, with revenue generated over time through microtransactions for additional content and in-game items. Titles like *League of Legends* and *World of Tanks* exemplified this model's success, offering easily accessible, engaging experiences that fostered long-term relationships with players. This era of gaming not only embraced a service model reminiscent of the software industry but also highlighted the importance of building communities, leveraging social networks, and engaging players through events and tournaments. This new model also redefined the measurement of success from "sales units" to average revenue per user (ARPU). Now, the focus is on creating enduring, dynamic gaming experiences that can evolve, supported by a model that allows for continuous iteration and engagement with the gaming community (Figure 1.3).

The emergence of new gaming studios championing the game-as-a-service model catalyzed unprecedented growth, propelling video gaming into the limelight of mainstream leisure activities with a worldwide reach. This period in the gaming industry was akin to a gold rush, characterized by an explosion of free-to-play (F2P) titles on PC and mobile platforms. The adoption of the F2P business model, coupled

FIGURE 1.3   The Game-as-a-Service era, with a shift happening from games primarily focused on unit sales to a model centered around player engagement.

with the capability to analyze the behaviors of millions of players, offered studios a competitive edge by allowing them to refine gameplay and enhance revenue streams strategically.

Interactive entertainment and the rise of social media have shifted the industry's focus from solely creating value through content to leveraging network effects. In this service-based era, success is increasingly determined by a title's ability to foster vibrant online communities. Players are drawn not just to play against non-player characters (NPC) but against each other, amplifying the social aspect of gaming. This paradigm shift underscores the importance of crafting experiences that cultivate positive network effects, where the value for consumers is significantly enhanced by the size and engagement level of the player base, rather than just the production values of the game itself. Moreover, the scale of F2P models necessitated the integration of social game mechanics to engage a vast, global audience.

As the gaming industry moves beyond initial economic hurdles and continues to enjoy widespread popularity, it's transitioning into a new phase where a game's success isn't solely determined by its quality or design, especially considering the market's saturation and the time constraints of contemporary life. The sheer volume of available content has paradoxically made it more challenging to discover games that appeal to the mainstream audience. This trend emerged with the rise of a new category: live-streaming. Gamers have always enjoyed watching others play, whether in arcades or at home, specifically, watching other people play video games became popular in the mid-2010s on platforms like Twitch. This category has since evolved into a critical component of how game companies market their content to audiences. It has also become a viable career option for a generation of video game fans and eager talent, who have started using Game-as-a-Platform to make money from it (Figure 1.4).

The surge in gaming video content owes much to the rise of F2P games, which helps acquire and engage players. This effective method for attracting and keeping players has made live-streaming a key component of live service games, leading to significant income increases for those creating gaming videos. This concept also paved the way for game studios to host and organize professional tournaments, a practice that dates back to the era of LAN parties. What has become a novelty is audiences sitting and watching others play competitively. To foster positive network effects, F2P publishers have implemented various strategies to acquire and retain players. Active investment in organizing tournaments has proven

2020s

FIGURE 1.4 The Game-as-a-Platform era, where collaboration with creators extends content creation beyond the capabilities of first-party game developers alone.

to be a crucial marketing tactic for these publishers, serving both to generate excitement and to help build a community around their titles. Esports has gained significant momentum thanks to the swift popularization of this new form of entertainment content.

The emergence of user-generated content, coupled with the rise of Roblox—an online game platform and creation system—has prompted gaming companies to enhance the capabilities of Game-as-a-Platform. Epic Games has made a significant move in this direction with the Unreal Editor for *Fortnite*. This tool introduces some Unreal Engine functionality to *Fortnite Creative*, including a proprietary coding language. The Unreal Editor allows *Fortnite* developers to create diverse experiences, aiming to earn a living in ways similar to opportunities available on YouTube.

Since the 1950s, video gaming has evolved from a niche hobby enjoyed by a handful of enthusiasts to a mainstream industry that bridges generations. This transformation underscores the effectiveness of releasing games with strong, broadly appealing intellectual properties (IPs). However, this strategy introduces its own set of challenges, including creative constraints imposed by licensors, the complexities of negotiating contracts for celebrity likenesses, and revenue-sharing agreements that can diminish profit margins.

Currently, we are in an era where the primary goal for gaming studios is to develop and secure their own IPs. The drive behind this ambition lies in the immense value that can be unlocked through licensing opportunities, adaptations into television and film, and a holistic engagement strategy. Studios that are ready to invest in and expand their IPs can reap significant rewards.

Moreover, games have transcended their traditional boundaries to become platforms that enable not just avid fans and developers to monetize content but also allow brands from various sectors to weave gaming into their marketing strategies. Industries such as fashion, sports, and music have begun to actively explore gaming as a channel for engaging with new audiences. Owning an IP does not merely open new revenue streams for studios; it also offers substantial benefits to other industries, creating a symbiotic relationship that fosters growth across the board.

Nintendo exemplifies the potential of gaming IPs to generate value beyond the gaming industry, through movie adaptations, theme parks, and crossover collaborations. This model demonstrates how gaming IPs can become cornerstone assets, propelling both the studios that create them and the broader ecosystem of industries looking to innovate in how they connect with their audiences.

Introduction to Live Service Games

2

Over the past decade, the gaming industry has witnessed a significant transformation with the rise of live service games. This shift from a focus on unit sales to one centered on player engagement marks a fundamental change in business models. Live service games are designed not just to offer a short campaign but to engage players for years, monetizing this sustained interaction through in-game purchases. This model now accounts for the majority of gaming revenue, attracting more developers to adopt it.

The move toward live services is driven by both developers and players. Developers benefit as they face lower risks associated with reduced development times and costs compared to traditional AAA titles. Additionally, they can incorporate ongoing player feedback into their updates, allowing for less polished initial releases but greater long-term returns through a strategy of rapid development and iteration. For players, the advantages include free-to-play options that let them try and play more games, as well as the enjoyment of social interactions and self-expression within the online community.

The core idea behind live service games is that spending money is optional—players can enjoy the game without paying. This requires games to engage players deeply, motivating them to spend voluntarily. The main measures of success here are the lifetime and average revenue per user (ARPU). Unlike traditional models that depend on initial sales, this engagement-based approach can lead to greater earnings over time by focusing on sustained player interaction.

Live services spread their revenue potential beyond a single launch event. Traditional games often depend heavily on initial sales close to release, with success hinging on immediate public reception. In contrast, live service games aim to earn consistently over the game's life. They enhance their longevity through regular updates based on player feedback starting right after release. For traditional games, the launch is the climax, but for live services, it's just the beginning. Each update in a live service game can generate excitement similar to a new launch, especially with new features or high-profile collaborations.

Live service games also have multiple ways to generate revenue. In-game purchases, including cosmetic items like skins or progress-based items like equipment, are crucial. Battle passes offer rewards that players earn over time, encouraging regular play. Some live service games charge for initial access if they already have a solid player base and brand loyalty, like *EA Sports FC*. Advertising is another revenue source, more common in mobile but expanding to PC and console games due to their regular engagement.

LiveOps as a discipline lies at the heart of live service games that change the player experience after the title goes live or receives updates without having to release a new version of the game. Gone were the days when developing a game, uploading it to the platform, and enjoying life was a sustainable business model for a game with a long lifespan. LiveOps has become an integral part of any Free-to-Play game and must be carefully planned starting with the design and ending with a go-to-market strategy. Game as Service transformed box game into a living organic game that is in constant evolution and Live Operations gives players a fresh experience every day.

LiveOps is a *practice* of introducing frequent and *data-driven events* to players without involvement of the game development team, aiming to maximize player *Lifetime Value*.

- Maximizing LTV, which extends both the duration and monetization potential of player engagement, is the ultimate goal of all LiveOps initiatives.

DOI: 10.1201/9781003427056-4

- Data plays a crucial role in LiveOps; it fuels the iterative nature of activities, which are continually optimized through analytics and A/B testing. LTV itself is a predictive metric, calculated based on data.
- LiveOps is a practice consisting of ongoing activities that are consistently available to players. These activities must be continually refined based on player feedback and aligned with the overall product roadmap.
- Events or campaigns serve as the fundamental components of LiveOps, forming the core of its strategy to engage players.

LiveOps has become increasingly popular as digital distribution and the prevalence of free games have significantly increased the number of games available. This shift has created a highly competitive environment where studios are compelled to keep players engaged with fresh content, timely updates, and ongoing support. LiveOps enables developers to effectively manage these demands, allowing for swift adaptations to player feedback and evolving technology trends.

Moreover, modern players have high expectations; they demand quick fixes to in-game issues and timely content updates. LiveOps strategies enable games to satisfy these expectations and maintain player interest through engaging content and immediate responses to feedback. Importantly, LiveOps provides vital opportunities for cost-effective content repurposing and enhancing core game features through events. It also opens up additional monetization avenues through subscriptions or battle passes, thereby securing the financial viability and success of games.

There are a lot of component parts and pieces that provide a holistic picture of live service games; nevertheless, when we talk about LiveOps, three main areas should be considered: acquisition, retention, and monetization. We will talk in detail about product metrics late, but first, let me briefly explain why these particular three areas define the scope of work for the LiveOps team. When it comes to live service game operations, in general, you should keep an eye on three relevant metrics:

Monthly Active Users (MAU) determines the overall success of a game and retention activities help keep it stable;

New Monthly Active Users (new MAU) shows how efficiently you work to attract new players and your acquisition activities support game audience growth;

Gross Revenue illustrates the financial success of a game and monetization activities allow you to develop a sustainable business.

What is acquisition? Acquisition involves bringing new users into the game and converting them into regular Monthly Active Users (Figure 2.1). Consider the entire internet as a potential source of users who could be persuaded to join your game. There are numerous platforms like Facebook Ads or Google Marketing Platform that offer a variety of ways to attract new users. These platforms allow for targeted advertising based on a wide range of player profiles such as age, location, and gender. The targeting can be based on algorithms that find similar users or on data provided by users on platforms like Twitch, Twitter, or Reddit.

In addition to online methods, traditional mass media channels like TV or radio, as well as offline events like exhibitions, brand collaborations, or promotional tours, also play a role in user acquisition. The integration of influencers through platforms like YouTube, TikTok, or Instagram has become a significant trend over the past decade. Importantly, the game itself is a powerful tool for acquisition; organic growth through word-of-mouth often brings in a very loyal audience. While these methods represent just a fraction of the possible ways to attract new users, finding effective strategies for continually introducing new players is critical for sustaining and growing the Monthly Active Users (MAU) .

What is retention? Retention focuses on keeping monthly active users (MAU) engaged by helping them master the game, set goals, make friends, and re-engaging those who haven't played in a while (Figure 2.2). Picture managing a large entertainment center where newcomers need guidance, regulars seek new challenges or skills to enhance, and those drifting away are reconnected through social

What is acquisition?

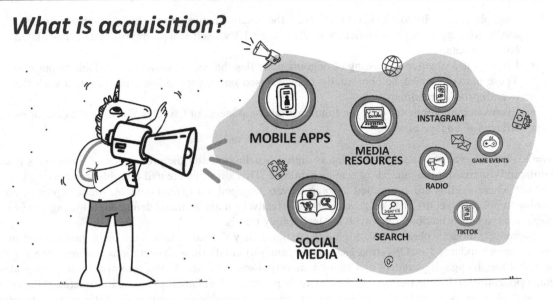

FIGURE 2.1 Acquisition involves bringing new users into the game and converting them into regular Monthly Active Users.

What is Retention?

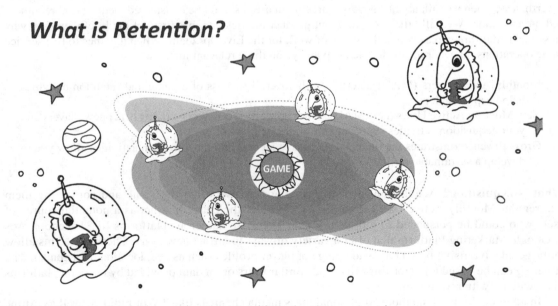

FIGURE 2.2 Retention focuses on keeping Monthly Active Users engaged.

interactions. As the manager, your job is to create engaging events that increase the number of active days per month or extend the duration of play sessions.

Now, imagine applying this concept in games globally across multiple regions, each with distinct cultural traits. This scenario demands tailored strategies to onboard new users and keep veteran players, who may have over 500 hours of gameplay, interested. Beyond just regional events and missions, it's crucial to analyze and refine the onboarding process for new players and address common issues that cause lapsed players to leave. Adding personalized tips and clear goal-setting can help reduce sudden player drop-offs.

What is Monetization?

FIGURE 2.3   Monetization involves generating gross revenue by leveraging players' gaming habits and financial behaviors.

Additionally, it's vital to continually assess and optimize how promotions and events are received to ensure they resonate well with the players and keep them engaged. These efforts are just a few key aspects of retention. Effective engagement is essential; without it, the game risks losing its player base entirely.

What is monetization? Monetization involves generating gross revenue by leveraging players' gaming habits and financial behaviors (Figure 2.3). Consider a manager of a chain of entertainment centers who must tailor pricing policies to the economic conditions of each region and adapt sales strategies to fit cultural nuances and audience sizes. Similarly, in gaming, if you can attract new players and keep your audience engaged with compelling content, they are likely to spend money.

The gaming industry offers various monetization methods tailored to different game types. For example, casual games typically have a large number of daily active users (DAU) and a higher rate of making purchases, although spending amounts might be lower at certain game levels. Mid-core games may have fewer daily users but can generate significant revenue from a small group of heavy spenders, often referred to as "whales," who may spend hundreds or even thousands of dollars. Additionally, many games utilize "Loot Boxes"—randomized selections of virtual items—as a primary revenue source. This strategy taps into the players' love for the excitement and chance of winning big, similar to casino. These are just a few ways games can be monetized, but integrating these strategies thoughtfully into game design from the start can significantly enhance the chances of releasing a financially successful title.

To effectively implement strategies within acquisition, retention, and monetization, it's essential to recall that the history of video gaming is shaped by three fundamental areas: technology, content, and distribution. These same three driving forces also guide the LiveOps discipline for precise game operations and audience management:

1. **LiveOps Practice:** This involves content production by understanding regional differences and tailoring activities to support the main game's key performance indicators (KPIs). For Monthly Active Users (MAU), this might include engagement events or campaigns to re-engage lapsed players. For acquiring new MAU, strategies could involve collaborations with celebrity influencers or guiding new players through their initial gaming experience. For boosting gross revenue, personalized offers or events outside the game can be effective.

Driving Forces

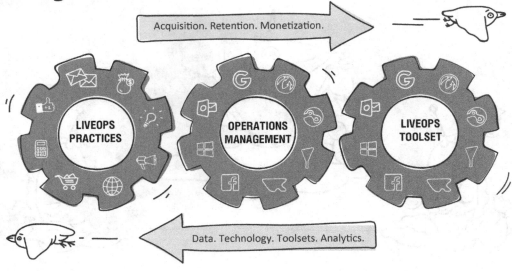

FIGURE 2.4   Three driving forces that shape LiveOps discipline for precise game operations and audience management.

2. **Operations Management:** This area encompasses Data, Store, or Campaign Management, and Data Sciences, which utilize both in-house toolsets and third-party platforms (e.g., Steam, Microsoft, or Apple Stores) to operate publishing and marketing, ensuring effective distribution of content to players.
3. **LiveOps Toolset:** This is an engine of LiveOps practice and an integrated solution leveraging technology that not only supports the game studio's internal functionality but also combines features from existing market platforms like Google, Facebook, or Microsoft.

Thus, on the one hand, we have "Practices for acquisition, retention, and monetization"; on the other hand, "Technologies, Data, Toolsets"; and in the middle is "operations management." (Figure 2.4). This arrangement clearly shows how critical it is for these three driving forces to work together to meet the needs of a live service game. Moreover, it is essential to outline the key elements of a successful LiveOps strategy, which are pivotal in orchestrating an engaging and profitable live service game:

- **Segmentation:** Vital for targeted promotions, segmentation involves categorizing players based on factors like location, age, gender, behavior, and preferences. This allows for precise promotion and tailored offers to different player segments, enhancing engagement and conversion rates.
- **Game Balance Management:** Central to maintaining player interest, this system enables adjustments in pricing, the introduction of new items, modifications to existing items, and the removal of unpopular ones. By managing these elements dynamically, LiveOps can keep the game fair and exciting.
- **Remote Configurations:** This technology empowers LiveOps to update and enhance the game's experience remotely without the need for players to download new updates. It streamlines the process of iterative improvements and ensures a seamless player experience.
- **Personalized Offers:** Crafting compelling offers is crucial for boosting monetization. These can range from first-purchase bonuses and daily rewards to exclusive gifts that attract new players and retain existing ones by continuously providing value.

- **Analytics:** Effective LiveOps requires comprehensive analytics to measure the success of different strategies and offers. By analyzing data, LiveOps can identify what works, what doesn't, and refine their approaches based on actual performance metrics.
- **A/B Testing:** This is a powerful tool for understanding player preferences and behaviors by testing variations of game elements. A/B testing helps in optimizing the player experience, thereby improving retention and conversion rates.
- **Event Implementation:** Engaging events that resonate with real-world happenings or in-game milestones can significantly enhance player engagement. Whether tied to global events, holidays, or unique in-game challenges, these activities help to keep the game environment dynamic and engaging.
- **Community Interaction:** LiveOps strategies must include active community engagement. Influencer and community management play crucial roles, acting as bridges between the players and the developers. This interaction not only improves player satisfaction but also provides valuable feedback for ongoing game development.

By integrating these key elements into the LiveOps strategy, game developers can ensure a vibrant, engaging, and continuously evolving gaming experience that meets the complex demands of today's gaming landscape.

Video Game Value Creation

3

Like in any business, in the gaming industry, success comes from value creation for players, employees, and shareholders. Value creation is essentially about giving something valuable to receive something else that holds greater value to you. The term is broad and takes into consideration both profit and loss (P&L); furthermore, it applies to players, owners, and employees. A methodical deep dive into the full range of value creation frameworks is beyond the scope of this handbook and would require a separate publication. This chapter will provide a general overview of the value creation in live service games (Figure 3.1).

Back in 1977, Rob Strasser, a big shot at Nike, whipped up a list of ten key "principles" for the company. He laid out what Nike expected from its employees and shared his vision for where the company was headed, also throwing in a heads-up about possible bumps along the way. He wrapped up the list with a punchy line: "If we do the right things, we'll make money damn near automatic."

In the world of LiveOps and video game creation, we take a leaf out of Nike's book. We see making money—the usual way to measure success—as something that comes after doing important things right. Focus on the right moves, and the cash will roll in on its own.

FIGURE 3.1 In the gaming industry success comes from value creation for players, employees, and shareholders.

DOI: 10.1201/9781003427056-5

For a game to hit it big, it needs to keep players coming back, offer fair deals in the game, and pull in a lot of new players. These are the big wins, and they're all based on solid facts and smart thinking. It's also super important to keep things running smoothly and sustainably, from game development to the business side of things.

Attempting to create something as iconic as Nike's manifesto may seem ambitious, but we're here to establish a series of guiding principles for studios aiming to launch the next big live service game and increase their chances of success. This includes understanding the production pipeline of a video game and specifically the value creation chain in live service games; methods to verify the effectiveness of your game strategies; and the intricacies of financial planning to ensure everything aligns with your business objectives.

GUIDING PRINCIPLES

Guiding principles outline an overall approach for overcoming specific challenges and serve as a compass, directing efforts and decisions without prescribing specific actions. Think of them as a strategic framework for addressing situations, one that capitalizes on or generates some form of advantage. Unlike a vision, which paints a picture of the desired outcome, guiding principles offer a roadmap for engagement. They help streamline focus, eliminating many potential but less effective courses of action.

Historically, traditional video games, often referred to as boxed games, follow a specific development cycle. In general, for boxed games, development teams work within a defined budget and adhere to a set release date, aiming to deliver a high-quality product that meets player expectations. After the game is launched—a milestone often celebrated with a well-earned break for the team—developers may shift to new projects, making revisits to the original game uncommon. This model, popular among many AAA titles, relies on the predictability of budgets, the allure of established franchises, and a commitment to delivering a polished product upon release. Production phases typically involve large teams, which may scale down after the game's launch. In contrast, live service games operate under a different set of seven guiding principles.

1. **Live Service Games Evolve Continuously:** Live service games are never complete, finished, or perfect; they're always in a state of evolution, adapting to player behaviors and growing with their audience and developers. Embracing change and maintaining agility is essential as player engagement may not always follow the intended design. This principle underscores the need for teams that are adaptable, curious, and empathetic both to players and fellow creators.
2. **Flexibility in Systems Design:** From the start, prioritize building systems that empower LiveOps teams to operate the game independently, minimizing the need for constant game developer involvement for updates such as in-game store changes, adding new missions or challenges, or setting up battle passes. Focus on designing for reusability and breaking down features into self-sufficient units.
3. **Commitment beyond Launch:** The challenge for live service games transcends the initial launch; it revolves around the ongoing creation of new content to satisfy the evolving demands of players. Collaboration between game developers and LiveOps teams is crucial in this endeavor, as it aligns content production with player expectations and operational capabilities. Understanding player preferences early and making iterative improvements based on these insights encourage a cycle of bold experimentation and meticulous execution.
4. **Guided by Insights:** It's vital to constantly seek out and analyze data. By regularly gathering insights and remaining vigilant against biases, teams can better understand player needs. Early in development, striving for consistency in data collection is more crucial than seeking perfection, with a balance between qualitative feedback and quantitative data to understand player behavior.

5. **Quality Perception Is Subjective:** Since players' perceptions of quality change over time and vary across different player types, making universally satisfying decisions can be challenging. Recognizing that it's impossible to please everyone helps in focusing efforts on impactful, business-smart choices.

6. **Revenue Follows Engagement:** Revenue should be seen as a result of successful engagement, not the primary goal. Instead, focus on early-stage qualitative measures that later evolve into quantitative KPIs. Understanding the game's strengths and limitations allows for more effective management of resources and expectations.

7. **Forecast Creatively, Manage Costs Wisely:** While revenue forecasts are inherently speculative, managing costs is within a team's control. Establishing a deep understanding of game systems, optimizing content pipelines, and setting realistic financial targets are key to navigating the unpredictable nature of game development revenues.

The gaming industry is fast-paced and quite often, it's hard to foresee or properly execute new or evolving technological trends or embrace successful business strategies or services. There is no guarantee that the gameplay mechanics you choose to apply, the operational strategy you choose to follow, and the event's design that you pursue will achieve product results that meet or exceed your expectations. The rapid evolution of our industry requires frameworks on how games can remain sustainable; therefore, the purpose of the game operations is to propose, deliver, and capture value in an efficient way.

In order to do this, behind any sustainable operational strategy, there must be a simple and straightforward promotion of the definite or emotional benefits that the game will offer, as well as the approximate time spent, contribution efforts, or price that it will charge each player's segments for these benefits. Therefore, before any game studio starts reflecting on innovations, it must first understand how the game is creating, delivering, and capturing value (Figure 3.2).

1. Understanding value through the lens of each player's segments to discover which **value propositions** are presumably to be of intense interest to some segments is the best way to create a compelling value proposition. Having identified a specific value proposition, we must make sure that this proposition "resonates" all over the game operations to help ensure that each action of the game serves to strengthen the chosen value.

2. The next element of any successful operational strategy is about how the game actually **delivers the value** it has promised to the players through highly engaging events, personal offers, or extra content. Implementing the core processes is critical to building efficient operations management of delivering decent value with a focus on the promotion of the value proposition at every stage of game operations.

3. Finally, **value capture** has paramount importance, and in some cases, a team may get away with not thinking about capturing value if it provides much of its new content through well-known techniques. That's why it is so important to know the underlying principles of revenue sources and pricing in value capturing from the combination of what we propose and how we deliver to ensure that operational decisions are creating real value.

The famous saying is, "Technologies can help but can't lead." A human being should decide what to do and lead game operations. The Human Factor of value creation is the team and its ability to build the most essential team habits enabled by a curiosity-driven spirit of game discovery that is an integrated part of sustainable game operations.

Building trust is the key to a successful player relationship. Recently trust—something which has always been essential for gaming—has been questioned several times in the players' community like security breaches, biases in AI, or the spreading of "fake news." Players will not open your games, use your service, or stream your content if they don't feel safe interacting with your brand. Trust is a crucial component in audience management.

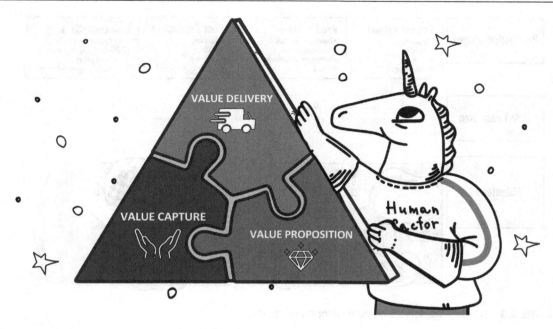

FIGURE 3.2 Fundamental enablers for value creation.

VALUE CREATION CHAIN

The game production process begins the instant a game concept is born and continues through to the release of the first version across platforms and further live operations (Figure 3.3). It's important to recognize that each game and each studio may have unique workflows. The approach to game production isn't universally fixed. As such, the specifics mentioned here may not align precisely with the processes at your studio, and that's perfectly acceptable. Before we delve into details, let's outline the general pipeline typical of live service game production, acknowledging that while there is no singular structure, most game development teams will encounter similar phases.

- **Ideation:** The game development process begins with ideation, emphasizing the generation of a unique game concept and a clear USP (unique selling position). This stage involves creating a pitch document to outline the game's concept and genre, along with a brief version of the game design document (GDD) for further elaboration.
- **Pre-production:** Pre-production is a phase focused on proving the game concept and preparing for full-scale production. It involves tasks such as prototyping the core game loop, answering critical questions, and scoping the project. Detailed documents like the GDD and technical design document (TDD) are created, and recruitment efforts are initiated to assemble the necessary team.
- **Production:** Full-scale development commences during the production stage. This iterative approach starts with a minimum viable product (MVP) and adds features and assets incrementally through sprints.
- **Post-production:** Post-production focuses on polishing and testing the game before launch. Backlog items are completed, excluding bugs, which are addressed during testing. This stage may involve three distinct phases leading up to the global launch: Technical Launch, Soft Launch, and Global Launch.

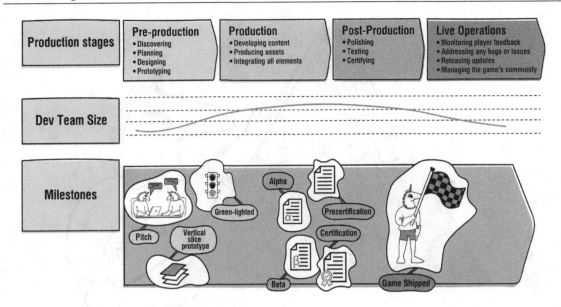

FIGURE 3.3   Five key live service game development stages.

- **Live Operations:** This stage focuses on sustaining and enhancing the game experience for players. It encompasses monitoring player feedback, swiftly addressing any bugs or issues, and rolling out patches and updates. Effective community management is also essential during this phase to maintain player engagement and support. Additionally, the development team often works on creating new content, features, and expansions to rejuvenate the game and retain the player base, ensuring the game remains dynamic and engaging for a long time.

A value creation chain is a concept that describes the entire chain of a game's activities in creating value during live operations. Analysis of these activities and relationships helps gaming studios understand them as a system of interdependent functions. If we take revenue as one of the metrics of value then as a rule of thumb that we're using, the revenue structure (see Figure 3.4) in the live service games is distributed by the principle 40/35/25 between base game, game updates, and live services.

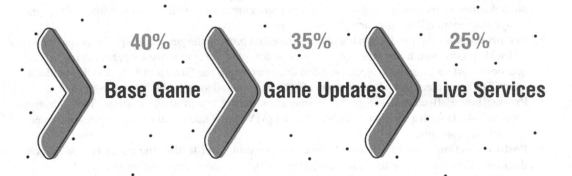

FIGURE 3.4   Revenue structure in the live service games.

Base Game: For every game, establishing systems that start adding value from the moment of release is crucial. This ability to generate value is fundamentally linked to its core gameplay mechanics, including the gameplay loops, the progression systems, or how it handles in-game currencies. Consider a game with a progression system measured in gameplay hours. Maintaining strong player retention through these systems creates value over the lifespan of a player's engagement, but this value is ultimately capped by the amount of content available at launch. At some point, players will have explored all the content the game has to offer, leading to a decline in engagement. The continued success and appeal of a game rest on its ability to constantly attract new players, introduce fresh content and gameplay mods, and effectively manage and repurpose its in-game resources.

To illustrate this with a non-gaming example, consider an entertainment park filled with a variety of rides, activities, and entertainment options. Such a park, by providing continuously engaging experiences for its visitors, holds the potential to generate value, but this potential is inherently limited by its initial setup. When Disney opened their entertainment park in Paris on April 12, 1992, Disneyland Park was brimming with rides, animations, and shops, all set within a meticulously designed environment. Despite its vast potential to draw in visitors and create memorable experiences, the park's ability to generate sustained value is constrained by its original design and concept, highlighting the importance of evolution and expansion in maintaining relevance and appeal (Figure 3.5).

Game Updates: Ensuring that the base game effectively retains players and that they are engaged with the core gameplay is crucial as the first step in the value creation chain. Once these fundamentals are firmly in place, the addition of extra content and new game modes becomes a viable strategy to enhance the player experience. These enhancements are integral to the ongoing process of value creation, providing fresh engagement opportunities and keeping the gameplay experience vibrant.

FIGURE 3.5   A base game, like a theme park, holds the potential to generate value, but this potential is inherently limited by its initial setup.

Before embarking on the development of this additional content, however, a comprehensive analysis is essential. It's important to thoroughly understand the socio-demographic characteristics of the players, their in-game behaviors, and any potential pitfalls that could affect their experience. Additionally, maintaining the economic balance of in-game resources is crucial. With a solid understanding of these factors, games can sustain a regular release cycle, ideally adding new and engaging content on a quarterly or even monthly basis, thereby ensuring a continuous stream of value creation through ongoing development commitment.

In the game updates part of the value chain, the value proposition is significantly enhanced through the development of new content that ties back to the base product's narrative or through collaborations with external brands. Additionally, introducing time-limited modes offers temporary yet engaging content that players can enjoy for a restricted period or number of attempts. These additions not only provide fresh engagement opportunities but can also refine the economic dynamics of the game by optimizing modes or enhancing in-game assets.

The delivery of this value primarily occurs within the game's development lifecycle—from concept through to consumption by players within the game client. This process imposes specific demands on operations management, including the need for a robust toolset, effective pre-production practices, meticulous quality assurance, and efficient release management. Beyond the immediate economic benefits derived from these updates, the development of extra modes also holds potential for generating indirect value. This could manifest in future products or partnerships, capturing benefits far beyond the initial scope of the current game update.

Game Updates play a pivotal role in maintaining player engagement, similar to how expanding an entertainment park keeps visitors interested and encourages return visits. Just as new and exciting attractions are essential for keeping an amusement park vibrant, so too are game updates for keeping a video game fresh and engaging. An illustrative example of this in the physical world is the expansion undertaken by Disney. On March 16, 2002, 10 years after opening Disneyland Park in Paris, Disney launched the Walt Disney Studios Park adjacent to it (Figure 3.6). This strategy of continuous expansion and renewal is crucial for sustaining interest and deepening visitor engagement, mirroring the dynamic nature of game updates in maintaining a video game's appeal and relevance over time.

Live Services: Live Services are a crucial element in the value creation chain, providing players with high-fidelity experiences that enhance and extend gameplay. By incorporating LiveOps techniques, these services utilize core gameplay dynamics as well as introduce new modes and content. The aim is to enrich the player's experience and foster engagement, which in turn facilitates additional value through sales in storefronts, personal offers, and other revenue-generating activities conducted outside the core game environment.

Within the scope of LiveOps, teams often implement weekly specials or culturally relevant events that help connect players with their peers or favorite creators. While these events themselves might not directly generate revenue, they offer joint event rewards and achievements that promote prolonged engagement. The strategy behind this is clear: the more time players spend immersed in the game, the greater the likelihood they will make in-game purchases, thereby indirectly driving revenue and enhancing the overall game's economic ecosystem.

In the Live Services part of the value creation chain, the value proposition stems from meticulous analysis of player preferences, regional cultural sensitivities, local influencers, and business partnerships. This analysis is then strategically aligned with in-game events, promotional sales, and additional content to maximize relevance and engagement. The process of delivering this value involves creating enhanced experiences across various platforms, including landing pages, game launchers, or third-party platform integrations. These elements work together to provide a seamless and extended player experience beyond the main game environment.

Value capture in Live Operations is methodically organized through a comprehensive pre-release protocol that includes the development of analytical methodologies, the establishment of data flow systems, storage solutions, and visualization tools. This setup culminates in the production of detailed reports and the collection of feedback from both players and stakeholders. This feedback is crucial for

FIGURE 3.6 Game updates, like new rides in a theme park, add extra content and new game mods to enhance the player experience.

making informed decisions that refine future strategies and operations, ensuring that each element of Live Services is optimized to contribute effectively to the game's ongoing success and player satisfaction.

Live Services in gaming can be likened to how an entertainment park like Disney transforms into a themed village, creating immersive experiences for visitors during special events. Just as game live operations continually refresh the game experience with new events and content, Disney transforms its parks to match seasonal festivities. For example, during the Christmas season, the park might turn into a winter wonderland with twinkling lights lining the streets and a giant tree that brings the spirit of Christmas to life (Figure 3.7). Similarly, for Halloween, visitors might find themselves immersed in a playful, spooky environment filled with adorable ghosts and themed decorations. These transformations are designed to enhance the visitor experience, drawing them back repeatedly, much like live services aim to keep players engaged and returning to the game.

FINANCIAL MODELS AND FORECASTS

Now that you've ensured the studio and its team are aligned with the guiding principles and have a good grasp of the production cycle and value creation in live service games, it's time to examine the fundamentals of the game's financial success. This involves confirming that the game not only starts with a solid concept but also has a business model and financial predictions that support its potential for future success.

Great games are also great businesses. Success in gaming hinges not only on creating exceptional experiences but also on achieving financial success. The sooner this realization is embraced by the team

FIGURE 3.7   Live services, like a theme park during the Christmas season, add in-game events, promotional sales, and additional content to maximize engagement and monetization.

and core players, the smoother the journey becomes. In essence, success boils down to building and managing the product profit and loss (P&L) statement.

Step 1: The team needs to align on what "good" looks like for them and for their investors or stakeholders.

During the pre-launch development phase, games typically require funding as they are not generating revenue. Historically, funding could come from internal sources, such as revenue from the studio's previous games, or external sources, such as publishers or venture funds. Publishers typically acquire game or distribution rights and compensate developers through royalties or revenue sharing. In contrast, venture funds invest in company ownership, expecting returns upon exit or through stock sales at higher enterprise values.

Understanding the incentives and expectations of capital providers is crucial for studios. Publishers prioritize the success of the game itself rather than the studio's profitability. Venture funds, however, focus on enterprise value, which encompasses factors like revenue, profitability (EBITDA), and market outlook, including innovativeness, culture, and public perception. Importantly, subjective factors heavily influence enterprise value, often acting as multipliers for revenue and EBITDA.

Back in late 2023, Electronic Arts had a Price-to-Sales (P/S) ratio of 4.81. Now, what that means is for every dollar of sales they made, their stock was valued at $4.81. On the other hand, by February 2024, Roblox's P/S ratio was 9.96. This suggests that for every dollar of sales Roblox generated over the past year, the stock was valued at $9.96.

This significant difference between the two companies' P/S ratios indicates that investors had more confidence in Roblox's future growth compared to Electronic Arts. Why? Well, it's likely because Roblox is seen as more innovative and technologically advanced. People believe Roblox has better prospects for making money in the future, so they're willing to pay more for each dollar of Roblox's sales compared to Electronic Arts.

Understanding investors' expectations is foundational to building successful video games. While sacrificing profitability for innovation may be acceptable with venture capital, it can be risky with publishers who prioritize game success. Thus, studios must prioritize financial management alongside game development to ensure long-term viability.

Step 2: Understand revenue potential of your game.

Reverse engineering revenue and breaking it down into smaller components—acquisition, retention, and monetization—is a valuable practice (Figure 3.8). By leveraging game design, past experiences, and budgets, developers can identify "goal posts" or ranges where each component is likely to fall compared to competitors.

Beginning with acquisition, several market indicators can aid in establishing these goal posts:

- To begin, the upper limit of a product's acquisition potential is often constrained by the platform or hardware base. For example, a game on a niche VR device cannot surpass the sales numbers of the VR units themselves. Similarly, a high-spec PC game has a more limited audience compared to a lower-spec one. Sources for such insights include market reports and first-party financial reports.
- Conversely, the lower limit is represented by a game with minimal virality that relies solely on paid user acquisition (UA). This can be calculated by dividing the marketing acquisition budget by the market cost per install ratio. Sources for this data include marketing agencies, aggregators, and industry peers.
- Within these boundaries, for premium products, there exists an attach rate over the platform base, determined by similar launches in the past. Historical data, such as recent installs of similar games, serves as a reliable predictor. Market research and industry intelligence providers are valuable sources of such information.
- Additionally, within these boundaries lies a combination of marketing and organic acquisition. Apart from paid media efforts, game teams can estimate the number of players acquired through recommendations or word of mouth. This estimation is influenced by factors such as the game's quality (rating) and Net Promoter Score (NPS). As a rule of thumb, an NPS of 30% would indicate that each player brings in 0.3 players organically, with an associated rating typically falling within the range of 7.4–8.1 out of 10.

By establishing goal posts and evaluating marketing potential and the quality of the game, the game team can estimate acquisition numbers, aligning them across launch and post-launch campaigns and creating different scenarios.

Retention, typically measurable in the late stage of development or during soft launch, can also be understood earlier by identifying retention patterns to make informed decisions.

- Competitors serve as the most reliable source of insights early on. Game teams can utilize market intelligence platforms or networks with peers to gain a ballpark understanding of acceptable retention rates for Day 1 (D1), Day 7 (D7), Day 30 (D30), and so on. Subjective evaluations

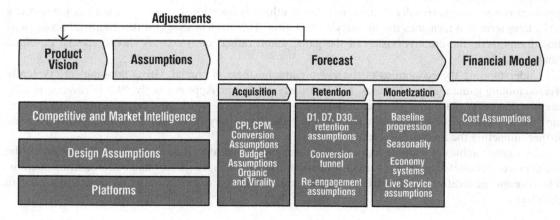

FIGURE 3.8   Game financial model and forecast validation framework.

from early playtesters can also provide valuable feedback by comparing the game to market references in terms of core gameplay loop, meta loop, and social loops, indicating higher or lower levels relative to the market.

- Playtime and short-term retention data from playtesters serve as another indicator. Statisticians have historically grappled with extrapolating results from time-censored data in areas such as drug control and automotive testing. Techniques like the Mean Cumulative Function (MCF) aid in this process by estimating the expected value of metrics over time, such as the number of game sessions, purchases, total playtime, and lifetime value. Additionally, the popular retention rate metric is derived from this estimate applied to the expected number of distinct days played.
- Furthermore, cohorting retention data is helpful. It's likely that initial users will retain much better than later users in the product lifecycle. Teams must account for the degradation of retention over time and continue optimizing for higher retention rates. However, it's inevitable that early metrics will be biased by the most engaged players who start first.

Finally, monetization represents both the most straightforward aspect and the one with the highest variance, necessitating the consideration of a comprehensive toolset and levers early on to fine-tune it effectively. As outlined in the value creation chain, monetization can be broken down into three main components:

1. **Base Game (Baseline):** This is driven by foundational product design and progression systems. It encompasses the initial structure of the game that encourages players to engage with monetization elements.
2. **Game Updates:** These involve the introduction of new content and features in the form of downloadable content (DLCs), season passes, game modes, and other expansions. Regular updates keep the game fresh and provide opportunities for additional monetization.
3. **LiveOps:** This aspect involves the implementation of regular, personalized, and special events within the game. These events are designed to enhance player engagement and offer opportunities for monetization through limited-time offers, exclusive items, and in-game purchases.

By understanding and effectively leveraging these components, game developers can establish a robust monetization strategy that maximizes revenue while providing value to players.

Step 3: Match the cost structure to the business potential.

All too often in the video game industry, the process is approached backward. Game teams often choose an idea they wish to pursue and then formulate revenue forecasts to cover their costs. This approach is not only financially imprudent but also ethically questionable, as it jeopardizes job security in the long term and tarnishes the industry's reputation. This does not suggest that financial projections should supersede the creative vision of the game team; rather, both aspects should coexist on equal terms.

Understanding the economics of the video game business is crucial. Gross bookings are typically divided among game makers, licenses, and first-party platforms. Approximately 30% of revenue is allocated to first-party platforms like Steam or the PlayStation Store, which have become the industry standard for platform fees. Additionally, common engines like Unity or Unreal incur engine license fees, further impacting the revenue structure.

As a game achieves a stable and consistent revenue trajectory, it becomes the cornerstone of the live service, necessitating a focus on unit economics. Live service games must demonstrate sustainable revenue generation compared to ongoing costs, making exploration of the revenue structure essential.

Cost of revenue, including platform fees and licenses directly applied to gross revenue, contributes to gross profit. Gross profit then covers operating expenses such as research and development, content and feature development, game marketing and sales, as well as other operational costs like office spaces and licenses.

Analyzing the economics ensures alignment across various aspects. Average revenue per monthly active user (ARPU) can be dissected based on new versus recycled content, core game progression, and ongoing research and development efforts. Revenue from new content should exceed R&D spending, while marketing and operations expenses should be lower than the cumulative new player acquisition multiplied by the lifetime value.

General and administrative costs lack a direct comparison within the revenue structure but require alignment. These functions often face reductions during business streamlining efforts, yet they are vital for business sustainability. Issues with human resource management, for instance, could lead to talent turnover affecting R&D or marketing efforts.

Functions such as legal or business development have a direct opportunity cost for the business if not properly managed, potentially leading to risks. Therefore, ensuring these functions are well-established is crucial for overall business success.

In the table below we present in broad strokes a skeleton of the P&L for a video game:

CATEGORY	DESCRIPTION	AMOUNT ($)
Revenue		
Gross bookings	Gross revenue from unit sales or in-app purchases	xxxxxxx
Other revenue	Additional revenue sources like licensing or subscriptions	xxxxxxx
Total revenue	Total income generated by the video game	xxxxxxx
Cost of Sales		
Licenses	Royalties for using game engines	xxxxxxx
Server costs	Costs for server hosting and SaaS licenses	xxxxxxx
1st party fees	Fees taken by 1st party platforms, such as Steam, Appstore	xxxxxxx
Total cost of sales	Sum of all costs associated with sales	xxxxxxx
Gross profit	Revenue minus cost of sales	xxxxxxx
Operating Expenses		
Research and development	Costs related to game development, including salaries and outsourcing	xxxxxxx
Marketing and sales	Expenses for marketing activities, PR	xxxxxxx
General and admin.	Overhead costs such as management, real estate, and administrative expenses	xxxxxxx
Depreciation and amort.	Depreciation of assets and amortization of intangible assets	xxxxxxx
Total operating exp.	Sum of all operating expenses	xxxxxxx
Operating income	Gross profit minus total operating expenses	xxxxxxx
Taxes	Estimated taxes owed based on operating income	xxxxxxx
Net profit	Operating income minus taxes	xxxxxxx

VALIDATION

Forecasts and models are constructed based on assumptions regarding retention, monetization, virality, user acquisition, and other components discussed throughout this book. Validation involves verifying whether the software the team is developing aligns with the assumptions that were made.

It's crucial to recognize that any validation conducted without real players is inherently biased. Even stages involving external audiences, such as alpha and closed beta testing, yield skewed results.

Validation of different metrics at various stages of product development can be achieved through the following methods:

- Acquisition:
  - *Incubation and Pre-production*: Conduct competitive analysis focusing on downloads and dynamics of similar games within similar genres and geographies.
  - *Pre-launch*: Monitor wishlists to gauge interest.
  - *Closed Alpha and Closed Beta*: Track community growth, such as Discord channel or newsletter subscribers. A sizable pre-launch community can serve as a direct-to-consumer marketing channel, providing confidence in achieving high acquisition results.
  - *CPI Testing during Soft Launch*: Conduct Cost Per Install (CPI) testing alongside the team's confidence and capacity to scale, validating marketing plans and Go-To-Market (GTM) strategies.
- Virality:
  - *NPS (Net Promoter Score)*: Collect NPS at various stages of development. Despite its subjectivity, NPS offers insight into the game's viral potential by indicating the likelihood of players recommending or promoting the game.
  - *Game Quality*: Seek mock reviews from journalists, streamers, and industry experts to assess the game's standing compared to competitors and its perceived quality.
  - *Referrals and Invitations in Closed Testing*: Establish social structures early in testing to collect data on virality, allowing iterative refinement of game design to maximize confidence at launch.
- Retention:
  - *Gameplay User Testing*: Conduct playtests focusing on core game loops, collecting telemetry and qualitative feedback to refine gameplay.
  - *Internal or Friends and Family Testing*: Regularly and consistently test accessibility, providing valuable insights at a low cost.
  - *Open Alpha or Alpha Weekends*: Gather quantitative data on Day 1–3 retention and potentially Day 7–14, constructing retention and engagement curves.
  - *Closed Beta Testing (CBT) and Soft Launches*: Assess Day 30 retention and engagement metrics.
- Monetization:
  - *Economy Design and Simulations*: Utilize spreadsheets or specialized tools like machinations.io to simulate progression systems and economy design, validating their potential to meet projections.
  - *Soft Launch*: Validate monetization with real players, typically conducted in the mobile space, as there are no equivalents in PC or console spaces.

Decision-making processes are susceptible to two fundamental challenges: **noise and bias** (Figure 3.9). Noise refers to the unwanted variability in judgments and decisions, stemming from differences in individual decision-makers, random variation, and contextual factors. In contrast, bias involves systematic errors or deviations from rationality, leading decision-makers to consistently favor one outcome or perspective over others. While noise introduces inconsistency and unpredictability into decision-making, bias produces consistent but potentially incorrect outcomes. To address these challenges, organizations can implement strategies such as standardization, decision aids, calibration, feedback mechanisms, decision hygiene, collaboration, and continual review. By reducing noise and bias, decision-makers can enhance the quality, reliability, and fairness of their decisions across various domains.

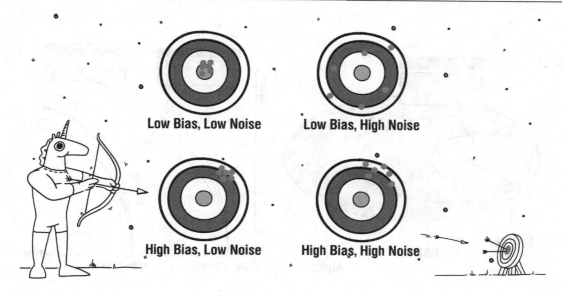

FIGURE 3.9   How noise and bias affect accuracy.

How to work with noise and biases during validation:

- **Test Consistently to Reduce Noise:** Changing methodologies adds noise to measurements. The challenge lies in balancing noise versus biases, which stems from inconsistency and unpredictability. Establishing standards in testing and measurement early on is crucial. While these standards may be far from perfect initially, this is precisely the scenario where perfection becomes the enemy of the good. Applying the same rules, albeit flawed, is preferable to constant changes aimed at improvement. Doing so avoids generating additional noise and ensures oversight of what truly matters.
- What's important is **incremental improvement rather than fixating on absolute metric values**. Absolute values tend to be biased, whereas concentrating on enhancing the specific aspects of your game for the right audience and grasping that formula is significantly more crucial than merely achieving desired absolute values devoid of consideration for noise, bias, and audience context.
- **Understand player personas and profile testers** to the best of your ability. Utilize player segments for weighting and results calibration. Leverage both qualitative and quantitative research to refine your target player categories, aligning them with desired gameplay, themes, and settings of the game, as well as cultural and demographic characteristics useful for future marketing efforts. Monitor metrics such as playtime and active days for each segment to assess how changes within the game, such as new features or content, resonate with different groups. This insight is essential for iterative development, ensuring that updates positively contribute to player satisfaction and lifetime value (LTV).

It's important to acknowledge that your early "free" users, in contrast to paid playtesters, are likely to represent your highest quality players overall, resulting in positively biased results. Therefore, it's reasonable to set higher absolute targets for metrics like retention and monetization, while also anticipating lower ROI on marketing efforts and reduced virality as the game scales.

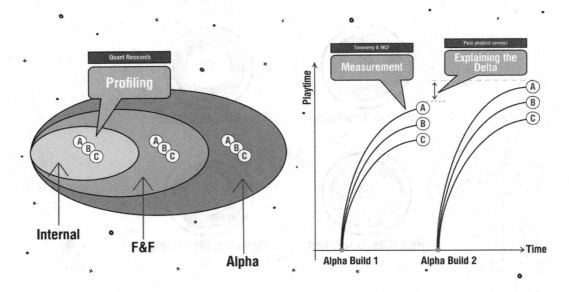

FIGURE 3.10   The iterative game development process, showing how profiling, quantitative research, and feedback from early internal phases to alpha builds refine game design and business strategy.

By meticulously profiling and measuring these aspects (see Figure 3.10) from the alpha or pre-alpha phase, utilizing quantitative research and telemetry, and adjusting based on post-playtest surveys, you establish a feedback loop that drives continuous improvement. This approach not only enhances the game's design and features to meet player expectations but also ensures that the overall business strategy remains robust, well-informed, and adaptable to the evolving gaming landscape.

PART II

Live Outside of Game Updates

The initial release is only the start of a live service game's lifecycle in the market. This part explores the application of traditional marketing frameworks to enhance and extend the player experience in live service games, emphasizing that a game is not just a product but an ongoing service. The role of LiveOps teams is paramount in understanding the game's target audience, crafting effective positioning, and setting content pricing that benefits both the game's profitability and player satisfaction. Effective promotions and a cohesive communication plan are also vital to maintaining player engagement and interest over time.

This part will provide a detailed guide on how to add additional value to live service games. It introduces "The 3 LAPs of Operations" framework, which is essential for transforming a generic gaming experience into a personalized player journey. By adapting strategies from the realms of product and service planning, communications, and go-to-market tactics, LiveOps can enhance player acquisition, engagement, and monetization.

Through practical examples and case studies, you will learn how to implement these marketing principles to keep your game competitive and engaging, maximizing the lifetime value of players and securing long-term success in the dynamic gaming market.

DOI: 10.1201/9781003427056-6

Live Outside of Game Updates

Generating Added Value

4

One of the most important focuses for LiveOps is an increase in the value of the game as a result of particular actions that may include extra or special events, personalization or partnership added by the LiveOps team to increase the willingness to pay. Just as in daily life, if you make a good product, the people will come to you, in the gaming industry the main driving force of the game is the game itself. Managing a live service game is strongly related to managing various types of cycles or player activity, monetization intensity, currency inflation and deflation. A game would typically have a handful of big events that create huge spikes in certain, if not all, game metrics, e.g., Christmas, Halloween, Black Friday, etc.

That being said, when it comes to LiveOps, the end goal of our activities is to generate added value with events outside of key development updates for base product, extra content, or modes. We classify those events in four categories: repeatable, personal, special, and out-of-game.

Repeatable Events are those that put the overall game in the center and occur daily, weekly, or monthly in one form or another (Figure 4.1). Their main focus is to maintain the stability of content consumption and the game economy by tweaking some parameters, such as conversion rates from one in-game currency to another, amplifying revenue during high seasonality, or compensating for a drop. Examples could be weekend specials that incentivize players to play even more or XP multipliers that wash out soft currency. There is plenty of room left for the shorter cycles, such as in-week seasonality (more time on weekends, less time on weekdays) or in-month seasonality (typically related to the salary payroll processing dates in various countries). Events to support that seasonality may need to be optimized and polished as much as possible and repeated over time.

Personal Events are those that put the player in the center and using predictive analytics profile the player's future behavior and preferences to support retention, monetization, or winback activities (Figure 4.2). In parallel we use a set of personal emotional triggers, such as "gained epic medal," to increase relevance and amplify the effect. Unlike repeatable events that adjust product KPI for the overall game, personal events are intended to optimize the content consumption or revenue flow on a player

FIGURE 4.1 Repeatable events are those that put the overall game in the center and occur daily, weekly, or monthly in one form or another.

DOI: 10.1201/9781003427056-7

FIGURE 4.2 Personal events are those that put the player in the center and using predictive analytics profile the player's future behavior and preferences to support retention, monetization, or winback activities.

FIGURE 4.3 Special events are those that highlight cultural or regional features, engaging a large number of players.

level. Each player may have a personal cycle that is related to his or her playstyle, game time patterns, and resource depletion. It may contradict the current seasonal events in a certain way, e.g., when a special activity is targeting heavy retention because of low season, the player may be active and instead appreciate additional discounts to support the gameplay.

Special Events are those that put in the center cultural or regional features like sports events, celebrations, historical reenactment, entertainment, parade, fairs, festival, or similar activities, engage a lot of players, and the conduct of events is reasonably likely to set the theme for weeks or months (Figure 4.3).

FIGURE 4.4 Out-of-game events focus on the human aspect, diversifying the leisure time of gamers when they are not playing.

Special events are content-rich, engaging, and visually attractive to the players; they stand out from the rest and are supposed to be highly relevant to what's currently happening in the player base and could be featured in the season passes.

Out-of-Game Events are those that put the human in the center. While not playing, a gamer is an ordinary human being with the needs to make their leisure time more diverse (Figure 4.4). By essence, traditional in-game channels are not relevant when players spend time outside of the game. Out-of-game events address exactly that. We can leverage different streaming platforms; content creators; or special BizDev collaboration that focus on external and popular cultural beats, such as new movie release, to remind players of the game's existence. For instance, during commuting, a human can watch popular content creators' competition on a streaming platform, level up the skill, plus earn goodies and then go back to the game as a player to spend goodies and use the skill. Players who are exposed to the game through these out-of-game events are more likely to spend additional time in the game. More time in the game means increased engagement and more revenue.

CALENDAR

With so many events occurring, it's essential to have a proper overview of everything planned. No matter how trite it may sound, the calendar is a great tool to see, schedule, and share all the above-mentioned types of events. LiveOps calendar, when established properly, helps to see, schedule, and share all the above-mentioned events (Figure 4.5). Furthermore, it could be a place of agile LiveOps practices to coordinate the team, projects, and processes.

Remember the value creation framework and the purpose of the LiveOps is to propose, deliver, and capture value. The primary value the LiveOps calendar has is the ability to organize value delivery via proposition from the above-mentioned types of events. In order to optimize value delivery operational processes, let's make sure we all have a solid handle on the core needs for all types of events.

Planning Horizon: The foundation of LiveOps calendar is the amount of future it takes into account: 1 month of specificity, and another 2 months of open-to-interpretation planning. For the first one you're

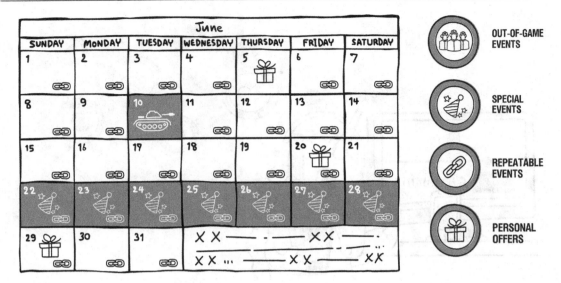

FIGURE 4.5 An example of a game calendar that includes all types of events.

looking for clear-cut aims and cementing repatriable and personal events to support product monthly KPI. For the latter two you're looking for ambition mixed with flexibility and real-world related special and out-of-game events in order to have plenty of time for content creation or contract negotiations. The obvious rationale is that, for the real-world and game-world happenings, your related content needs to come at relevant times.

Balanced Tempo: The salience of modulating event intensity helps to avoid player burnout, or simply put, timing is everything. Planning out your releases isn't just a boon for efficiency; it's actually the only way to get things done at all. So establish the right rhythm, keep it flowing, and make it something your team and your player base can depend on. With LiveOps events, you need to find a middle ground. It's not enough to just release new events that are more of the same. You've got to provide enough exciting, unexpected value to your players while ensuring they stay rested.

Proper Event: Looking at verticals like real-world holidays, real-world major events and happenings, and already established game-world events (and adjacent releases, like movies of the same universe), you'll need to pick the what of LiveOps events. Christmas is approaching—are you doing winback activities with streamers to amplify visibility? The World Cup is coming up—are you throwing in funny betting to incentivize players come back to the game after watching the match? You need to know, on a timed basis, what type of content you'll be giving your audience. And you need to know it well in advance, so you can get the wheels turning for delivery. The calendar is how you do that.

The calendar is the house where plans are made and the team's thoughts are gathered. LiveOps team polishes and nurtures descriptions in a catalogue for repeatable events, establishes clear metadata for personal offers, including triggers and conditions, and aligns special events with products and marketing beats. This may seem obvious, but many teams overlook it, and it turns into the inability to see every project, campaign, or event in a single calendar or failure to keep stakeholders in the loop.

Creating Player's Path 5

When you operate a big game in a large and distributed team, there is a significant challenge. LiveOps has frameworks and operational processes in their disposal to visualize the monthly or quarter plans as really simple and quite straightforward, but then it comes to players who open a game to have fun and face an enormous amount of information (Figure 5.1). Over time, events, campaigns, or collaborations have become much more diverse and complex, which brings the following operations challenges:

- Players possibly encounter an overabundance of monthly events: game updates, regional news, community events, surveys, and more.
- Players encounter communications that are isolated or perhaps irrelevant to their gaming experience.
- Players encounter numerous landing places and access points, such as the website, launcher, stores, and event pages. This can overcomplicate their gaming experience.

Each player's game progression is formed of hundreds of paths that they have been exploring, and it's always important to place the right emphasis on their resulting experience. We want to give each player some kind of promise that, if they stick around in the game, we'll listen to and understand them. We'll evolve the player's generic experience into one that feels like their own unique experience (Figure 5.2).

The game comes first, and there is always a game generic path for all players. Our primary goal is to support this path in premium and in-game shops and to produce in-game and regional events to promote engagement.

However, we can pave each player's individual path through the promotion of relevant content and events. Doing this gives us the power to overcome those aforementioned operational challenges posed by excessive quantity of information, isolation (without context of other game events), and irrelevant content. We need to consider all content that players interact with as data points that can provide us valuable

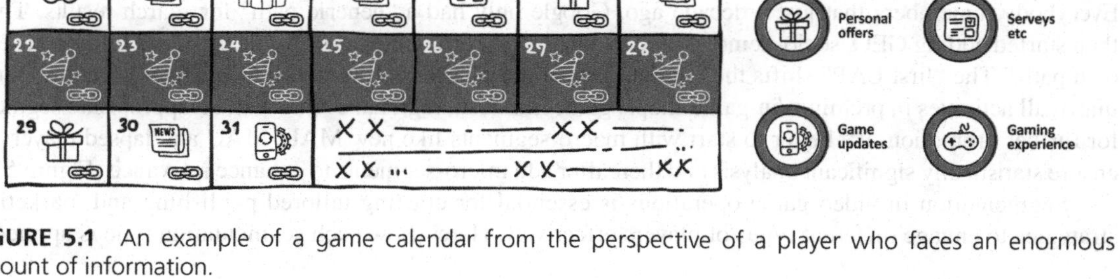

FIGURE 5.1 An example of a game calendar from the perspective of a player who faces an enormous amount of information.

DOI: 10.1201/9781003427056-8

FIGURE 5.2 Helping players navigate the generic game path and create their own experiences enhances engagement.

insights. This could be data from items they interact with in any of the game stores, the in-game missions they take on, regional events that they engage with, and so forth. All of these data points taken together give us a picture of each player. We can use that profile to build a path that's more specific and relevant to them:

- There is no point in promoting every single in-game personage (vehicle, champion, character); it's only worth promoting those that are relevant to the player's level and preferences.
- It can be effective to actively promote special events to players with progression on game assets connected to those events.
- It makes sense to highlight different items to different players. For example, expensive items should be specifically promoted to "whales"—the players we mentioned in a previous module who tend to significantly spend.

We're talking about an evolution from generic to personalized player experience. This is termed the "three LAPs of operations": live around the player, live around the proposition, and live around promotion.

LIVE AROUND THE PLAYER

Everybody remembers that just a decade ago, Google only had a "generic path" for search results. They then started adding GEO, socio-demographic, behavior, and other indicators for the sake of building "user's own path." The "first LAP" shifts the relationship toward player-centric, which means that LiveOps teams match all activities in premium/in-game shops, game missions, regional events with an appropriate segment for further promotion. It's better to start with macro-segments like new MAU, MAU and lapsed players to ensure statistically significant analysis and thereafter add micro-segments to enhance relevance (Figure 5.3).

Segmentation in video game operations is essential for crafting tailored publishing and marketing strategies to engage different types of players effectively. Here's how each segmentation type is applied:

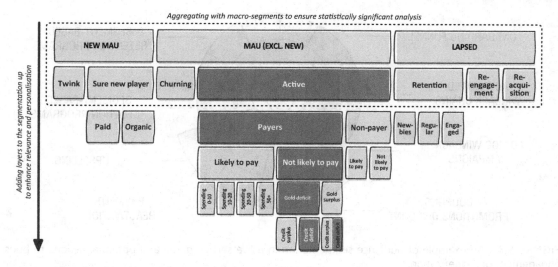

FIGURE 5.3   An example of audience segmentation in a live service game.

- **Marketing Segmentation** involves understanding who the players are and what drives them. This includes analyzing demographics such as age, gender, and location, which provide a statistical overview of the player base. Additionally, psychographics are examined to gain insights into players' psychological attributes like interests, lifestyles, and values, which help in predicting player preferences and behaviors.
- **Motivational Segmentation** delves into the reasons why players are drawn to a game. This can include motivations like seeking challenges, escapism, social interaction, or competition. Using frameworks like those offered by Quantic Foundry, developers can pinpoint the key leitmotifs that attract different audiences to their game, aiding in designing features that resonate with various player segments.
- **Behavioral Segmentation** focuses on how players have interacted with the game in the past. This approach studies patterns of player behavior to identify distinct groups or clusters. A common application of this is in monetization strategies, where players are categorized as Whales (high spenders), Dolphins (moderate spenders), and Minnows (low or non-spenders) based on their spending behaviors.
- **Lifecycle Segmentation** categorizes players according to the progress they've made within the game. Players can be segmented into groups such as beginners, mid-level players, and those at the endgame stage. This segmentation helps in understanding how engaged players are over time and allows for tailored content that suits their stage in the game lifecycle, ensuring sustained interest and engagement.

When the game reaches a stage of maturity and when enough data is collected to build robust segmentation and models, we advise to transition from descriptive to predictive segments—those indicating likely behavior of the player in the near future (1–4 weeks). This approach provides more clarity on the offer design and will be explained in detail in Chapter 14. Descriptive segments are useful from a reporting point of view. It helps you to keep track of your game economy health (How does the share of "Whales" evolve? How did their average check evolve?). But it has limited interest from an operational perspective: "I know that this guy is a Whale, so what?" Predictive segments are still useful for a health check but are also easier to work with from an operational perspective: "This player is likely to stop playing within the upcoming days because of a decreasing sessions length, what can we do to boost his activity?" (Figure 5.4).

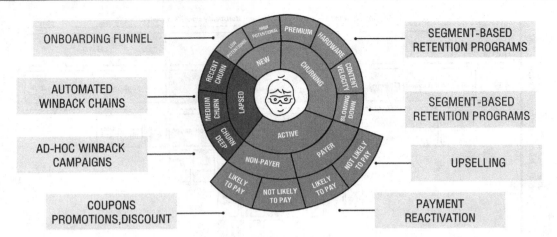

FIGURE 5.4   An example of audience segmentation in a live service game and potential actions to boost engagement or monetization.

Newbies: Perhaps the simplest and the hardest segment to work with are newbies. It is the simplest because the user experience and the observations are typically very easy to collect; the offers are relatively easy to come up with and the first-time user experience (FTUE) is something the game designers dedicate a lot of attention to. Yet, for almost the same reason it is very hard to make a continuous and sustainable impact in this segment outside of the "must" campaigns that should be really a part of the FTUE from the early days of the game. Such campaigns may include player retargeting along the funnel, first-time conversion packs, referral and recommendations for engaged newbies. New players may have different expectations from the game; it is hard to understand that with little to no data about newbies.

Lapsed: This is a category of players who are not actively playing at this moment. The definition of activity normally varies across the industry, titles, genres, etc. Some products decide on a calendar range, such as a 30-day period. For example, if a player didn't make it in MAU of the current month but played before, he or she may be considered as lapsed. As much as it is comfortable for the business modeling and reporting purposes and provides a clear definition for the stakeholders, such an approach doesn't contribute much to the audience management strategies of how to engage with these players. The data can provide a pretty good idea about the probability of certain audience segments returning to the game. For instance, experienced players with months of inactivity may have a higher likelihood of return than a player who played one session a week ago.

- **Recent or Highly Engaged Churners** still remember very well the experience of the game and the emotions are still fresh.
- **Casual Low-Engaged Churners** may remember the game as something from the past and would occasionally return to see how the game evolved in recent times. These guys may typically return for new game modes or new content. Most big game beats have the potential to re-engage—to spark this emotion in lapsed players that would make them want to play again. They need to be content-rich and use broader media to target, as it's unrealistic to expect these players to check our emails. The emotions may be nostalgia, thrill, FOMO, etc.
- **Disinterested** are the truly lost players. Winning them back may sometimes require even bigger effort than new user acquisition. The difference in value, marketing, onboarding between someone who played an hour 5 years ago and someone totally new is that the former may still remember the password. This is the territory of brand marketing.

The lapsed category deserves additional sub-segmentation especially as the game matures. Unpacking it, defining strategies, and analyzing appropriately is a key to effective inactive audience management.

Churners: Player with high likelihood to *leave* the game. This inclination can be observed if the player has been reducing the number of games per day and the number of active days, or if the player's friends had left the game shortly before. In general, it is very hard to stop churn; however, identifying the reason could help retain those players via monetary (giveaways, discounts) or engagement (goal setting) practices.

Non-payers, Likely to Pay: Typically, when a player experiments the game for the first time, we can understand their level of engagement compared to other players from the same time cohort through data. Those with higher comparative levels are usually those with higher likelihood to become your paying players in the future. A first-buyer offer could be designed and suggested at some point of this early experience.

Non-payers, Not Likely to Pay: In the freemium economy this segment will probably be the biggest one. Most of the players will not spend a cent in your game for various reasons; and past a certain point in the player journey, it becomes hard to unlock conversion for these players. However, as we will discuss in the monetization part further, a value of the player is not only in the money he or she brings directly, but also in other contributions, such as referrals (bringing other players, aka virality), creation (contribution to the content of the game), support for other players. Even a player not bringing additional players or contributing to content generation is valuable in a multiplayer game: he contributes to keep the amount of concurrent users (users active at the same time of the day) high, and thus contributes to keep the matchmaking algorithm performance good, allows the developer to avoid using bots, and contributes to the retention (then monetization) of all players by increasing the sense of belonging to a community (think about it: if you login into a multiplayer game and see that only few hundreds of players are active, would you still play this game? Would you spend some money into a game in which you are not sure it will still be alive in 2/3 months?) Don't put a cross on your non-payers, but rather seek for ways to create value through them in a different way.

Active Payers (Likely to Pay): Some players, over time, will start showing a certain pattern of what they purchase and at what frequency or cadency. This information can be used for upselling offer by diversifying the typical basket or by promoting high price points with bonuses and discounts.

Active Payers (Not Likely to Pay): An active player who was previously paying may now be showing signs of not paying in the future. While most players don't follow a consistent payment pattern, they may pay for a few months and then stop for a while, eventually falling into the non-paying category. At this point, they require reactivation to encourage them to start paying again. One common way to reactivate non-paying players is to offer them exclusive discounts or access to rare content. This can incentivize them to start paying again and potentially re-engage with the game. Additionally, if a player has churned for a long time and is unlikely to come back, offering them access to rare content can still trigger their interest and prompt them to return, even if it's just to grab the content for later use.

Resource Deficit: Excessive promotions and high density of events could lead to some players lacking resources to progress at the pace they are used to. This is a specific case of high likelihood of payment where offers should be oriented toward resource packages and currencies.

Resource Surplus: The opposite scenario may result from the economic design of certain features or sales being too generous, leading to players getting significantly more resources per minute spent or per dollar paid. Such states in the economy may result in revenue drops and reduced number of payers. The focus of LiveOps in this case should be in resource depletion and washout through all possible means—promotions, discounts, events, and challenges.

It's important to note that all segmentation practices degrade over time and need to be constantly readjusted. This is simply because the context is always changing, and the data and models get more advanced. In the long run, this evolution would lead to a truly one-to-one personalization where offers and strategies are adjusted and customized for every individual player.

LIVE AROUND THE PROPOSITION

The value proposition, encompassing the combination of offers and messaging, should center squarely on delivering value. It's important to recognize that different player segments perceive value differently, and LiveOps might also attribute unique values to specific items.

The "second LAP" shifts your operational processes toward sorting and matching items, events, news, and updates from a "generic path" to align with the "player's own path." (Figure 5.5). Once you have determined segmentation, it means that you've identified specific triggers and conditions for transitions between segments. One of the challenges for LiveOps teams is to find a value proposition for each segment and cover these segments with appropriate items (which could be a regular product, special offer, hint, or additional highlight about a current game event). For example, you can adjust each monthly plan if you notice that you don't have enough propositions for active players who are likely to spend less than $10, or if there is a game event that better fits particular vehicle/vessel/champion owners, you should plan additional promotions for this segment.

The job of the LiveOps team is to disassemble and analyze what the value proposition for players is at any given point in time. The value for a player can be deconstructed into four layers:

- **Functional:** Quite simply, features and utility. For example, specific weapons can be used in battles and give the player access to different strategies of simply giving them more power, and that power, as well as other stats like accuracy or durability, can vary from weapon to weapon. Different vehicles can have different speeds; upgrades can have varying levels of effectiveness on what they modify. Focusing on this aspect gives players a better understanding of the gameplay and meta gameplay value of different items and how they compare to each other.
- **Financial:** This can refer both to real-world value and the ability to generate more resources in the game. For example, premium account often gives players the ability to farm more resources. The entire battle pass system has its basis in the financial value it offers—players get more resources for the same level of activity if they have a paid battle pass.
- **Intangible:** This component concerns rarity, comfort, confidence, and trust. It's often combined with certain financial or functional characteristics to make them more impactful. For

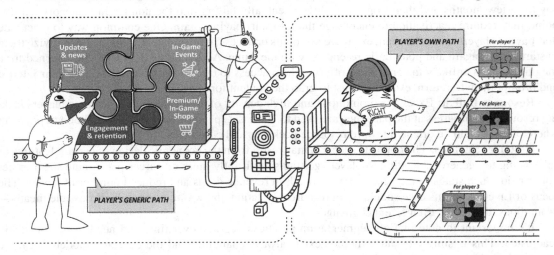

FIGURE 5.5 Match content from the game's generic path and personalize it for each segment to enhance engagement and monetization.

example, "try before you buy" offers the intangible value of the guarantee that you know what you're getting. This aspect typically increases conversions in the decision-making journey. Many subscriptions appeal to consumers' need for comfort and security when it comes to how easy the cancellation process is.

- **Emotional:** Finally, the emotional aspect is the one that can't be easily or practically replicated within the ecosystem. It addresses deep emotional motivations, such as a sense of belonging, grace and glory, a higher purpose, and so on. This is usually the part that can drastically increase the willingness of players to pay without inflating the utility (Figure 5.6).

Let's consider an example of a character in an RPG game:

- It has a certain functional value—this character moves faster and is good for scouting or looting items in the arena. For certain players who like this kind of gameplay, this is an important value.
- Its financial value is also clear—the price point is what a player would expect to pay for this.
- Nothing particularly distinguishes this character from other similar scouts. It's replaceable, and the willingness to pay is likely to be at the price level or lower.
- To encourage players, the LiveOps team may offer free money back if the character doesn't satisfy the player during the first week. This intangible value creates a sense of security.
- Finally, let's imagine this character has an emotional value that speaks to the player. For instance, it could be supporting a cause, such as charity, or it could have a skin from the player's favorite content creator.
- By adding those intangible and emotional components, the character will likely be sold at much higher conversion and quantity than without them.

Propositions made around functional and financial values are usually priced around what kind of utility they provide—this is a great example for commodities: consumables and currencies of all sorts. The willingness to pay rarely exceeds the level historically set for this kind of items and it's hard to generate significant surplus. It doesn't mean anything bad—as we've seen and will be seeing through this book, commodities are essential components of game economy.

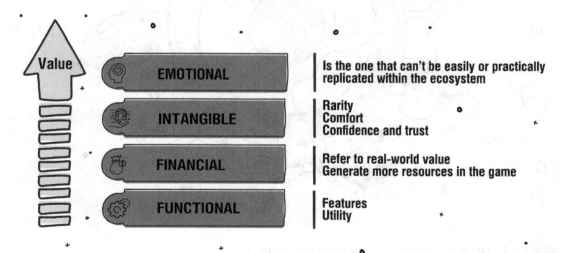

FIGURE 5.6   Four layers of value.

LIVE AROUND THE PROMOTION

As soon as segmentation and appropriate value propositions have been identified, we should move on to the "third LAP" and develop a communication plan to promote products or events to players. The next challenge for the LiveOps teams is to support the positioning, messaging, and designing of communications, as well as gathering and processing players' feedback (Figure 5.7).

There are two main aspects that should be kept in mind creating a communication plan:

Omnichannel: With the rise of communications capabilities (launcher notifications, in-game promo, email, banners, SMS, messengers, etc.), players should have a completely unified and integrated communication experience from the first touchpoint to the last. "Unified" means cohesive creative design in all channels and "integrated" means adjusted next message/channel in response to player's behavior.

The channels are not equal in terms of the coverage, target segment, conversion, impressions, and therefore impact. In the table below we list and compare existing channels in the mix of the Live game promotions.

FIGURE 5.7   Omnichannel and reginal relevant communication.

CHANNEL	PROS	CONS
In-game promo 	The most contextual, as by definition all target audience are active players, therefore typically provides the best conversion for monetization and retention activities.	Can quickly become the most abusive to the player experience if the interactions are not timed and personalized enough. Also, it's rather useless for winback activities.
Launcher promo 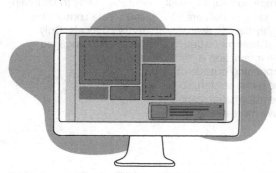	Notifications in the Windows/MacOS tray are visible, small enough to be quickly read, but large enough to be informative. A great channel for winback or re-engagement.	Most of the games don't have a launcher and/or use Epic store, Steam, or similar platforms for distribution.
Email 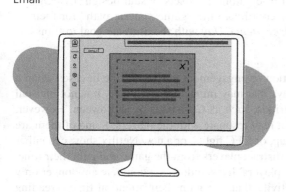	Cheap, reliable, highly personalized. One of the few channels to reach the players who lapsed a long time ago.	Old and unpopular, not required in many games. Typically, it has a very low conversion rate as well.

(Continued)

CHANNEL	PROS	CONS
Social media 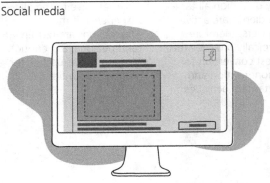	With the help of custom audiences, it provides a way to reach the lapsed audience in an alternative way to email.	Expensive, requires a lot of integration work for some CRM systems. It typically uses emails or other user identifications for matching, which is often low. A big chunk of internet browsing is now happening on mobile—a point to consider.
Mobile apps 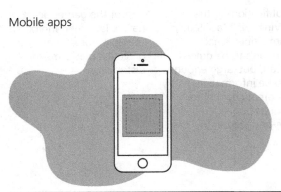	Companion apps as well as game portals are highly flexible ways to deliver messages. The interaction is happening outside of the game session, so the information can have more details.	Requires teams to maintain and create content for those channels. Only suitable for engaged audience.

Regional Relevance: It doesn't necessarily mean re-creating all assets' visual design. LiveOps teams need to step in and make sure that they coordinate the "game generic path" for their regional cultural or emotional triggers like *Independence Day* with the ultimate goal to transform them into serial and sequential events.

A regionally relevant event may be used for monetization or engagement purposes, like in cases when a big country or region is having a series of bank holidays that may impact the activities. It is not unusual to have activity and revenue spikes during holiday periods, such as Christmas or Halloween. However, there are a lot more of smaller or more niche events that may resonate with the players. Some of them are purely cultural while others, such as Football World Cup, or UFC fights, or a new Netflix show can either represent an opportunity or a threat, because they may distract players from the game and gain their time.

In a way, when a game becomes big enough in the players' lives, it does not compete any longer only with other games, but it competes with any other activity that can gain their attention time—reading books, watching TV series, going out. This requires a very careful approach from the operations team not to burn out players, find opportunities to remain in the attention of the audience even outside of the game.

The Three LAPs of Operations

6

Building on our discussion of evolving player experiences from generic to personalized, we now focus on refining these ideas into a practical framework. Known as the "Three LAPs of Operations," this strategy centers around living around the player, the proposition, and the promotion. This approach will serve as an integral methodology, enabling LiveOps to enhance player engagement and sustain game success through focused audience management.

For anyone starting out or looking to improve an existing game, it all starts with a solid foundation. It's essential to clearly understand the what, why, and how of what you're doing. This means knowing exactly what your game aims to achieve, why it matters to your players, and how you'll deliver on those promises.

- WHAT ARE YOU DOING? Your goal is to forge lasting bonds with your players, turning brief encounters into enduring relationships.
- WHY ARE YOU DOING THIS? The aim is to nurture a symbiotic relationship where both parties—developer and player—benefit continuously.
- HOW ARE YOU DOING THIS? This involves identifying distinct player characteristics and customizing interactions to resonate with those specific traits.

With these guiding principles established and in order to have sustainable value creation, we outlined the Three LAPs of Operations (3LAP) framework (Figure 6.1) that answers the following questions:

1. **Who Is the Target Audience?** The idea is to have segments which are small enough and stable within at least 1 week/month. Determine who your target audience is and divide them into actionable segments. This allows you to tailor experiences based on various attributes like progression (measured by the number of battles), engagement (active days per month), and monetization (real money spent). The goal here is to clearly define segment boundaries and prioritize which ones to address first.
2. **What Player's Problems Do We Solve?** As soon as differences between segments have been uncovered, we should find a value proposition for each one within the following areas: engagement, onboarding, winback, and monetization. Address the core issues your players face. Enhance engagement by increasing session durations, boost monetization by refining conversion strategies, improve winback retention, and optimize onboarding to retain new players longer. Values like care, trust, connection, and recognition should be central to your offerings, turning features like game recognition, support reminders, and social connections into compelling reasons to stay engaged.
3. **What Exactly Is Offered?** As soon as value has been identified, we should determine product and price. And price shouldn't be only the money, it could be player's time or any type of advocacies. Innovative pricing strategies, such as offering refunds or rewards based on gameplay milestones, can significantly enhance perceived value.
4. **What Should the Offer Look Like?** As soon as the product has been set up, we should come up with a creative idea. When presenting your offer, simplicity is key. Focus on the main value through clear messaging and visuals, and strategically time your promotions to maximize impact.

DOI: 10.1201/9781003427056-9

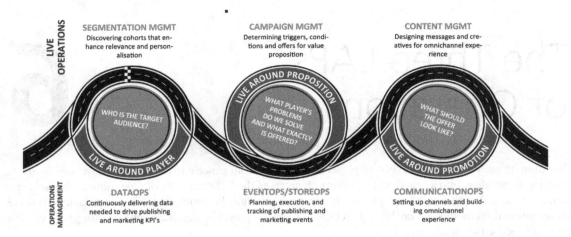

FIGURE 6.1   The 3LAPs of Operations framework.

In live service game operations, there are many intersections between publishing, marketing, operations, and development. The "3LAPs of Operations" framework connects Live Operations and Operations Management responsible for delivering value to the game through technology.

- While LiveOps is discovering cohorts that enhance relevance and personalization, DataOps should continuously deliver data and maintain segmentation.
- While LiveOps determines triggers, conditions, and offers for a value proposition, EventOps/ StoreOps should continuously manage storefronts, set up events, and launch campaigns.
- While LiveOps is designing messages and creatives for an omnichannel experience, CommunicationOps should continuously set up channels and build this experience.

On the horizontal dimension, we have three LAPs of questions-driven progression and on the vertical dimension, we have some kind of bridges for each of the LAPs between LiveOps and Operations Management responsibilities.

PART III

LiveOps Techniques

The part on LiveOps techniques presents methods for making Free-to-Play games financially successful. It explains that games need to continuously attract new players, ensure these players stay interested over time, and find ways to earn revenue from the player base. By creating a game that players are excited to join and want to keep playing, developers can encourage a natural growth in their user base. As players become invested in the game, some will choose to spend money, which the game can then reinvest in attracting more new players. This funnel (Figure III.1) is sustained by incorporating in-game events and tailoring experiences to individual player preferences, which enhances the game's appeal and longevity.

Navigating the dynamic world of live services games hinges on a single, yet multifaceted metric: the Lifetime Value (LTV) of its players. While LTV serves as the ultimate "North Star" for product decisions, it's worth noting that calculating this metric can sometimes be a complex endeavor due to the various methodologies involved. We'll delve deeper into the intricacies of calculating LTV in Chapter 14. For the scope of this chapter, however, think of LTV less as a numerical value and more as a guiding principle.

We explore the role of Acquisition in shaping the LTV. The "Virality" component reminds us that a player's value isn't just in their wallet; it's also in their network. Effective acquisition strategies ensure that the cost per player remains lower than their LTV, a fundamental tenet of a profitable model.

Next, we tackle the critical issue of Engagement. A game's revenue model is only as robust as its ability to retain players over time. This is where the "Retention" variable in the LTV equation comes into play. Strategies that extend player engagement ultimately inflate their lifetime value, making retention a focal point of any successful LiveOps strategy.

Monetization is an integral aspect of the LTV function. It addresses critical variables such as the "Percentage of Payers" and "Spending," yet it does so in a way that naturally complements a well-designed

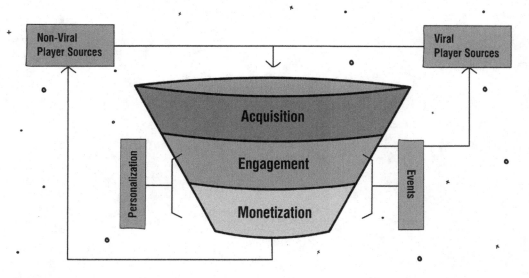

FIGURE III.1 Acquisition, engagement, and monetization funnel.

DOI: 10.1201/9781003427056-10

game. The true art lies in creating a balance between free and paid experiences that not only attracts players but also nurtures them into becoming long-term, valuable members of the gaming community.

Game event is a time-limited experience that seamlessly combines core gameplay features with new mechanics to optimize both player engagement and monetization. It offers the flexibility to tweak the game's economy or retention on the fly, all without necessitating developer involvement.

Personalization serves as a dual engine for both retention and monetization within the gaming ecosystem. By crafting a tailored experience, you not only heighten player engagement, thereby increasing retention, but also create a pathway for players to find value in premium offerings. This enhanced user experience often translates into a greater willingness to spend, thus positively impacting two key components of the LTV function.

By diving deep into each of these facets, we aim to provide a comprehensive toolkit for optimizing the LTV of your players. As the saying goes, "you can either increase the number of customers or the value of those customers." In the world of live service games, achieving a high LTV means succeeding in doing both.

Acquisition 7

The distribution of video games has transformed from a predominantly physical process involving publishers, manufacturing of media like cartridges and discs, and retail distribution, to a digital-centric model facilitated by the internet. Historically, developers and publishers would produce a master copy for manufacturing, relying on retailers for game visibility and sales. Notably, companies like Nintendo continue to utilize physical sales for their first-party titles, highlighting the ongoing relevance of physical distribution. However, the shift to digital distribution has streamlined game delivery, reducing costs and enhancing efficiency. This shift also parallels a move from traditional brand marketing to acquisition strategies focused on digital platforms, leveraging influencers and community engagement for marketing.

To give this some perspective, historically AAA video games, much like Hollywood blockbusters, follow a rigorous marketing cycle. These games are often announced years in advance, building anticipation through a carefully curated mix of content, social media buzz, and public relations activities, all bolstered by hefty marketing investments and widespread media buying. The intensity and scale of these campaigns can be staggering. For example, the 2014 release of the game *Destiny* was accompanied by an enormous marketing budget. This budget encompassed a high-profile live-action trailer featuring the likes of Peter Dinklage, set to Led Zeppelin's music, and a massive TV-ad campaign estimated at $6.7M focused heavily on *The Simpsons* marathon and the NFL.

Apex Legends, created by Respawn Entertainment and published by EA, is the opposite example, exploding onto the gaming scene with a bang. It quickly became the #1 most watched title on Twitch in February 2019, garnering a whopping 63.7 million live hours watched within 10 days after its release. Approximately 21% of core PC gamers in the US played *Apex Legends* within the first week. This video game made history by launching without any typical marketing strategies. The reason why I chose *Apex Legends* is that their launch was an early indicator of where marketing is heading as Generations Z and Alpha continue to grow and technology shifts toward engagement strategies. They strategically leveraged a keen understanding of emerging influencer marketing and the virality effect to ignite organic growth.

Live games are constantly being updated by their nature and user acquisition is an ongoing process. It's not just about catching the attention of players anymore; it's about drawing in individuals who will actively engage with the game and contribute to its community. When it comes to methods for acquiring players, we can broadly categorize them into three streams:

- **Paid user acquisition (UA),** which involves scaling up the player base through media buying and advertising campaigns. This can be done on third-party platforms such as social media networks like Facebook and Instagram, search engines, or video content platforms like YouTube. Paid UA allows for targeting, ensuring that the right message reaches players who are most likely to be interested. However, relying on paid UA might not be cost-effective or sustainable as a long-term growth strategy.
- **Earned user acquisition (UA),** which stems from the games appeal and generates buzz. This includes opportunities to feature the game on gaming platforms like Steam and Epic Games Store, collaboration with influencers, and receiving positive media coverage. Each of these second-party channels for promotion is earned through the game's quality and appeal. Influencer marketing requires human management to establish authentic connections with content creators who can genuinely endorse the game to their followers. Platform relations require

DOI: 10.1201/9781003427056-11

business team and development efforts to integrate a platform's priority features and technology to obtain editorial support. Press outreach translates into positive publicity through traditional news releases, story pitches, press conferences, and other strategies that build friendly relationships with reporters, editors, bloggers, and other media representatives.

- **Owned user acquisition (UA)** takes advantage of the game's internal channels and own player base. This may involve content marketing on game's websites, video content creation, or fostering a vibrant engaging community. It encompasses utilizing word-of-mouth promotion where satisfied players become advocates for the game, bringing in new users through their networks.

This chapter delves into five key components of video game distribution that are essential for understanding user acquisition strategies: platforms, business models, media mix and segmentation, intellectual property (IP) and partnerships, and the roles of influencers and community. Additionally, we explore the concept of virality, a significant yet elusive driver of growth, emphasizing its potential impact on expanding the player base. While not exhaustive in covering the vast landscape of video game marketing, this segment prioritizes aspects most pertinent to Live Operations, highlighting the nuanced process of managing influencer marketing campaigns as a detailed case study that may serve as a model for other acquisition efforts.

The focus here isn't to prompt marketers to completely rethink their product launch strategies, but to shed light on the complexities of media buying and the broader scope of activities, including offline advertising, typically managed by marketing departments. Given that LiveOps doesn't encompass these broader marketing activities, the aim of this chapter is to outline critical factors for an effective user acquisition strategy. It further illustrates how LiveOps can tap into viral growth by enhancing player engagement and leveraging collaborations with influencers, thereby contributing to a comprehensive approach to drawing new players into the game.

PLATFORMS

Traditionally, video game distribution has revolved around platforms, with industry giants such as Sony, Nintendo, Microsoft, and previously Sega playing pivotal roles in promoting titles and shaping the industry. The PC, owing to its decentralized nature, initially stood apart, but with the emergence of platforms like Steam, it too has transitioned toward a more centralized and aggregated approach.

Platforms typically charge game companies fees or revenue shares for access to aggregated, high-quality gaming audiences. While platforms offer a wide range of services including payments and social features, audience reach remains their primary driver of success.

The platform mix is thus a key driver of game growth, with availability across multiple platforms maximizing audience reach. However, this comes at a cost—both financial and operational. Financially, platforms may charge up to 30% of a game's revenue in fees, sometimes exceeding the game maker's own margins. Operationally, publishing on platforms means relinquishing full ownership of the audience. Platforms may restrict game makers from maintaining their own premium shops, account systems, conducting price discriminations and discounts, or employing certain technologies (e.g., Steam's stance on blockchain). From a business perspective, platforms are generally uninterested in games building relationships with players outside of their ecosystems.

Nevertheless, the platform-driven growth of games cannot be disregarded due to the size and quality of the audience they offer. This is particularly true for console and mobile platforms, where technical constraints may limit alternatives. (Note: At the time of our writing, mobile third-party app stores are subject to legislative discussions.)

Even on the PC, where self-publishing is feasible, it comes with its own set of challenges. Developers must bear the costs of maintaining a launcher, commerce infrastructure, and data centers. Moreover, significant user acquisition efforts are required to drive traffic to the game's website and guide users through the conversion funnel. However, notable successes such as *Palworld*, *Enshrouded*, as well as earlier titles like *V-Rising*, *Valheim*, and *Stardew Valley* demonstrate the potential for success by simply placing a game on platforms like Steam, without significant marketing investment.

What are the important things to keep in mind when platforms are part of your game's growth strategy?

1. **"The winner takes it all": Ratings and recommendations** serve as the primary drivers of growth on platforms. Algorithms that determine game placements in recommended sections or top charts rely heavily on metrics such as installation numbers, player engagement, and overall satisfaction. The more players install and enjoy your game, the higher the likelihood it will be featured in recommendations, thus attracting even more players to try it out. High ratings not only boost visibility but also contribute to a higher conversion rate from awareness to wish list to installation. Conversely, low ratings and a toxic community can quickly diminish momentum and negate the positive effects a game might receive from platforms.

2. **Eventfulness and featuring** are also key factors in driving visibility on platforms. Games that receive frequent updates and quality enhancements often garner higher visibility through news announcements, banners, and targeted customer relationship management (CRM) efforts. Events, sometimes accompanied by discounts, provide an excellent opportunity to re-engage existing players and monetize their continued involvement in the game, while also attracting new players through platform promotions.

3. **Seasonality** plays a significant role in platform dynamics. Platforms facilitate many-to-many relationships between a diverse array of publishers, developers, and a broad audience. Consequently, large, successful games tend to monopolize audience attention during major events and updates, potentially overshadowing smaller games. Therefore, conducting competitive analysis and closely monitoring market trends become essential for timing and prioritizing events to maximize visibility and player engagement.

Platform-based operations can be a viable strategy on PC, and many games have achieved sustainable success this way. Operating through platforms may not even be a choice, especially in the case of consoles or mobile devices. While all the points mentioned above are relevant to these devices, competition manifests in different areas such as business models, media and marketing, IPs, and community engagement.

BUSINESS MODEL

The choice of business model is a crucial aspect that influences not only the future monetization potential of a game but also its acquisition potential and room for optimization. We explore the interplay between Freemium, Subscription, and Premium models. Each approach presents a unique pathway for user acquisition and revenue generation, tailored to different player preferences and market dynamics. The discussion extends to the operational nuances of implementing these models, their market positioning, and their impact on user acquisition. The aim is to provide insights into the effectiveness of each business model within the evolving framework of live service games, setting the stage for a deeper understanding of their roles in the user acquisition.

Freemium

Freemium models have emerged as quintessential elements in the landscape of Live Services games, with the entirety of their revenue being garnered through active, ongoing player engagement and acquisitions. At its core, the Freemium business model is pivotal for strategies aimed at user acquisition. By granting access to the game at no cost, developers open the doors wide to a vast potential audience, anyone with an internet connection, a suitable gaming device, and a penchant for the game's genre, thereby broadening the acquisition funnel significantly.

Gone are the days when the mere absence of a price tag was a sufficient draw for gamers. In today's saturated market, free games abound across all genres and quality levels, making it evident that simply removing the price barrier is not enough to secure a competitive advantage in player acquisition. Freemium games must be easily accessible, ready for optimization, and incorporate scale as a critical factor.

Scale: Perhaps one of the most significant decisions occurs even before the game's launch: determining the target audience and understanding its social demographics. Ultimately, this choice influences the size of the user base the game can attract and dictates the product design needed to satisfy the preferences and needs of the target segment. Competition within the segment is also a critical factor to consider, particularly in highly saturated genres like *First-Person Shooters* (FPS). Numerous sources, ranging from free sources like streaming statistics and Steam data to more sophisticated and sometimes costly market research, can inform this decision-making process, allowing for a more tailored approach.

Epic Games targeted a wide demographic with *Fortnite*, aiming for a broad appeal across age groups and gaming preferences. Their decision to incorporate elements like building mechanics alongside traditional shooting gameplay contributed to its massive success and ability to attract a diverse player base. Riot Games strategically targeted the competitive gaming community with *League of Legends*, understanding the potential for growth in the emerging esports scene. By offering a free-to-play model and focusing on regular updates and competitive events, they built a large and dedicated player base.

Accessibility: Understanding the scale of your potential target audience and deciding to adopt the Freemium model necessitates a streamlined process to maximize user acquisition efficiently. The acquisition funnel is a marketer's critical tool in the freemium realm, enabling the team to discern optimal acquisition and onboarding strategies. If we consider video game distribution from the final stages of software development to the initial interactions with players, the freemium strategy largely revolves around streamlining this process. Simply removing payment barriers isn't enough; it doesn't provide a competitive edge against other freemium games. Eliminating other obstacles—whether they're platform-related, concerning user experience, or psychological—can significantly enhance the free-to-play acquisition strategy. For example, improving game accessibility can involve launching a "light" version for swift download, letting players begin immediately as the full game loads in the background. This strategy accelerates entry, enhances user experience by offering instant gratification, and reduces wait times, thereby streamlining the acquisition process.

Roblox is a platform that hosts a multitude of user-generated games across various genres, all accessible for free. Its accessibility lies in its cross-platform compatibility, allowing players to access the platform and its games on PC, mobile devices, and consoles. Additionally, Roblox's simple user interface and intuitive game creation tools enable players of all ages to create and share their own games easily. This accessibility has contributed to Roblox's immense popularity, making it a favorite among gamers worldwide.

Optimization: Central to this is the understanding that the acquisition funnel acts as a critical radar for optimization throughout the entire user journey, from initial contact via acquisition channels to engagement milestones like the first login or battle. Success in the free-to-play model hinges not just on the product but significantly on the team's ability to leverage every stage of this process, integrating data points for comprehensive analysis. As the game and its strategy evolve, teams must remain agile, using insights on audience behavior, channel performance, and other variables to refine their approach. Sustaining a robust free-to-play strategy necessitates a dedicated investment in the team's capabilities, encompassing not only their expertise but also their ability to use insights and tools effectively, fostering a culture of continuous improvement and strategic adaptation.

Supercell continuously optimizes *Clash Royale* by analyzing player data and adjusting gameplay balance and monetization strategies accordingly. Regular updates and balance changes keep the game fresh and engaging while ensuring a fair playing field for all players. King, the developer of *Candy Crush Saga*, utilizes data analytics to optimize the game's monetization strategy. By analyzing player behavior and purchasing patterns, they can tailor in-game offers and promotions to maximize revenue without compromising player experience.

Subscriptions

Subscriptions offer access to a catalogue of games in exchange for a regular subscription fee. Similar to platforms, subscriptions grant access to audiences while imposing a fixed fee, the distribution of which to game developers occurs based on platform subscription agreement with a game. Typically, this involves a distribution model based on overall player engagement: the more players engage with a particular game, the greater share of the subscription revenue it receives. Subscriptions present a viable avenue for games to reach audiences they might not otherwise access. For instance, even renowned titles like *League of Legends* are now available on platforms such as Xbox Game Pass, demonstrating the potential for one of the world's largest free-to-play games to tap into the subscriber base of Game Pass.

Developed by Rare and published by Microsoft Studios, *Sea of Thieves* is an open-world multiplayer pirate adventure game. Initially launched in 2018, the game received mixed reviews regarding its content and depth. However, after being included in Xbox Game Pass, *Sea of Thieves* saw a significant increase in its player base. The subscription model allowed players to try out the game without committing to a full purchase, leading to increased engagement and a thriving community. Over time, Rare continued to support and expand the game with regular updates and new content, further fueling its growth within the subscription service.

Alternatively, subscription is a good option for a game that is retaining and very engaging but may lack some monetization options, for instance, in genres that typically serve a younger audience or genres that are not typically fit for monetization techniques. Think about things like cozy games; for instance, it's not a great option, and if there is no monetization, there will be no lifetime value generation. Similarly, free-to-play games are viable options for subscriptions to reach large audience numbers and potentially to get higher shares of subscriptions because of their super high engagement phase and playtime while still being very monetization-friendly to the player base.

In today's market, there are numerous subscriptions that have appeared. Subscription by Netflix, game subscription services by Apple Arcade, and Microsoft Game Pass are just a few examples. Subscriptions lie at the intersection of acquisition, retention, and monetization in the gaming industry. From an acquisition perspective, subscriptions offer a solution to the financial barriers associated with gaming. By paying a monthly fee, players gain access to a library of games without the need to purchase each title individually. This model is particularly attractive to younger audiences or individuals with limited disposable income.

From a product strategy standpoint, the acquisition avenue for subscriptions becomes more compelling for games approaching the end of their lifecycle or those struggling to leverage other acquisition options effectively.

Subscriptions provide game teams with a relatively straightforward way to generate lifetime value from their players. Yet this LTV is capped. It's crucial to recognize that once subscribers commit, it becomes challenging, if not impossible, to surpass this revenue threshold. Additionally, there's the challenge of competing with other games available within the subscription service. Therefore, the attractiveness of subscription models is heightened for games lacking a scalable organizational system or those that have already recouped their investment and are in the twilight of their lifecycle.

The appeal of subscription options for customers is undeniable. It's essential for game teams to carefully consider their target audience and ensure alignment with the subscription platform in terms of target demographics. Sometimes, subscription platforms offer a minimum guarantee, which serves as a baseline investment ensuring developers recoup their initial investment.

Premium

Premium business models for selling video games are among the oldest in the industry and continue to be a dynamic category. This vitality partly stems from premium games adopting live service features and incorporating lifetime value aspects in addition to the initial purchase price. Charging an upfront cost for players to start playing the game significantly contributes to the game's lifetime value and ensures sustainability for the game maker and the company's economy in the long run, even if the game transitions to supporting the game with live service months later.

Additional appeal of the premium business model emerged as a response to the rising popularity of the free-to-play model. The free-to-play games have been flooded with questionable practices from its inception, utilizing dark patterns such as gambling and *Gacha* loot boxes, and often lacking transparency. Consequently, players have grown to value the straightforwardness of paying once for a premium game without the expectation of future payments. This aspect significantly attracts the premium game audience, particularly on platforms like Steam, where payment methods and player details are readily stored, thereby eliminating a major payment obstacle that used to exist.

Another strategy adopted by some premium video game teams for user acquisition is gradually decreasing the price of a premium game until it becomes free to play. This approach allows the game team sufficient time to create enough content to sustain the game in a free-to-play model. For instance, *Destiny 2*, initially launched as a premium title, made a significant pivot toward the free-to-play model with the introduction of *New Light*. This version allowed new players to experience a vast portion of the game's content without upfront costs, including access to a variety of planets, strikes, and PvP modes, effectively rejuvenating the game's user base. Similarly, *The Sims 4* employed a transitional strategy by initially offering the game at a premium price before making the base game free to play. This shift opened the door for a new wave of players intrigued by the life-simulation game. By lowering the entry barrier, EA aimed to attract a broader audience, hoping to monetize through the extensive catalogue of expansions, game packs, and stuff packs that add depth and variety to the game experience.

The success of a premium game launch and its user acquisition largely depends on the game team's ability to forecast sales accurately. Operating a premium game entails significant risk due to the volatility and unpredictability of the initial audience. This is influenced by factors such as game quality, target audience, marketing campaigns, publisher reputation, and others. For games that can successfully predict the size of their audience, the premium model can provide a competitive advantage. Consider games like *EA Sports FC*, *NHL*, or *Madden*, which have annualized release cycles. Knowledge about previous releases enables the game team to accurately estimate the number of copies of the next version that will be sold.

Pricing is a crucial component of premium game acquisition. When considering pricing, two key factors must be taken into account: price sensitivity at launch and price elasticity for the game's lifespan, especially in relation to life service acquisition. Price sensitivity refers to the extent to which the price of your game affects players' willingness to purchase it. It is useful to understand price sensitivity, whether it's at the product launch, a significant milestone, or when considering changes to the game that necessitate a price review.

In the context of video game pricing, the Van Westendorp Price Sensitivity Meter (PSM) offers valuable insights through its four key questions and derived metrics such as Points of Marginal Cheapness (PMC) and Points of Marginal Expensiveness (PME).

The model's initial questions probe consumers' perceptions of price thresholds, determining the price points at which a product is deemed too expensive, too cheap, a bargain, or starting to get expensive. Derived metrics such as PMC and PME provide additional granularity, indicating the price range where consumers perceive the game as too cheap or too expensive, respectively.

By leveraging these insights, video game developers and publishers can tailor their pricing strategies effectively:

- They can avoid underpricing by identifying the PMC, ensuring that the game's price doesn't signal low quality or value.
- Similarly, understanding the PME helps in setting a price that maximizes revenue without deterring potential buyers, striking a balance between perceived value and affordability. This comprehensive approach empowers companies to set prices that resonate with consumers' perceptions and market demand, ultimately optimizing sales and profitability in the competitive video game industry (Figure 7.1).

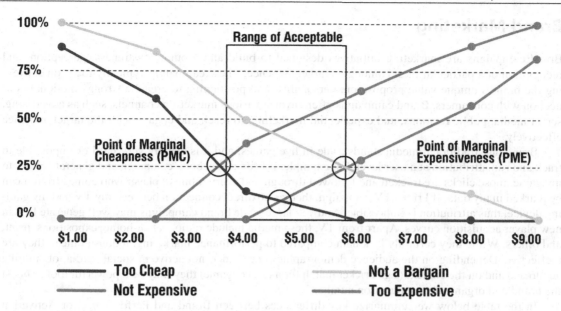

FIGURE 7.1 The Price Sensitivity Meter (PSM) helps determine the psychologically acceptable range of prices for a single product or service.

Price elasticity, on the other hand, gauges the extent to which your sales or installations will be impacted by changes in price. This metric proves particularly valuable when devising discounts and price promotions. Continuously monitoring elasticity over time aids in comprehending the optimal frequency for price adjustments.

If discounting or running a price promotion by 20% results in a 30% increase in installations, it indicates that price elasticity is working in your favor. Perhaps an extreme case of price elasticity that adds freemium spine on premium model is demos. A demo is a limited version of a game intended to let interested gamers try it before purchasing. It's important to note that unlike in freemium live service where FTUE is consistently polished and optimized, premium demos don't usually follow the same trajectory and just offer a very limited window into the game—usually just a few levels or features. This puts a risk on conversion if demos are not good, or don't accurately capture the good parts of the game. Nevertheless, they can be incredibly helpful for new franchises that players may have concerns about.

MEDIA MIX

The choices of platforms and business models are strategic decisions. There is little to no room for maneuvering when those choices are made. What allows games to scale on an ongoing basis are marketing campaigns and activations. These are more traditional media buying and advertising practices that we will try to unpack in this part of the chapter.

As a disclaimer, the topic of media buying and advertising is a complex one and we will only be able to touch the surface in this book. However, we will try to provide the necessary elements for LiveOps professionals to better understand the marketing acquisition angle of the product management. In a later part on influencers we will cover more tactical aspects of marketing campaign management, which are applicable to other media with caveats.

Brand Marketing

Brand campaigns are marketing initiatives designed to build and promote awareness, perception, and recognition of a particular brand among its target audience. These campaigns typically focus on conveying the brand's unique value proposition, personality, and positioning to create a strong emotional connection with consumers. Brand campaigns often involve various marketing channels, such as advertising, social media, public relations, and experiential marketing, to reach and engage with the target audience effectively.

Brand and traditional media stands aside in live games, and it is usually very hard or impossible to track and run attribution at a user level. For example, if I run a Facebook campaign and generate clicks to my game, those clicks are tracked and followed through and every (almost) player who comes from it can be marked in my data. If I run a TV campaign, there is no direct connection between my TV and my gaming device, thus attribution is impossible. And yet, large-scale brand campaigns may well generate lifts in new player acquisition curves. Apart from TV, these media include radio, out-of-home, expositions, print, and others. While they certainly lack data compared to performance marketing, it doesn't mean they are ineffective. Depending on the audience demographics (e.g., older, not active in social media, or running ad blocks) and on the context (e.g., cricket match for a cricket game) they may be a powerful tool to boost the brand and organic user acquisition numbers.

In the table below we summarize key differences between Brand and Performance, or Activation campaigns.

ASPECT	BRAND CAMPAIGNS	ACTIVATION CAMPAIGNS
Focus	Long-term brand equity and recognition	Immediate sales or responses
Goal	Build emotional connections and brand perception	Drive short-term results
Emphasis	Storytelling, brand identity, values	Promotions, discounts, direct response tactics
Channels	TV, print, digital display	Email marketing, social media ads, search ads
Success metrics	Brand awareness, perception, loyalty	Sales, leads, click-through rates
Impact	Slower, sustained influence on consumer behavior	Quick, direct impact on consumer behavior

Game companies have a sort of love-and-hate relationship with Brand campaigns. On the one hand Brand campaigns lack established and widely accepted measurement methodology like digital activation campaigns (we will discuss challenges with those in the future). This makes performance-driven marketers skeptical of the efficiency of brand campaigns. On the other hand, the video industry has been historically very big on events, such as PAX, Gamescom, Tokyo Games Show, Paris Games Week, etc. The importance of gaming press and journalism is also undeniable. It is hard to attribute a clear ROI to press relations and events; however, they are widely considered as essential especially when launching AAA games.

For many games and channels the brand advertising is simply irrelevant. Consider a hyper-casual mobile space that is incredibly saturated with audiences pretty much contained within the segment and re-targeted from one game to another for snackable content without much of the emotional connection.

For bigger brands with long-lasting ambitions and live service approach, brand building is crucial. And while strong brands can be built without large investments in media buying, like in the case of *League of Legends*, that was driven by the community rather than media spend. Although Riot did invest heavily in esports which can be arguably considered as a branding activity.

So what makes brand media a viable option to support user acquisition? While figuring this out is beyond the goal of this chapter, here are a few points that can add perspective on this:

1. **Choose brand media when other options don't work**. It is incredibly hard, if not impossible, to tell compelling stories that create lasting impressions with performance ads and search engine marketing. Mass-reach channels and quality content are particularly effective in capturing attention and resonating with audiences.

   Naughty Dog's marketing campaign for *The Last of Us Part II* relied heavily on compelling storytelling through cinematic trailers. These trailers, released on mass-reach channels like YouTube and social media platforms, created lasting impressions with audiences by showcasing the game's emotional narrative and high production values. The intense and immersive storytelling captured the attention of both gamers and non-gamers alike, generating significant buzz and anticipation for the game's release.

2. **Find a sweet spot between seasonality, cost of media, and target audience indexing**. It's important to remember that in traditional brand media the cost is driven by other actors rather than video games competitors. These channels are commonly used by luxury brands, car manufacturers, fashion, retail chains, consumer products, etc. *World of Tanks* is one of the games that leveraged TV advertising effectively to grow the audience. In the early days of scaling in the West, the *World of Tanks* marketing team ran brand campaigns regularly and successfully. The key element was strategic media buying at periods with lower cost for consumer brands while the target audience was actively playing the game. In January, for instance, players were actively playing with higher engagement rate, but media cost was lower following a busy and expensive end-of-year period.

   Nintendo's marketing strategy for *Animal Crossing: New Horizons* capitalized on seasonality and strategic media buying. The game was released in March 2020, coinciding with the onset of the COVID-19 pandemic and global lockdowns. Nintendo leveraged this timing to target audiences seeking escapism and social interaction during quarantine. By strategically running brand campaigns during periods of increased engagement and lower media costs, such as summer vacations or holiday seasons, Nintendo maximized its reach and audience engagement.

3. **Integrate cross-channel campaigns**. Combine mass-reach channels with other marketing channels for a cohesive brand experience. Look at effects across both organic users, re-engagement, and decreased cost per acquisition for performance channels.

   Epic Games' marketing approach for *Fortnite* involves integrating cross-channel campaigns to create a cohesive brand experience. For example, when promoting in-game events or new content updates, Epic Games utilizes a combination of mass-reach channels like social media, influencer partnerships, and traditional media outlets to reach a diverse audience. By leveraging multiple marketing channels simultaneously, *Fortnite* ensures maximum exposure and engagement across different demographics, leading to increased organic user growth and decreased cost per acquisition.

4. **Optimize creative content.** Coming up with a whole new brand creative each time is akin to gambling—it is expensive and very unclear if it will deliver. Use digital channels to understand what works before investing heavily. Don't come up with a whole new creative, but rather develop on top of what already works. Maintain a presence with consistent yet new content to build and reinforce brand awareness over time.

   Activision's *Call of Duty* franchise employs an iterative approach to creative content development. Rather than constantly reinventing the wheel with each marketing campaign, Activision builds on what works. By analyzing data from digital channels such as social media engagement, website traffic, and player feedback, Activision identifies successful themes, narratives, and visuals. They then incorporate these elements into new marketing materials while refining and optimizing them based on performance metrics. This iterative process allows *Call of Duty* to maintain a consistent brand presence while continuously evolving and adapting its creative content to resonate with audiences.

In conclusion, while brand campaigns in the gaming industry face skepticism due to challenges in measurement and attribution, they remain an integral part of marketing strategies, particularly for larger brands with long-term goals. Events, gaming press, and community engagement are crucial for building strong brands, even if their ROI is difficult to quantify directly. Figuring it out provides a competitive advantage and path from being a niche product to a cultural phenomenon.

Performance Marketing

The growth of premium economies in the early days, especially on mobile, was fueled by performance marketing. Being able to attribute marketing acquisition and understand the corresponding lifetime value of those players, and if the latter value is higher than the cost per customer acquisition, marketers could easily scale their efforts. However, this process relied heavily on accurate attribution, which was particularly strong in the early days of mobile. Contrastingly, attribution has always been a problem in the console and PC space. Instead of direct attribution, marketing technologists in these sectors utilized an approach called fingerprinting. This method matches certain attributes of potential customers, such as their IP address and device ID, with similar attributes within the game. While effective, fingerprinting has always had a significant margin of error, which has been exacerbated in recent days due to rising privacy concerns and data protection legislation. Additionally, policies such as the IDFA from Apple have pushed mobile companies away from direct attribution to fingerprinting technologies for marketing attribution. Many industry slowdowns can be directly associated with the challenges of fingerprinting and marketing attribution. In the current context, without a reliable and commoditized marketing analytics solution, understanding what works and what doesn't in the growth strategy of game titles presents a valuable competitive advantage.

As we established, every new player has an average value they may contribute to the live product. This is the **lifetime value (LTV)**. Depending on the nature of the product, it could be discounted by the cost of support of every player, as well as by deducting interest rates on capital. But all in all, the notion of LTV allows marketers to contribute to the business by bringing users into the game for a cost lower than LTV (Figure 7.2). The cost per acquisition (CPA) and relevant average LTVs should be measured by geographies, target segments, and, if the scale allows, by channels and campaigns. Strategically the dynamics of CPA and LTV will be showing the maturity and saturation of the market with the existing product setup.

Over time, the cost per acquisition (CPA) tends to increase as marketers are compelled to reach out to segments of the population that are either less interested or less engaged in the gaming ecosystem. Simultaneously, the lifetime value (LTV) of these players tends to decrease since their level of interest is often reflected in lower retention rates and spending within the game.

A critical factor intertwined with CPA and LTV is the **payback period**, which is the duration expected for the marketing investment to break even. This period can vary widely depending on several variables such as the type of game, the platform it's available on, and the economic conditions of the company and market. Some companies may anticipate a quick return, expecting marketing efforts to pay off within weeks or months, which is often the case for mobile games with rapid user turnover and quick gameplay loops. On the other hand, games with a more extensive content offering and a dedicated player base may have a much longer payback period, extending to years.

This payback period is a strategic gauge that influences marketing decisions significantly. If a company operates with a short payback period mindset, marketing strategies will focus on rapid user acquisition and immediate revenue generation. Conversely, with a long payback period, the emphasis shifts toward building a solid player base over time, nurturing player engagement, and gradually monetizing through in-depth content and services. Each approach has its own set of financial implications and risks, and choosing the right strategy is crucial for sustainable growth and profitability in the gaming industry.

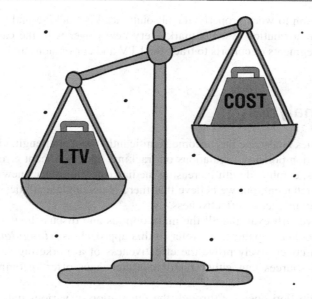

FIGURE 7.2 The cost of user acquisition should be lower than the player's lifetime value (LTV).

Performance media is a broad term, but it usually covers social media advertising, affiliate marketing, and search engine marketing. Each of the channels is very complex and has particular pros and cons:

- **Search Engine Marketing (SEM):** Search Engine Marketing, often abbreviated as SEM, presents marketers with a highly targeted advertising platform. Through SEM, marketers can place ads directly within search engine results, ensuring immediate visibility to users actively searching for relevant keywords. One of the key advantages of SEM lies in its pay-per-click model, which allows marketers to exercise precise control over their budgets and measure the return on investment (ROI) effectively. However, SEM can be competitive and costly, particularly for popular keywords. Marketers must continuously optimize their campaigns to maintain visibility and combat click fraud, which can impact campaign performance and ROI.
- **Social Media Advertising:** Social media advertising offers marketers a powerful way to reach targeted demographics with precision. Platforms like Facebook, Instagram, Twitter, and LinkedIn provide advanced targeting options based on user interests, demographics, and behavior. Social media ads are often more cost-effective compared to traditional advertising channels, offering wide reach and engagement opportunities. However, social media advertising comes with its challenges, including ad fatigue among users, dependency on constantly evolving platform algorithms, and variations in ad performance based on the audience and platform.
- **Affiliate Marketing:** Affiliate marketing operates on a performance-based payment model, where marketers pay affiliates based on the results they achieve, such as sales or leads. This approach makes affiliate marketing a cost-effective way to reach new audiences through affiliate networks. Marketers benefit from wide reach and scalability, leveraging affiliates' marketing efforts to promote products or services. However, managing affiliates and ensuring their marketing efforts align with brand standards can be challenging. Additionally, there's a risk of affiliate fraud, where affiliates may engage in unethical practices to inflate results, impacting campaign performance and profitability. Commission fees associated with affiliate marketing can also eat into profits, requiring careful monitoring and management of affiliate relationships.

For paid user acquisition to work properly, the absolute need is tracking and attribution. Without going into much details, the attribution systems mark every new player with the campaign they came from. This allows to build segments or cohorts to track the LTV and conversions and to zoom into this segment specifically.

Media Mix Analytics

The marketing analytics landscape has become significantly more challenging in recent years due to the rise of privacy protection policies, regulations on tracking, and significant error margins in fingerprinting technologies. This, combined with increasing media costs, introduces new risks for the video game business. It's a bold statement, but we believe that there is no single analytics solution that can provide complete confidence in marketing effectiveness.

In this section, we will examine all the main options and discuss how a combined approach can help build trust in media campaigns. We refer to this approach as *triangulation*, which suggests that no single source can conclusively prove the effectiveness of a marketing campaign. However, when used together, these sources can either instill confidence or offer recommendations for potential improvements.

Marketing attribution operates through the integration of various data streams, including marketing touchpoints and in-game events, to provide an understanding of campaign effectiveness on the funnel. Touchpoints connect user interactions with marketing efforts, such as clicks on ads or referral links, while events represent actions users take in-game, like installs or first logins, or on owned platforms, like game purchases or community sign-ups. Goals are defined events or event combinations that describe desired user actions. The process begins with the collection of events and touchpoints, followed by matching events to goals and attributing them to relevant touchpoints. This data is then utilized for reporting and insights on campaign performance, helping in real-time optimization and audience segmentation. Touchpoint tracking involves implementing trackers with specialized links and pixels to monitor campaign performance across different channels. In-game integration enables tracking of user actions within the game, providing crucial data for assessing user acquisition, retention, and engagement. Ultimately, in-game users are matched with external users based on touchpoint data. This matching algorithm is called fingerprinting that works by collecting various data points from a user's device, such as browser type, operating system, screen resolution, installed plug-ins, and IP address, and combining them to create a unique identifier or "fingerprint" for that device. This fingerprint can then be used to recognize and track the user's activities across different websites and devices, even if cookies are disabled or cleared.

Incrementality measurement is a method used in marketing to determine the true impact of advertising or marketing activities. It aims to assess whether certain outcomes, such as sales or conversions, occurred solely because of the marketing efforts.

Traditionally, incrementality measurement involved conducting experiments where a control group is exposed to the marketing activity while another group is not. However, modern incrementality measurement has evolved to utilize advanced data analysis techniques and platforms. These methods allow marketers to measure incrementality without the need for complex experiments, often by leveraging causality modeling and time series analysis. This approach analyzes various factors, including seasonality and operational changes made by marketers, to isolate the impact of marketing activities.

The main challenge of incrementality measurement is data collection about all things going on in and around the game. There may be external factors that are not visible but the system would be creating false positives.

Quantitative research in this context can typically be best run as a part of newcomer surveys. A newcomer survey serves as a tool for developers to gather feedback from players who are new to their game. These surveys typically encompass questions regarding various aspects of the player's initial experience, such as the ease of learning game mechanics, first impressions of graphics and gameplay, effectiveness of tutorials, encountered challenges, and suggestions for improvement. Our recommendation is to integrate top-of-the-funnel components into such questionnaires to study how players learned about the game, through what channels, and what convinced them to start playing, etc.

Each method has pros and cons, and most important blind spots that can put in question marketing campaign effectiveness or even the strategy overall. The table below summarizes various cases of marketing analytics triangulation and provides recommendations and possible interpretations:

ATTRIBUTION	INCREMENTAL IMPACT	QUANTITATIVE RESEARCH	INTERPRETATION
▦	▦	▦	Robust evidence of campaign effectiveness. It's recommended to continue this campaign provided even marginally positive ROAS.
▦	▦	☐	Likely an effective activation campaign. Long-term brand impact is not evident. Push for ROAS maximization and consider aligning such campaigns with stronger brand and emotional beats.
▦	☐	☐	Trackable impact through attribution systems, but a lack of impact on the overall acquisition trajectory and player reporting. It is likely that this campaign is cannibalizing organic traffic. The recommendation is to temporarily switch it off entirely or in certain geographical areas and monitor the impact.
☐	▦	▦	Likely an effective campaign lacking a trackable funnel. Consider introducing additional activation elements, such as invite codes, social media support, landing pages, etc.
☐	▦	☐	Possibly an effective campaign lacking a trackable funnel or an external event influencing the acquisition. Research all communications and community activities around the game. If there is no evidence of any external events, consider adding activation elements.
☐	☐	▦	Likely a post-effect of previous brand beats. Consider these insights when planning future brand beats.
☐	☐	☐	Robust evidence of campaign ineffectiveness. Stop and re-evaluate all components of this campaign.

Finally, there are Marketing Mix Models (MMMs). MMM is a statistical analysis method used to evaluate the effectiveness of various marketing elements in driving performance. It aims to identify and quantify the impact of different marketing activities, such as advertising, promotions, and pricing strategies, on key performance indicators (KPIs) like installs. MMM involves analyzing historical data to understand how changes in marketing variables correlate with changes in business outcomes.

Somewhat similar to incremental measurement, this is an analytical approach as opposed to tracking (tech) or survey (research). Incremental measurement zooms into the granular campaign window, while MMMs provide more of a macro view aiming to understand long-tail brand impact better.

These models are not a panacea. While theoretically effective, there are significant risks associated with relying solely on this approach. One major disadvantage of Marketing Mix Modeling (MMM) is its reliance on historical data, which may not fully capture rapid changes in consumer behavior, market dynamics, or technological advancements. This limitation can lead to inaccuracies in predicting future outcomes and optimizing marketing strategies, particularly in video games where trends and player preferences evolve quickly.

IPS AND PARTNERSHIPS

A great year for gamers was 2023. An unprecedented quality and quantity of video games were released. Among the best performing games in revenue, one could find *NBA 2K*, *Hogwarts Legacy (Harry Potter IP)*, *Baldur's Gate 3 (D&D IP)*, *Marvel's Spider-Man 2*, *Madden NFL*, *Star Wars Jedi: Survivor*, *Monopoly Go*, *EA FC* (ex-FIFA)—all of which are based on intellectual properties not native to video games. *Fortnite*, one of the biggest live services, released a Lego partnership expanding as well as a series of events featuring Eminem, The Weeknd, Lewis Hamilton, and Lady Gaga. Overall, there were more than 75 collaborations for *Fortnite* in Chapter 4.

In all of these cases the use of IPs had both a product and distribution impact.

On the distribution side, the use of IPs stretches the target audience of the game to include the fans of IPs. *Kim Kardashian: Hollywood* released in 2024 by Glu Mobile rapidly gained popularity due to its unique premise, which allowed players to experience the glamorous lifestyle of Kim Kardashian herself. The IP was a catalyst for all things marketing in this case—the game team effectively leveraged social media platforms, allowing players to share their in-game achievements and progress with friends, all in synergy with Kim Kardashian.

On the product side, intellectual properties simplify FTUE and understanding of game mechanics. It's fairly expected how Spider-Man moves and behaves or what the ultimate goal of *Monopoly* is. Game makers can leverage this cultural and common knowledge to create more elegant and streamlined experiences.

What makes a partnership good from the user acquisition standpoint?

1. First and foremost, a good partnership is one that **does not alienate the existing audience**, and it's important to check if your current audience is feeling positive or neutral about it initially. Moreover, a good partnership **expands the audience** by reaching players who couldn't be reached otherwise or doing that more efficiently.
2. There is a **mutual interest and a mutual benefit** for both parties. This will likely impact the cost structure and the quality of execution.
3. **Synergy with other user acquisition levers**—media mix, business model, influencers. Partnerships can become incredibly more powerful if the content they provide can be leveraged in marketing campaigns, picked up by owned and adjacent influencers.
4. Furthermore, **effective partnerships should grow LTV**. They provide ongoing support and updates to maintain player interest over time. Regular content drops or expansions related to the collaboration can keep the game fresh and encourage continued participation from both new and existing players.

Fortnite has scaled partnerships to an extent that we haven't really seen in the video games industry before. Here is a snapshot of the types of partnerships executed in *Fortnite* in recent years that adds perspectives on types of integrations and sources of inspiration:

TYPE OF PARTNERSHIP	DESCRIPTION	EXAMPLES
Franchise Collaborations	Collaborations with entertainment franchises	Marvel, DC Comics, Star Wars, Ghostbusters
Celebrity and Influencers	Collaborations with individual celebrities	Travis Scott, Marshmello, Ninja
Event Based	Partnerships centered around special events	Marshmello Concert, Star Wars Premiere
Brand Collaborations	Collaborations with consumer brands and companies	Nike, Ferrari, Moncler
Cultural and Pop-Culture	Collaborations inspired by cultural icons	*Stranger Things, Borderlands 3, Alien*
Gaming and Esports	Collaborations with gaming franchises or esports	*Rocket League, Halo, Street Fighter*
Seasonal Collaborations	Partnerships occurring within specific seasons	NFL Super Bowl

High-profile collaborations generate buzz both within the gaming community and in mainstream media. The excitement surrounding these partnerships often leads to increased social media discussions, media coverage, and word-of-mouth referrals, further amplifying network effects and, importantly in the case of *Fortnite*, simplifying further partnerships.

In the following section we will uncover how execution of acquisition integration can look like on the example of influencer marketing.

INFLUENCER MARKETING

Influencer marketing is type of earned user acquisition strategy that blends traditional celebrity endorsements with current, content-centric marketing approach. This method has rapidly gained traction in the last decade as a result of dwindling ad inventories and reduced interest in conventional advertising, coupled with the rise of ad blockers. By tapping into the power of player engagement, influencer marketing leverages the enthusiasm of players who are keen to share their gaming experiences or collaborate with influencers whose audiences intersect with trending games, effectively enhancing the reach and appeal of a game.

Promotion with influencers is native and intrinsically part of the content produced. As a matter of fact, it is unblockable by ad blockers. Its efficiency allows marketers to reach precise targets, engaged and committed to follow their favorite influencer's opinion. Influencer marketing allows marketers to run performance-driven campaigns that are trackable and can be combined with organic outcome such as Brand Awareness and Brand Consideration.

Influencer marketing is not about quick results: it's about demonstrating your authority and credibility within the industry; it's about becoming synonymous with whatever it is that you offer, like Hoovering the floor instead of vacuuming it. On YouTube for example, a content including a promotion of a brand and product may stay forever on the platform and will ultimately keep providing results to the company. It's even more true for evergreen content which tends to be continuously rewatched, shared over years.

Influencer campaign is affordable for each company and the scope of potential creator activations is massive from nano, micro influencer to macro, AAA ones. However, the disciplines don't follow the same codes of traditional advertising. It is human management and requires lot of resources to reach the right creators, convince them, and brief them in a way that the promotion of a brand or product is well spread but still in a native way, in the influencer's own style. Thinking the influencer will repeat a script given by the company is one of the biggest mistakes done by marketers when tackling this discipline.

Influencer Marketing Canvas

The Influencer Marketing Canvas is a tailored adaptation of the Business Model Canvas, designed by industry professionals to assist teams in comprehending, organizing, and strategizing their influencer marketing efforts. This user-friendly instrument provides managers with the ability to visualize their plans more clearly, thereby facilitating improved decision-making (Figure 7.3).

Goal

The goal serves as a specific target that must be attained to ensure the success of your campaign. It directs your efforts toward making informed decisions and taking the necessary actions to achieve the desired outcome. Depending on the current needs of the game, there are several potential types of campaign goals: acquisition, retention, winback, monetization, and brand awareness or consideration. Establishing a concrete goal from the outset enables the influencer manager (IM) to determine the most suitable creator or influencer to collaborate with, identify the type of content required, and pinpoint the most appropriate and effective platform for content promotion.

The targets for influencer marketing campaigns can vary based on the specific goals and objectives of the brand or campaign. Below is a short list of some of the most common targets defined in influencer marketing including actions to leverage growth potentials and how to find insights within existing player base.

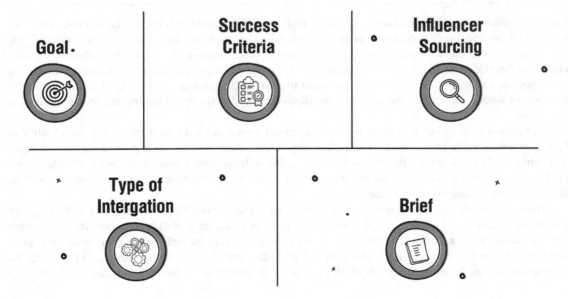

FIGURE 7.3 Influencer Marketing Canvas.

TARGET	WHERE'S INSIGHTS?	WHERE'S GROWTH POTENTIAL?
Brand Awareness. It focuses on increasing brand visibility and recognition by activating larger audiences and new demographics.	Evaluate the current player base and their familiarity with games like yours.	Collaborate with gaming influencers to introduce your games to new audiences on platforms like Twitch or YouTube. Engage influencers to create walkthroughs, tutorials, or reviews to attract gamers who may not have discovered the games yet.
Audience Engagement. Boosting engagement metrics such as likes, comments, and shares on social media platforms. This helps in fostering a sense of community around the brand.	Analyze player interactions within the current gaming community.	Use influencers to organize multiplayer events, challenges, or tournaments that encourage both existing and new players to engage with the game and each other.
Lead Generation. Driving traffic to the brand's website or landing pages, encourage followers to sign up for newsletters or participate in contests.	Evaluate the effectiveness of current in-game promotions or referral programs.	Leverage influencers to showcase exclusive in-game content or limited-time promotions, driving new players to sign up and try our games. Utilize influencers' unique referral codes and links to track and reward new player acquisitions.
Game or Content Promotion. Showcase and promote specific game or content, ultimately driving sales and conversions through influencer recommendations.	Assess the response to recent updates, content, or in-game purchases.	Collaborate with gaming influencers to showcase new features, extra content, or in-game items. Provide influencers with early access to exclusive content to generate excitement and entice new players to explore your games.
Social Media Growth. Increase the number of followers on social media platforms and improve the overall social media presence and influence.	Evaluate current follower growth on social media platforms.	Engage gaming influencers with large and diverse audiences to promote your games on various social media channels. Encourage influencers to share user-generated content and engage with their followers to drive increased visibility and interest.

Acquisition: In this case, the IM will focus on finding influencers whose audience aligns well with your game but has not yet been extensively exposed to it. Influencer marketing can contribute to user acquisition by leveraging influencers' reach, authenticity, and ability to create engaging content. Below you can find some of the ways that influencers can help to achieve your acquisition goals.

- **Audience Expansion:** Collaborating with influencers with a follower base aligned with your target demographic, expanding your reach to new audiences.
- **Authentic Recommendations:** Influencers' authentic endorsements build trust with their audience, encouraging potential users to try your game or content.
- **In-Depth Reviews and Demonstrations:** Creating detailed reviews and demonstrations through influencers to educate potential users, addressing queries and facilitating informed decisions.
- **Exclusive Offers and Promotions:** Using influencers to promote exclusive offers and time-sensitive promotions, creating a sense of urgency and encouraging immediate user action.
- **User-Generated Content:** Encouraging influencers and their followers to generate and share user-generated content, showcasing real-life experiences and expanding brand visibility.

By focusing on the techniques above, IM can collaborate with influencers to expand their reach and foster a deeper connection with the gaming community. Each approach has the potential to significantly impact the user base of a game, as seen in the following case studies:

- Ninja (Richard Tyler Blevins born June 5, 1991) and *Fortnite*: Ninja's streams, characterized by his dynamic personality and engaging gameplay, catapulted *Fortnite* into the limelight, contributing to a surge in the game's user acquisition. His influence is quantifiable; after his stream with rapper Drake in March 2018, *Fortnite* saw unprecedented growth, leading to hundreds of thousands of new players joining the game. Ninja's *Fortnite* stream with Drake smashed Twitch viewership records, attracting over 600,000 concurrent viewers.
- PewDiePie (Felix Arvid Ulf Kjellberg born October 24, 1989) and *Minecraft*: When PewDiePie revisited *Minecraft* with a new video series in 2019, it revitalized the game's popularity. The series, which combined his signature humor with the creative possibilities within *Minecraft*, drew millions of views and new players, contributing to a significant increase in sales and user acquisition. YouTube's 2019 Rewind paid homage to top creators, notably highlighting PewDiePie's impact on *Minecraft*'s popularity. Acknowledging the previous year's backlash, YouTube shifted focus to celebrate the year's standout moments, including PewDiePie's *Minecraft* series. His return to the game coincided with a surge in viewership, marking a significant year for *Minecraft*. PewDiePie's "Minecraft Part 1" alone amassed over 34 million views, underscoring his influence on the game's success on the platform.
- Shroud (Michael Grzesiek born June 2, 1994) and *Valorant*: Shroud's participation in *Valorant*'s early access, coupled with his reputation as a skilled former CS:GO player, generated high anticipation for Riot Games' new shooter. His streams around the game's release in April 2020 provided viewers with a professional's insight, driving *Valorant*'s closed beta to reach peak viewer counts on Twitch and a substantial initial player base. In August 2020, Shroud marked a triumphant comeback on Twitch, drawing 516,289 viewers on his first day back and nearly surpassing Ninja's record of 600K concurrent viewers.

These influencers, through their authentic content creation and strategic partnerships, have proven to be powerful allies in reaching new audiences and achieving user acquisition goals. Their success exemplifies the potential for well-aligned influencer collaborations to not only entertain but also to drive substantial growth in a game's player base.

Engagement: Here, the IM will primarily aim to engage audiences that are already familiar with your game, such as existing players. This could involve working with Community Contributors or regular paid influencers who have previously generated significant acquisitions for the brand. Here's an exploration of the key aspects of influencer marketing in these efforts:

- **Rebuilding Trust and Credibility:** Influencers contribute to (re)building trust by endorsing the brand positively, especially among players who may have lapsed or had negative experiences. Influencers also share authentic testimonials that help overcome hesitations, encouraging previous players to re-engage.
- **Personalized Communication:** Influencers enable the creation of personalized and targeted messaging for winback efforts, addressing specific concerns or highlighting new offerings. Furthermore, they engage directly with their audience, hence providing a more personal touch to win back customers and encourage repeat purchases.

Through targeted collaborations, IM seeks to harness the influencers' capability to rebuild trust, deliver personalized communication, and highlight new game features or improvements, thereby deepening the engagement levels within the existing player base. The following examples illustrate how strategic partnerships with influencers have significantly bolstered engagement metrics:

- The Destiny Community Summit marked a transformative engagement strategy by Bungie, inviting Stefan "Datto" Jonke, a luminary within the *Destiny* community, for an in-depth dialogue about *Destiny 2*'s trajectory. Datto's involvement played a critical role in reshaping player perceptions and catalyzed significant improvements in the game's direction, as evidenced by the positive reception from both influencers and the broader player community.
- BlizzCon has consistently served as a platform for Blizzard Entertainment to engage with the *Overwatch* community, inviting esteemed influencers to discuss forthcoming features, balance adjustments, and new maps. The influencers' participation in BlizzCon panels not only amplified excitement for upcoming updates but also restored faith among players.

Through personalized communication and direct involvement in community dialogues, influencers have become indispensable in rekindling player enthusiasm and loyalty. These case studies exemplify the transformative potential of influencer partnerships in not just entertaining an existing audience but significantly enhancing engagement and commitment within the game's community.

Monetization: In this domain, the focus of the Influencer Manager (IM) shifts to not just drawing players to the game but also enhancing revenue streams. This involves identifying and partnering with influencers whose content not only resonates with your game's existing user base but also inspires spending within the game, whether through direct in-game purchases or the promotion of premium content. The goal here is to harness the persuasive power of influencers to demonstrate the value of the game's monetized features, enticing players to invest in their gaming experience. Here we will delve into how influencer marketing can be instrumental in driving monetization for your game:

- **Upselling and Cross-Selling Opportunities:** Influencers can effectively promote upsells or cross-sells, showcasing complementary content or premium features to maximize revenue from existing players. By implementing influencer-driven affiliate marketing programs, games allow influencers to earn commissions for driving sales and contributing to monetization goals.
- **Showcasing New Features or Offerings:** Influencers display new features, updates, or offerings, driving interest and encouraging previous payers to explore the game's latest content. Influencers create urgency by promoting limited-time campaigns or exclusive access for returning players, driving immediate engagement and monetization.

Influencer Managers can effectively drive revenue while deepening the game's engagement with its community. Influencers' unique ability to showcase a game's monetized features in an authentic and compelling way can translate directly into increased sales and enhanced player investment. The following real-world examples illustrate how integrating influencers into a game's monetization strategy can lead to remarkable outcomes:

- *PUBG* and Influencer Weapon Crates: In a unique collaboration, *PUBG* players had the opportunity to purchase exclusive weapon skins designed by popular streamers Shroud (Michael Grzesiek) and DrDisRespect (Herschel "Guy" Beahm IV). The Ghosted Crate by Shroud and the Speed and Momentum Crate by DrDisRespect custom skins reflected the personalities of their namesakes.
- *World of Tanks* and HandOfBlood: *World of Tanks* introduced a novel addition to their in-game commanders with the inclusion of Maximilian Knabe, better known as HandOfBlood, a prominent German YouTuber and live-streamer. This new commander brought HandOfBlood's distinctive voice and character to the game, invigorating players and fans with a unique gaming experience. Available in three exclusive bundles, players could acquire this special commander by purchasing the Rheinmetall Skorpion G, the historic Tiger 131, or on his own.

These examples underscore the influential power of well-executed influencer collaborations in monetizing a game's content. By showcasing game features and exclusive offers, influencers can compel their audiences to make purchases, proving that authentic partnerships extend beyond engagement to have a tangible impact on revenue. Their success demonstrates the significant role that influencers can play in not only expanding a game's community but also in contributing to its financial success.

Success Criteria

A collection of key performance indicators (KPIs) that serve as a means to assess the effectiveness of a campaign in achieving its intended results. For instance, when considering a campaign focused on acquiring new active players, the most crucial KPI is the Cost per Acquisition. Once the campaign is launched, it's essential to keep track of the initial cost per acquisition (within the first 6 days) for each published post or video.

- **Re-engagement Rate:** Percentage of previously inactive players who re-engage with the game.
- **Conversion Rate of Winback Campaigns:** Percentage of re-engaged players who make a purchase.
- **Cost-per-Action:** the total cost spent to receive the required actions by your players (first login, first battle, first purchase, etc.)
- **Player Feedback and Sentiment:** Qualitative insights into player sentiment, gathered through surveys, comments, or reviews.
- **Return on Ad Spend (ROAS) for Winback Campaigns:** Revenue generated from winback campaigns compared to the amount spent on those campaigns.
- **Affiliate Marketing Commission Payouts:** The total amount paid to influencers through affiliate marketing programs.
- **Return on Investment (ROI) for Monetization Campaigns:** The profitability of the monetization campaigns in relation to the investment.
- **Audience Reach:** Maximizing the number of unique views through influencers.
- **Impressions:** Number of unique plus recurring views a post generated.
- **Engagement Rate:** Level of interaction with the content, indicating the impact of a post.
- **Social Profile Growth:** Increase in followers on your game's social media profile due to influencer campaigns.
- **Trackable Assets (Coupon Codes and Custom URLs):** Utilization of personalized coupon codes and URLs for tracking interactions.
- **Sales:** Number of sales generated directly from influencer campaigns.
- **Social Sentiment:** Public reaction and sentiment toward the campaign on social media.

However, it's equally important not to overlook the long-term acquisition impact that may span months or even years. By analyzing the data from individual posts or videos, noticeable patterns may emerge. One particular video might yield substantial results rapidly but have a limited long-term effect after a month, whereas another could initially underperform yet deliver consistent acquisitions over an extended period.

The marketing funnel is another way to track the success of campaigns that signifies the journey of users from initial awareness into the end goal. Marketers leverage various tracking software to closely analyze user behavior. At a technical level it can help optimize the campaigns and address potential obstacles in their UA journey. The funnel for Influencer User Acquisition (UA) campaigns, specific to PC game titles, might consist of multiple measurable steps (Figure 7.4).

As we go deeper into the user journey we can see further funnel events, like first in-game purchase or first real-money transaction; however, those metrics specifically align with retention and monetization objectives.

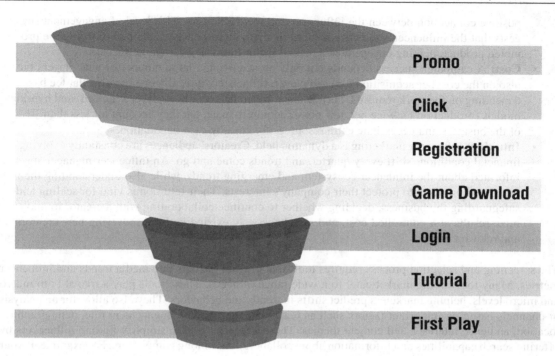

FIGURE 7.4   The funnel for Influencer User Acquisition (UA) campaigns, specific to PC game titles.

Influencer Sourcing

Even with the numerous tools accessible for marketers to identify suitable creators based on factors such as gender, demography, location, engagement, and content type, there remains an element of risk involved. The onus falls on the marketer to carefully evaluate the advantages and disadvantages in order to ensure a successful campaign, considering factors like financial conditions, content type, existing synergies between the brand and product, and the target demographics. To pinpoint the ideal talents that align with your goals and target audience, it is crucial to focus on the following key aspects:

- **Relevance:** Examine the creator's performance on platforms where you want your game to be promoted. Does the target audience meet your company's requirements in terms of genre, demographic distribution, geographic distribution, and content type? How many followers does the creator have? What are the trends in terms of views? How engaged is the audience in terms of likes, comments, and reshares? How often does the creator release content and promote brands?
- **Reach:** This quantitative measure varies across platforms, reflecting the influencer's ability to draw viewership. Key metrics to consider include the average views on YouTube videos over both short and long terms, and the average concurrent viewers (CCV) on Twitch streams. Reach provides a broad understanding of the influencer's potential to expose your game to a wider audience.
- **Engagement:** The frequency and quality of audience interaction with the influencer's content are telling indicators of their ability to engage and influence their community. High engagement rates, characterized by a significant number of reactions or comments, suggest a strong,

positive connection between the influencer and their followers. This level of engagement suggests that the influencer's audience is more likely to be responsive and open to trying the promoted product, making engagement a pivotal factor in driving campaign success.

- **Cost:** A campaign success depends not only on acquiring a large number of new players but also on the cost per acquisition for each player. Influencers typically operate on a flat fee basis, depending on the work required. Performance-based fees (per new player acquired) and hybrid models (production fee+fee per new player acquired) exist, but they account for less than 10% of the business and necessitate extra resources for case-by-case negotiation.
- **Intuition:** Influencer marketing is a dynamic field. Creators' audiences are constantly evolving, financial conditions shift every quarter, and trends come and go. An influencer manager stays informed about the influencer ecosystem and emerging trends, while also understanding their brand and products to protect their company's interests. Their intuition is vital for scaling and safeguarding the business, deciding whether to continue collaborating with a creator to maximize results at a controlled cost, and simultaneously expanding by discovering new creators and relevant niches.

The screening and selection process requires tools that provide insights into media trends and influencer metrics. Many tools in the market cater to a wide range of needs. These tools play a role at both macro and micro levels, helping marketers predict shifts in trends and behaviors. They also allow for an analysis of channels based on important factors such as reach, channel growth, engagement rate, demographics, location, audience interests, and content themes. These platforms aim to simplify finding influencers by offering search capabilities and information about collaborations among competitors. For example, if your focus is on streaming platforms like Twitch, you can rely on freely accessible online tools that provide insights into key stream metrics. These metrics include concurrent viewers, peak viewership numbers, follower growth rates, and content trends.

There are also influencer marketing platforms that offer services handling all aspects of campaigns from start to finish. These platforms automate outreach campaign execution, content creation, and payment management. This holistic approach can be particularly beneficial for expanding operations or managing campaigns with less resources involved. However, it's essential to recognize the downsides of relying heavily on automation. It can introduce risks to the quality of campaigns and brand safety. When there's a lack of involvement in selecting influencers and overseeing their content, it can negatively impact the quality of traffic. Therefore, balancing automation and strategic oversight is crucial to maintaining brand integrity and ensuring campaign outcomes.

Finding the right talent for influencer marketing campaigns is a multifaceted process that involves various strategies, each with its unique advantages and challenges. Each method, from direct engagement to utilizing intermediary services, presents a balance between time investment and financial cost, highlighting the importance of choosing the approach that best aligns with your campaign objectives and resource availability.

- **Do Everything by Yourself:** You explore the platforms and social media, identify the candidates, contact them, negotiate, sign contract with them. Finally, you brief them, and pay after campaign is released. You handle every single step of the process. This option is ideal to set good and direct relations with the talents. It remains very time consuming. The market is more and more structured. Most of the macro and AAA influencers now have agents to handle their business.
- **Use Third-Party Platforms (Tubular, SullyGnome, Upfluence):** They can streamline the influencer selection process, offering valuable insights and aiding in the discovery of new, untapped influencers by saving time and guiding research efforts. While these tools excel in sourcing and providing direction, they rarely support campaign execution such as setting up campaigns, drafting contracts, or processing payments directly. For those needs, specialized campaign execution platforms are available, capable of managing a wide array of campaigns

simultaneously, including mass briefing, contractualization, and payment. However, while these platforms offer convenience and efficiency in campaign management, they still require dedicated resources for effective execution and come with additional costs.

- **Use Third-Party Agencies:** In addition to helping you save time during some steps of the process, they extend capabilities by allowing you to get recommendations and extra ways to reach out to influencers you couldn't contact otherwise: provide list of influencers they are already in touch, recommend influencers based on campaign they ran with them in the past, provide knowledge of the market in general (being in general working with multiple companies on different challenges). Staying in touch with agencies will also contribute to pull new project opportunities and last-minute deals to you. The utilization of third-party agencies can indeed offer substantial benefits to your brand, necessitating an additional budget. However, it is crucial to select agencies judiciously and remain vigilant against engaging too many intermediaries. Excessive layers can lead to multiple fees, dilute the clarity of your campaign's brief and objectives, and render the campaign impersonal, ultimately diminishing its effectiveness.

Type of Integrations

Influencer marketing offers a wide range of advertising formats that are closely linked to the product type we want to market. Whether it is an Instagram post, Twitch branded stream, or YouTube dedicated video, the choice of platform and type of integration need to be tailored to the target audience and the goal of campaign.

We cannot effectively promote makeup products on a tech channel, and conversely, gaming hardware is not a suitable fit for beauty channels. Although it seems obvious, some marketers still opt for quantity over quality without checking correlation between the product and the channel or platform. The ideal platform and social media channels for your game will depend on your objectives and the nature of your activities.

- **Ongoing Activities:** For acquisition purposes, you'll be looking at YouTube for its capacity to provide immediate and long-term results. For brand awareness, Instagram, TikTok, and Facebook are among the preferable social media with an audience relevant to your title.
- **Time-Limited Activities:** Generally, it's advisable to utilize platforms and social media channels that can deliver quick results for limited-time campaigns. Twitch is a relevant channel for time-limited activities as it provides immediate attention and is required to take instant action to enjoy a specific time-limited beat. Some platforms, like YouTube, may not be ideal for short-term promotions, as they can be costly to generate an immediate impact. Additionally, this approach may cause frustration for viewers who discover a promotion after it has ended.

As the influencer marketing landscape continues to expand, the primary platforms for campaigns are becoming increasingly saturated, resulting in heightened competition and elevated costs. One of the principal challenges in influencer marketing is striking the right balance between adhering to the indispensable trends dictated by each platform and consistently exploring novel, disruptive opportunities to stand out from competitors.

When implementing ongoing influencer marketing initiatives, it's crucial to stay informed about which strategies are effective, which have lost their effectiveness, and which remain profitable, all while keeping your objectives in mind. When initiating influencer activities for your game, you will naturally begin by collaborating with creators within the same target audience as your product. While it is essential to work with these influencers regularly, it's also important to avoid overexposure, which could lead to diminishing returns in terms of attracting new customers.

After establishing these initial relationships, it's time to expand your horizons and explore other paradigms that offer synergies with your product, ultimately broadening the scope of opportunities to reach your target audience in new ways. For instance, a game set during World War II could benefit from partnerships with military or history-themed social media channels. To differentiate your product further, you may consider exploring lifestyle, entertainment, or other relevant channels.

To effectively engage your target audience, you may need to adapt the promotional strategies based on the channel and the resources available to influencers. As the topic is broad, we will focus here on influencer marketing in gaming and consequently two main platforms that offers horizontal formats and at the same time show the biggest effectiveness in acquisition marketing.

YouTube is still the dominant and most influential social media platform that offers a wide range of marketing formats:

- **Let's Play Content:** Collaborate with an influencer who features a variety of games on their channel to create a video dedicated solely to your game, showcasing gameplay elements, tips, and tricks.
- **Entertainment Content:** This approach, while potentially more costly and risky, opens up avenues for unique integrations, such as real-life shooting sessions, constructing a wooden tank, or organizing brand-themed battles on water. Additionally, venturing into dedicated non-gaming videos creates opportunities for strong synergy between influencers' video content and game. In these scenarios, the influencer manager often plays a more active role in the video creation process, ensuring content aligns closely with the game's vision. With their high-quality production and viewership, such campaigns not only captivate audiences but also significantly enhance brand awareness, showcasing the game in diverse and engaging contexts.
- **Livestream:** This is the most "on hand" experience we can get from influencer. Sponsored dedicated stream may last from 1 hour to even 3 hours and creates authentic and interactive connection with the audience. Due to its real-time nature and as opposed to the previously mentioned formats where we always get the preview of the promotion, here with live streams we need to rely on creators' creativity and common sense. However, to make a stream successful we need the right approach and full engagement of the creator. That said, we can use different tactics that boost the streamer's motivation. To name a few, it can be performance-based payment model or the use of on-stream live counter showing campaign goal progression.
- **Mono Content:** If you aim to promote your game on a channel that focuses on a single game (e.g., *Minecraft* or *League of Legends*), consider a non-dedicated integration, where the influencer embeds a 60–90 second promotion of your game within their existing content. It can be linked to the video topic (for example, military history or tech channels) but can be also unconnected (like for entertainment or comedy content). It should contain the main information about the product, game visuals, benefits of the invite code, and strong call-to-action, the more personal and original the better. With the saturation of sponsored content and lack of creator's engagement, integrations may at times lose their expected acquisition effectiveness. This approach may not yield the same results as dedicated integrations, so pricing negotiations should reflect this difference.
- **Interconnected content** aims to explore additional verticals that resonate with target segments pertinent to our product. The underlying strategy involves identifying audiences engaged in related areas, such as those interested in PC or monitor reviews, under the assumption they might be inclined to explore PC gaming. By integrating our game into such non-dedicated content, we achieve complementary exposure at a lower cost.

Twitch as opposed to YouTube focuses exclusively on live-streaming:

- **A dedicated live stream** as explained above is an excellent way to create authentic and impactful campaigns.
- **In-stream integration**, besides fully dedicated stream we can opt for more affordable options which are in-stream integrations.

- **Steam branding** is a format that should accompany both dedicated streams and integrations. It can be also a stand-alone campaign of time-limited passive Twitch branding. Its main goal is to boost brand awareness, but it also has solid potential to support user acquisition. Twitch branding includes chat bots with CTA, on-screen animations, banners, or commands.

There are many other places and formats where your acquisition marketing campaigns can benefit from. YouTube community posts, use of influencers, Discord servers, or exploring other streaming services like Kick, Trovo, or Facebook gaming can be a great addition to the standard platforms. It's all about having your mind open to new trends and keeping up to fast-growing and changing influencers' ecosystems.

Brief

Once we identify the right talent, go through the administration processes, and negotiate the terms of our cooperation, the next step is to share the campaign details and its requirements with the partner. And here comes an influencer brief that serves as a guide for creators by outlining the details of a specific campaign. It is essential to offer a concise brief, as influencers may not read it in its entirety, and the key aspects of the brief, such as the objectives, could be overshadowed.

Additionally, it is important to refrain from dictating what the influencer should say. An effective brief typically includes the primary goal of the campaign, guidelines on what to do and avoid, relevant assets for display, clickable links (if applicable) for directing viewers to a specifically optimized funnel that monitors performance, supported accounts (for let's play content), and a required disclosure of sponsored content. The longer and the more complicated the brief is, the chances of influencer being discouraged or simply not complying with it become higher. The brief for gaming influencers should be adjusted to the specific type and format of the campaign and include the following:

1. Campaign objective (user acquisition, winback, brand awareness, etc.)
2. Overview of the campaign. Start/end dates of the campaign and overview of the content requirements (deliverables and content quality)
3. Talking points. Key points or messages that should be communicated by the influencer, in his own words
4. Incentive. Detailed information about the incentive/invite code (specific to the product we promote)
5. Tracking mechanism. Tracking link guidance and call-to-action tips
6. Dos and don'ts. Clear partnership disclosure in line with local legal regulations, brand safety measures
7. Additional notes. Any other relevant information, like contact details, approval process, etc.

By focusing on clarity and conciseness, the brief ensures that the essential elements of the campaign are communicated efficiently, reducing the risk of misunderstandings or non-compliance. Ultimately, a well-executed brief not only facilitates a smooth collaboration but also enhances the potential for achieving the desired campaign outcomes.

VIRALITY

The concept of virality plays a key role in the strategies used to acquire users in live service games. This is achieved through recommendations and in-game invitations, amplified by user-generated content on YouTube and Twitch. Personal recommendations are powerful but difficult to measure as they occur outside the game when players share their experiences with others. On the other hand, in-game invitations are more measurable. It involves existing players directly proposing the game to potential new players within the game's environment using features like email invites or social media notifications. The true measure of virality in live service games lies in their ability to foster player-driven growth autonomously without relying on marketing campaigns. When a game naturally compels players to share their experiences and invite others it achieves sustainable expansion of its player base.

The K-factor (Figure 7.5) serves as a metric for measuring virality. It represents the number of players each existing player brings into the game. Calculating the K-factor accurately poses challenges due to ways players can introduce others to the game. However, the true worth of the K-factor lies in its ability to compound player base growth to how interest accumulates over time. When a game's K-factor reaches or exceeds 1, each player brings in more than one player on average, potentially leading to exponential growth. This self-propagating expansion, fueled by the game's appeal, surpasses what can be achieved through paid marketing or organic discovery.

Careful consideration is necessary for in-game invitations to avoid negative perceptions. While these invitations can be a tool for acquiring users and fostering virality, excessive use or aggressive tactics can backfire. If a game prompts players excessively to invite others, it runs the risk of appearing desperate or spammy, which can diminish the perceived value of the game. Overexposure may turn users into skeptics or even critics. It is important to restrict the number of invitations a player can send, ensuring that each invite holds significance and is more likely to be accepted. In-game invitation mechanics should be seamlessly integrated into the user interface without being intrusive. Aggressive prompts or pop-ups could have an impact on making the game seem desperate. Ideally, invitations should function as a background feature that players can access when they genuinely wish to share their gaming experience.

A great example of this can be seen in the "Recruit a Friend" program of *Final Fantasy XIV*. The campaign is designed in a way that carefully considers the benefits and frequency of invitations, making sure it doesn't create any perceptions. When a new player uses a code and subscribes to the game, both parties receive rewards within the game. These rewards increase based on how the new player continues their subscription, which encourages bringing in players who are likely to stay engaged for a long time. By limiting the number of players sent invitations, each referral becomes more thoughtful and deliberate, encouraging selectivity and genuine interest among friends who are invited to join. Moreover, the referral rewards are meticulously designed to be desirable without disrupting the game's balance. This ensures that while they are attractive, they don't provide advantages that could disturb the gameplay experience.

FIGURE 7.5 K-factor measures how many additional users each existing player brings to the game.

Viral Game

When it comes to creating viral games, it's crucial for them to have the ability to foster connections among players and reward those connections. Simply having appeal isn't enough; these games need an environment where players find value in being part of a community. This is accomplished through three features embedded within the game:

- collaborative (enabling shared experiences),
- competitive (providing a platform for player rankings), and
- communicative (facilitating idea exchange and discussions).

These components create a sense of community, motivating players to involve others in the game and enhancing enjoyment. However, if these features are merely added as an afterthought to boost popularity without improving gameplay, they may discourage players from attracting them. The successful integration of functionalities occurs when they are seamlessly woven into the core development stages of the game. A game is intrinsically social and viral, or it isn't. Superficial viral strategies like invitation mechanics often lead to temporary growth only.

A game that revolves around collaboration, competition, or communication possesses the ability to go viral. Players naturally feel inclined to invite others in order to enhance their gaming experience. For a game to truly go viral, it should initially focus on creating an individual experience for players, which would then be expanded upon to include social features that foster a sense of community. Square Enix's *Final Fantasy XIV* has successfully integrated these elements into its core gameplay, resulting in an interconnected community:

- Collaboration, such as dungeons and raids, is essential for overcoming challenges and progressing further.
- Competitive side offers a thrilling environment where players can test and compare their skills against others.
- Communication is facilitated through guilds and chat systems, allowing players to exchange ideas and strategies and socialize with one another.

A noteworthy feature is the "Novice Network," which caters to newcomers by initially focusing on personal experiences. This system gradually introduces players to the aspects of the game while smoothly transitioning them from solo play to communal interactions. Experienced players who act as mentors within this network not only enrich the player's experiences but also contribute to nurturing an inclusive community environment.

Encouraging Viral Champions

While increasing the number of invitations can be effective, care must be taken to avoid them being perceived as spam, which can tarnish the game's reputation. A balanced approach involves controlling the number of invitations a player can send, focusing on quality over quantity. This could mean restricting players from sending repeated invites to the same user or group, thereby maintaining a high invitation rate without misuse. Diversifying the format and channels for these invitations can also help. It shifts responsibility to players, encouraging them to choose their invitation methods and recipients wisely.

Incorporating game-like elements that reward players for hitting certain milestones or achievements can naturally encourage them to share their progress and experiences. This not only increases the game's visibility but also fosters a community spirit, encouraging others to join in on the fun. It's often more beneficial to invest in your player base rather than spending heavily on traditional marketing. This approach can be more effective and financially prudent than conventional advertising.

World of Warships partnered with PayPal for a limited-time offer, giving players an exciting opportunity to earn up to €20 for each friend they successfully invited to join the game through the new Recruiting Station. This approach not only incentivized existing players with a tangible financial reward but also added a competitive edge to the recruitment process. The most successful Recruiter, the player who invited the most friends, stood to win an additional €10,000, creating a high-stakes environment that spurred players into action. This strategy highlighted a creative blend of financial incentives and competitive spirit, driving player engagement and expanding the game's community.

Remember, the goal isn't just to increase the number of invitations sent but to enhance overall player engagement and retention. Incremental improvements to existing invitation mechanics, rather than adding entirely new ones, can be more effective, especially after the game's launch. It's crucial to ensure that these features add value to the player experience and don't make players feel like mere tools for marketing. Players are more likely to stay committed to games that demonstrate a commitment to enhancing their gaming experience.

Amplifying Viral Engagement

It can be effective to create a sense of artificial scarcity to make invitations more valuable. When players have a limited number of invites to send, each invitation becomes a decision, making the game itself appear more valuable. This idea not only rewards conversions but also reinforces the game's inherent value on a fundamental level. It encourages players to choose who they invite based on the quality of their network, promoting a thoughtful and meaningful approach to invitations. As a result, the process of going viral takes longer as users take their time considering whom to invite rather than sending out invites.

Implementing this sense of scarcity doesn't have to be permanent. It can be adjusted dynamically over time, aligning with how the game progresses, and ensuring that the engaged players are able to act as advocates for the game. For example, players could earn invites through gameplay or as part of the game monetization strategy, where they receive a limited number of free invites but can purchase additional ones.

One noteworthy instance where an invite-only strategy was employed is during Riot Games' closed beta launch of *Valorant*. To create a sense of exclusivity, the beta version of the game was only accessible through limited invites. Players had to watch Twitch streamers who had access to drops in order to receive an invite. This process required linking their Riot and Twitch accounts, adding a level of engagement. By making beta access scarce and only available through invites, Riot Games successfully generated excitement and desire for *Valorant*.

However, there is usually an inverse relationship between the number of invitations sent and their conversion rate. When a game inundates its player base with invitation options, each invite becomes less likely to lead to a new player joining the game. Hence, although boosting conversions is generally a move, it's crucial to strike a balance to prevent overwhelming players with an excessive number of invitations.

Virality focuses on how players are introduced to the game, while engagement reflects their ongoing involvement and satisfaction. Typically, these elements exhibit a positive correlation: a game that keeps players engaged over time is also more likely to be recommended by them to others. Addressing either virality or engagement independently can lead to short-term gains but might not sustain long-term growth. Instead, game development should prioritize the core gameplay experience, enhancing both engagement and virality. This relationship between virality and engagement is crucial for the sustainable growth and success of live service games.

What Kills Virality?

Virality is a fragile aspect of game success, sensitive to various negative influences and is easily disrupted by various factors that can cast a shadow over its success. At the forefront are pay-to-win mechanics, which sow seeds of discontent within the gaming community. This model, where financial input overshadows skill and effort, often leads to widespread criticism. When word spreads that monetary investment trumps merit, it naturally repels potential newcomers who value fair play and equal opportunity.

Equally damaging are invasive promotional tactics embedded within the game's environment. Excessive pop-ups, persistent upselling, and intrusive ads not only mar the immersive experience but can also provoke a wave of negative responses from the player base. Rather than acting as a bridge to further content, these aggressive strategies can become barriers, deterring players from engaging with the game and dissuading them from introducing the game to others.

Technical robustness is another pillar of a game's virality. Bugs and glitches that persistently plague gameplay can rapidly taint a game's reputation. Players flock to games for their seamless experiences and the escape they offer from reality. When these experiences are riddled with technical failings, the likelihood of players recommending the game decreases significantly, as the game becomes known more for its flaws than its features. The power of virality can sometimes take an unfortunate turn, as seen with the launch of *Cyberpunk 2077*. The anticipation for the game turned into widespread disappointment when players encountered numerous glitches and bugs. The game's release in 2020 was quickly overshadowed by a flurry of viral videos showcasing the myriad of technical issues. This digital chaos ignited the ire of fans worldwide, turning virality into a vehicle of frustration and mockery.

The implementation of paywalls presents yet another hurdle to virality. When key content or progress is gated behind additional payments, it can create a chasm between the game and its players. The frustration stemming from blocked access to significant game aspects can lead to a reluctance among players to endorse the game to others, curtailing the organic spread that is vital for a game's growth.

The community plays an indispensable role in a game's virality. A toxic environment can quickly erode the social foundation that many games rely on for their appeal. New players are less likely to join, and current players may leave if the community is rife with hostility, bullying, or exclusionary behavior. This negativity can spread beyond the confines of the game itself, into forums and social media, creating a widespread perception of an unwelcoming player base. When the community becomes a deterrent rather than a draw, it not only stifles the virality but can also severely impact the game's overall retention and growth.

Engagement

8

Imagine launching a video game that not just breaks sales records but also becomes a sensation in culture. That's exactly what happened with *Grand Theft Auto V.* When it was released on September 17, 2013, *GTA V* took the world by storm. It shattered seven Guinness World Records. It became the best-selling and highest-grossing video game in 24 hours; moreover, it became the fastest entertainment property to reach $1 billion in earnings.

The *Grand Theft Auto* series had already garnered a following since its game in 1997. However, it was *GTA V* that set standards in the gaming industry. The excitement among players was visible as they eagerly awaited its release. Before its launch date, players enthusiastically promoted the game through forms of user-generated content (UGC).

This enthusiasm extended beyond the game into real-life communities. Streets were adorned with murals inspired by *GTA* and players organized events to celebrate this game. Online platforms were flooded with thousands of gameplay videos shared by players showcasing stunts and detailed explorations of the open world within the game. These videos quickly became a sort of currency, among players solidifying *GTA V*s position in culture.

Back in 2013, the modding community embraced *GTA V* with a level of enthusiasm. Players were able to create game modes, character models, and various other modifications that showcased their creativity and extended the lifespan of the game beyond its initial release. These mods weren't just tweaks; they were additions that completely transformed the gaming experience.

The fact that *GTA V* was able to inspire such a creative engagement from players speaks volumes about the game's design and the strength of its community. The game provided a platform for players not only to play but to express themselves in countless ways blurring the lines between being a gamer and being a content creator. As a result, an energetic and self-sustaining community emerged—one that not just played but also actively promoted, expanded upon, and truly lived within the world of *GTA V* in ways that even the developers might never have imagined.

Player engagement has become an aspect of the gaming industry as it significantly impacts how long and deeply players immerse themselves in games. This is not just a passing trend; the fact that increased engagement leads to player purchases demonstrates its power in enhancing the gaming experience.

For teams focusing on engagement, the challenge lies in creating and maintaining a game environment that emotionally resonates with players. It entails constructing a world where players feel like they are part of a community. The ultimate goal is to provide experiences that enable players to express themselves, accomplish their in-game objectives, and find fulfillment.

Engagement is a result of experiencing good emotions over a period of time. In the real world, engagement is what comes before marriage, an ultimate form of loyalty (in theory and religion). People get engaged after a series of positive moments with each other, creating this intangible tie. Engagement in gaming mirrors the dynamics of real-life relationships, where ongoing positive interactions result in outcomes such as loyalty, cross-purchasing, active selling, and co-creation. Engaged players often go beyond playing the game; they share their gaming experiences on social media platforms and streams, effectively becoming advocates for the game. This external engagement, driven by a sense of belonging and identity, expands the game's reach (Figure 8.1).

Conversely, negative experiences can damage the connection between players and the game, leading to disengagement and weakening their bond. LiveOps teams must navigate these landscapes with care. To truly understand how players engage with a game it is important for LiveOps teams to focus on

DOI: 10.1201/9781003427056-12

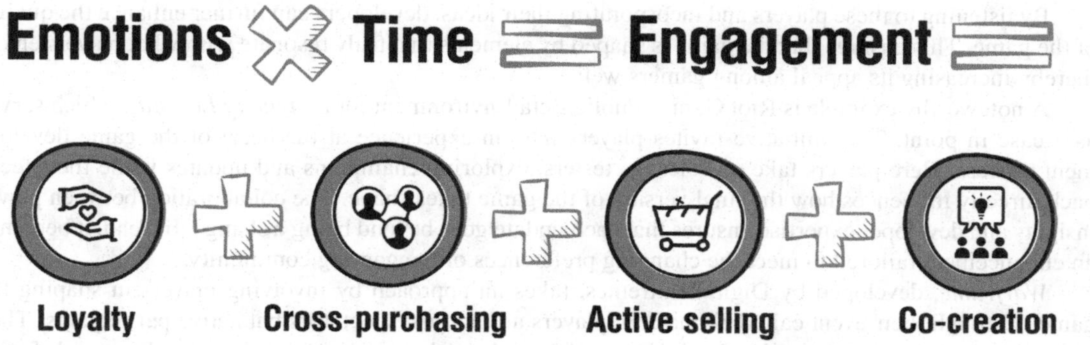

FIGURE 8.1 Positive engagement results in outcomes such as loyalty, cross-purchasing, active selling, and co-creation.

nurturing drivers that align with players' intrinsic needs and the overall goals of the game. This includes understanding why players connect with the game, what keeps them coming, how their emotions affect their in-game behavior, and who forms the core of the game community. By tapping into these aspects of engagement LiveOps can create experiences that deeply resonate with players. This increases the likelihood of long-term success and profitability.

THE VALUE OF ENGAGEMENT

Engaged players bring value to a game in different ways. First, they actively participate in shaping and improving the gaming experience, leading to enhancements that appeal to a player base. Second, engaged players tend to explore and purchase a variety of in-game products. Third, engaged players use word-of-mouth recommendations to attract new players and strengthen the games community. Lastly, engaged players generate content that can match the quality of professional work.

The success of a game's revenue model depends on its ability to keep players engaged for a time. This is where the "Engagement" factor in the lifetime value (LTV) equation becomes crucial. Strategies encouraging players to stay involved with the game ultimately increase their value over time, making engagement an important focus for any live service game. By creating a connection with the game and fostering a strong community, more players are motivated to participate in the in-game economy.

Lifetime value is a measure that encompasses different aspects. Each of these four boosters plays a role in increasing player loyalty, enhancing their value, attracting new players, and promoting quality user-generated content. Now, let's explore each of these aspects in detail and learn how to assess the value of each booster.

Boost 1: Increasing Loyalty

When players have a connection to a game, they often want to contribute to its improvement. They might come up with ideas for features or ways to enhance the gameplay experience. By sharing their ideas players can provide insights to developers about what they enjoy and what they would like to see in the game.

Some players are incredibly passionate about the product. They don't just play the game; they feel like they are part of the development team, driven by their desire to help make it the best it can be. These dedicated players hold importance because they genuinely care about the game's progress and its continuous improvement.

By listening to these players and incorporating their ideas, developers can further enhance the quality of the game. This ensures that the game is shaped by elements that truly resonate with what players enjoy, thereby increasing its appeal among gamers well.

A noteworthy example is Riot Games Public Beta Environment for *League of Legends*, which serves as a case in point. This initiative invites players into an experience at the heart of the game development process. Here players take on roles, as testers, exploring champions and updates while their feedback directly influences how the final version of the game takes shape. The collaboration between player insights and developer expertise ensures that each update goes beyond being a change. Instead, it becomes an enhancement tailored to meet the changing preferences of the gaming community.

Warframe, developed by Digital Extremes, takes an approach by involving players in shaping the game. Through their event called TennoCon, players are not just spectators but active participants. They engage in workshops and panels where they can freely share their ideas and visions for the game's future alongside its creators. These events break down barriers between players and developers, fostering a connection and understanding between both parties.

Zenimax Online Studios showcases how player feedback plays a role in refining *The Elder Scrolls Online*. By implementing an in-game ticketing system players have the opportunity to report bugs and issues contributing to an enjoyable gaming experience. This system not only resolves gameplay issues but also creates a collaborative environment where players feel valued and heard.

The enduring success of any title hinges on the loyalty and passion of its core audience. To truly comprehend the value these core players bring, it's essential to first identify who they are and track a spectrum of metrics. For in-game behavior, this includes the resilience to pricing shifts, the number of active days per week or month, and the average duration of gaming sessions, which paint a picture of the player's in-game commitment. Out-of-game contributions are with metrics like the volume and influence of player-suggested content and the frequency of their social advocacy for the game. Furthermore, it's important to consider the frequency and quality of contributions made by core players to enhance the game's knowledge base through forums, wikis, and bug reporting.

It is crucial to keep track of the growth and retention of the core player base. Metrics like how many new players join the core audience and how well these core players stick around over time provide an understanding of their long-term dedication to the game. By focusing on these metrics, LiveOps teams gain an understanding of how fostering player loyalty contributes to enhancing the game's lifetime value. Through strategies that encourage forms of player engagement, LiveOps can cultivate an active player community, leading to overall success and longevity for the game.

Boost 2: Leveraging Cross-Promotion

Cross-promotion serves as a strategy utilized by gaming studios to encourage players to delve into and enjoy games or content, within their portfolio. It's not about making transactions; it's about creating a sense of satisfaction, retention, and engagement within the gaming community. When players become completely absorbed and involved their behavior goes beyond playing the game—they actively seek out. This behavior is more than cross-purchasing; it's what we can call self-adoption.

In this context self-adoption occurs when players develop a trust and connection with the game and its universe. Engaged players don't just play for the sake of playing; they form a bond with the game that naturally leads them to explore and embrace features, expansions, or in-game items.

It's important to differentiate self-adoption, which is driven by player involvement and engagement, from selling methods driven by marketing techniques. The former relies on the depth of player engagement. When a game successfully fosters this level of engagement, the benefits are significant. Self-adoption led by players proves to be more profitable than traditional cross-selling strategies.

The reason is quite simple. Getting people to adopt something focusing on engagement requires investment in terms of marketing and sales efforts. Blizzard has found a way to do this effectively by offering rewards within their games, which helps build loyalty and trust among engaged players while also piquing their curiosity for the experiences that Blizzard has in store. They take it a step further by implementing a strategy where *Overwatch* players who are also subscribers of *World of Warcraft* get rewards. This approach ensures that players become deeply immersed in Blizzard's captivating gaming universe, motivating them to explore games in their catalogue. It's clear that Blizzard truly understands player behavior and preferences as they provide incentives that align with what players are interested in.

Valve has also embraced this concept by integrating its game portfolio with the Steam platform. For example, if you own games like *Half Life* or *Portal* you have the opportunity to unlock items in *Team Fortress*. This feature encourages players to delve into games created by Valve.

The focus here is not only on the lifetime value of individual titles but on the methods employed by gaming studios to encourage players to explore and enjoy games or content within the overall studio portfolio. This approach goes beyond increasing sales numbers; it aims to enhance player satisfaction, retention, and deeper engagement within the studio games. Cross-selling relies on understanding the preferences and needs of players and using that knowledge to provide tailored recommendations for products or content.

Various metrics can be utilized to assess the effectiveness of cross-selling. One important metric is the conversion rate, which measures the percentage of players who decide to try additional games and further make the first payment after being exposed to new content. This metric helps determine how successful cross-selling techniques are in converting players into buyers. Another valuable metric is cross-playtime across a studio's game portfolio. This metric tracks how much time players who engage in cross-promotion spend playing titles offered by the studio.

By prioritizing player engagement and establishing a connection between the player and all the games in the portfolio, these strategies highlight how organic adoption, fueled by player participation, can be more lucrative and sustainable compared to marketing-driven cross-selling. By implementing cross-promotion techniques, LiveOps teams can transform engaged players into advocates who actively explore their game portfolios.

Boost 3: Encouraging Advocacy

When players have a great time they often share their excitement with others. On the side if players come across negative aspects in a game they're more likely to express their discontent publicly. In the gaming world its widely known that players tend to talk about negative experiences than positive ones. Estimates suggest that players who share positive gaming experiences usually talk to around 5–10 people while those sharing negative experiences might tell 10–15 people.

However, these numbers are usually based on expectations when the game is enjoyable and meets basic standards. While these experiences are positive, they don't tend to create buzz. On the other hand, when players have an exceptional gaming experience that goes beyond mere satisfaction and becomes truly memorable, things change. In some cases the outstanding quality of the gaming experience becomes a story worth sharing. Players become advocates who not only share that they had a good time but passionately endorse the game itself. Their recommendations go from statements like "It was fun" to enthusiastic endorsements like "You absolutely have to play this game; it's absolutely incredible!" The endorsements gain their strength not from the sheer number of people they reach but also from the genuine enthusiasm and authenticity behind the players' recommendations. When engaged players actively promote a game, they become an asset for game studios, essentially transforming satisfied players into an enthusiastic and voluntary sales force.

Let's take a look at *PUBG* (*PlayerUnknowns Battlegrounds*) as an example. This game experienced a rise in popularity largely driven by player recommendations and the buzz within the gaming community. Players eagerly shared their exhilarating experiences and unforgettable moments from the game across platforms, including social media and gaming forums. The organic spread of enthusiasm among players played a role in fueling the game's growth. Statistics indicate that a substantial number of *PUBG* players were referred through word of mouth, surpassing the impact of traditional advertising efforts. While specific numbers may vary, it is widely acknowledged that active promotion by *PUBG* players played a pivotal role in driving exponential growth and widespread adoption of the game. This phenomenon exemplifies how satisfied players who are captivated by a gaming experience can become some of the most effective advocates for a game.

When players are thoroughly satisfied with their gaming experiences, they naturally become supporters who eagerly share their enjoyment with friends and fellow members within gaming communities. This word-of-mouth promotion often has a profound impact than any advertisement or marketing campaign. To measure the effectiveness of this advocacy, you can use metrics that capture the nuances of player recommendations and their influence on a game's growth and revenue.

Referral program metrics are crucial in this regard. By keeping track of how players share the game, we can understand how far their recommendations reach. We see this in games where players use in-game tools to invite others or show off their gameplay on media. Equally important is monitoring the number of visits or downloads that come directly from these player referrals. This gives us insights into how effective word of mouth is at attracting players. The conversion rate of these referrals is also significant as it tells us how well these recommendations turn into players. Additionally, evaluating the increase in revenue attributed to player referrals helps us measure the impact of this advocacy and reveals how player recommendations can contribute to a game's success. This is complemented by the cost-per-acquisition metric, which compares how efficient it is to acquire players through referrals compared to marketing strategies. This emphasizes the value of encouraging active selling.

Another important metric is the Net Promoter Score (NPS), which measures how likely players are to recommend the game to others. A high NPS indicates player advocacy, which is crucial for games that rely on community and player satisfaction for growth. Conducting surveys can help measure the NPS and provide insights into player satisfaction and their potential to advocate for the game within the player base.

By utilizing these metrics, LiveOps teams can gain an understanding of how player satisfaction leads to increased lifetime value for the game. This approach highlights not only creating engaging gameplay experiences but also fostering a community where players feel motivated to share their experiences, thereby expanding the game's reach and influence.

Boost 4: Fostering User-Generated Content (UGC)

UGC has emerged as an element that enhances player engagement and enriches the overall gaming experience. UGC can be found both within and outside the game environment. Outside the game it takes forms such as blog posts, live streams, memes and tutorials where the gaming community shares insights and strategies. Inside the game itself, players tweak game mechanics, characters, and levels. These modifications not only extend the game's lifespan but also ensure its constant freshness and appeal to both existing and new players.

For game developers promoting UGC brings benefits. It helps foster a community spirit while also ensuring that games remain relevant long after their initial release. Mods have particularly demonstrated their power in this regard by allowing players to express themselves and actively contribute to the evolution of games. This creates a sense of ownership and belonging among players.

On the one hand players engage with UGC for various reasons including expressing their creativity and enjoying social interactions with fellow gamers. They cherish opportunities to customize features within games while also seeking recognition from both their peers in the gaming community as well as developers themselves. In some cases, these player creations even become parts of games—opening up avenues for royalties or collaboration opportunities.

The Elder Scrolls V: Skyrim. stands out as an impressive example of how players can come together to shape the game. One remarkable aspect is the modding community, particularly the Beyond Skyrim project. Through this effort players have expanded the game universe well beyond its original boundaries. They have crafted lands, stories, and characters, effectively expanding the lore and providing fresh experiences for players worldwide.

This level of involvement demonstrates how UGS not only improves the gaming experience but empowers players to make their own mark on the game world. These initiatives highlight the impact of

UGC as it transforms games into evolving platforms driven by community creativity and passion. The Unreal Editor for *Fortnite* truly stands out in how it measures UGC and player engagement value.

- Player Popularity measures the ability of UGC to attract players and bring back those who have stopped playing. This metric is crucial as it reflects the appeal of UGC and its ability to expand the player base.
- Player Retention is another metric that shows how well UGC keeps players coming. Consistent playtime and a high rate of returning players indicate content that resonates with the audience.
- Time Played rewards creators based on how much time players spend in their UGC, emphasizing the importance of creating immersive and engaging content. A popular mod that keeps players engaged for periods not only enhances individual gaming experiences but also significantly contributes to the overall health of the game ecosystem.

By incorporating these metrics, LiveOps teams can quantitatively assess how UGC impacts player engagement and contributes to a game's lifetime value. This approach assists developers in nurturing a vibrant UGC community that actively contributes to the game's long-term sustainability and achievements.

STRATEGIES FOR ENGAGEMENT

In previous chapters we discussed how value creation encompasses all the activities involved in adding value to a game, from its concept to its live operations. Similarly, engagement is developed through a chain of steps, starting with the core gameplay and then getting enhanced with elements like meta-game, economy, and extra content. Eventually, it matures through live services. This layered approach ensures that initial engagement is firmly rooted in the game's core offering, which is crucial for retaining players in the run.

Player engagement with the game usually resembles a heartbeat chart—with spikes, declines and growth zones, seasonality and rhythm. At a high level, it consists of three components—baseline generated by base game's retention, updates with extra content or new game modes, and live service that maintains eventfulness in between (Figure 8.2).

Baseline is driven by games' installs and retention curve. First-time user experience, gameplay, setting, and pacing define early retention. Day 7–14 retention is driven more by the game's meta, gameplay variety, and depth. Day 30+ will typically be driven by social more than everything.

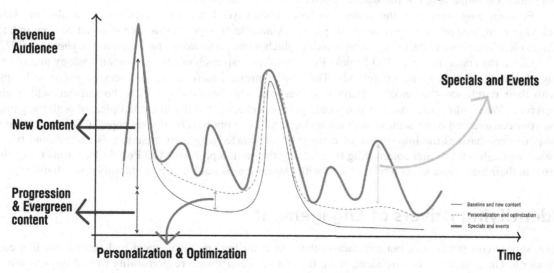

FIGURE 8.2 Correlation of player engagement depends on new content, personalization, and special events.

The truth about baseline engagement is that it will be going down over time as the incoming audience declines both in quantity and quality (tip: look at retention per time cohort to understand this dynamics). Therefore, it's important to consider regular injection of engagement with updates. Season passes, DLCs, new game modes all provide a great opportunity to boost re-engagement and extend the game's lifetime.

Product updates being driven by development effort have a major limitation—they usually require significant investment of time, content production, and engineering resources to execute. And this profit-and-loss equation doesn't always warrant high frequency and scale. Therefore, it's wise for game teams to invest in strategies that could add engagement. Strategies, like encouraging player self-expression, capitalizing on momentum, or fostering team involvement, can revitalize the player experience. These strategies provide valuable tools for re-engaging players and revitalizing the game's ecosystem. This ensures that the chain of creating engagement keeps moving forward, fueling both player lifetime and game lifetime value.

Empowering Team Engagement

To drive player engagement effectively it is essential for the organization from game developers to customer support teams to share a common vision. It is crucial for everyone involved to understand the importance of fostering an engaged player community.

To achieve this goal, comprehensive training and coaching sessions are necessary. These sessions could include workshops that focus on designing games with players in mind, where developers work on creating features that directly address player feedback and preferences. It would be beneficial to invite a group of players to participate in these workshops either virtually or in person as their real-time feedback and ideas can be invaluable. Additionally conducting workshops where the development team delves into player data and analytics can help them gain insights into player behaviors, preferences, and pain points.

However, mere understanding is not sufficient; the team must embody engagement through their actions. The staff at a game studio should genuinely be enthusiastic and positive about their work and the games they develop. If they are not excited or willing to share aspects of their games with their personal networks, it is unlikely that players will become engaged either. This principle is illustrated by a case where a significant number of employees do not play their games.

Leadership also plays a role in fostering player engagement. The leaders and directors at the top level should lead by example showing a sincere and strong dedication to the game and its community. This approach from the top helps foster an atmosphere where active player involvement is not simply a target but rather a genuine result of the studio culture.

Ensuring engagement in the gaming industry goes beyond providing experiences; it also involves acknowledging and addressing issues as they arise. A notable example of this approach can be seen in CD Projekt Red's response to the criticism surrounding glitches and performance problems with *Cyberpunk 2077*.

Given the concerns raised CD Projekt Red has taken responsibility by issuing an apology and offering players the option to request refunds. The team expressed their desire for every player to be happy with their purchase—"we would always like everyone who buys our games to be satisfied with their purchase. We would appreciate it if you would give us a chance, but if you are not pleased with the game on your console and don't want to wait for updates, you can opt to refund your copy." CD Projekt Red's response emphasizes the importance of companies acknowledging their mistakes. By addressing these issues through refunds and committing to resolving the game's problems CD Projekt Red aims to regain trust in their brand and foster a relationship with players that is built on accountability and reliability.

Identifying Drivers of Engagement

You should constantly seek out any factors that can contribute to engagement and any factors that can hinder it. Once these factors are identified it becomes a management responsibility to find ways to leverage or eliminate them.

When the COVID-19 pandemic emerged, Epic Games saw an opportunity to utilize *Fortnite* as a platform for events and collaborations. The game hosted concerts, movie screenings, and formed partnerships with brands transforming it into a social space. This strategic shift attracted a more diverse audience, including non-players who were intrigued by the cultural events happening within the game's universe. By aligning with events and partnering with diverse brands, *Fortnite* showcased how games can effectively serve as mediums for communication and engagement that go beyond traditional gaming audiences.

Sometimes the initial sources of engagement can hinder the growth. Let's take the example of *Pokémon GO*, an augmented reality game developed by Niantic. We can easily observe elements that drive engagement in the game. Its success lies in its ability to tap into players' desires for exploration, social interaction, and collecting Pokémon in the world. By introducing features that blend virtual elements with physical exploration, further engagement can be encouraged, captivating millions of players.

However, alongside these aspects *Pokémon GO* also faced challenges. Concerns regarding player safety and trespassing became significant as enthusiasts ventured into properties or unsafe areas during gameplay. Additionally public disturbances arising from gatherings at PokéStops as well as issues related to cultural sensitivity when placing game elements in sensitive locations. Addressing these concerns required not only refining the mechanics within the game but also educating players and engaging with non-players affected by the real-world impact of the game. Efforts to improve safety features, respect cultural boundaries, and build relationships within the community played a vital role in keeping the game's momentum going and making it appealing to a wider audience beyond just the players.

In both *Pokémon GO* and *Fortnite*, understanding and influencing both players and non-players are key factors in fostering engagement. Game developers and LiveOps need to go beyond improving the in-game experience. They should also deal with the social, cultural, and safety considerations of their gaming worlds. By doing this they can establish a lasting gaming ecosystem that engages and retains a range of players.

Leveraging Engagement

Dedicated players can become advocates for the game by actively promoting it because of their connection and enthusiasm toward the games. Such support from players, which isn't driven by commercial motives, often carries credibility that direct marketing messages from the game studio can't. Game studios can effectively promote their games by investing in community building and engagement efforts, such as organizing fan events or creating interactive platforms.

When planning events to encourage player engagement it's important to tailor them to appeal to the target audience. An excellent example of this approach is Valve Corporations *Dota 2* Short Film Contest. This contest aligns perfectly with *Dota 2*s spirit by encouraging community members to create films related to the game. These films often showcase a blend of humor, creativity, and deep knowledge of *Dota 2*, reflecting the passions and skills within the *Dota 2* community. This event has become a part of *Dota 2*s strategy, for engaging with its community significantly contributing to the game's popularity and cultural impact.

In the world of F2P live service games there exists a small group of players commonly known as "whales" who contribute a significant amount of revenue. Gaming teams treat these players like members of a club offering them privileges such as access to private parties, personal community managers, and the chance to meet esports celebrities. However, game developers also strive to engage an audience that goes beyond the most dedicated players, including their friends and family. This creates a sense of inclusivity and belonging within both the player and non-player communities.

A great example of this strategy is Wargaming Fest: Tanker Day, which is a celebration organized by the creators of *World of Tanks* to honor the national Tanker Day. This event truly showcases their dedication to engaging with the community as it attracted 250,000 attendees from 28 countries and had 2.6 million viewers worldwide. During this festival passionate players were given opportunities for self-expression, participation in gaming activities, and complete immersion in their game's universe. Events like Tanker Day demonstrate how gaming companies not only nurture their players but also create inclusive experiences that celebrate and engage their entire player base.

Each step taken to foster player engagement—such as encouraging team participation, leveraging momentum, and empowering player self-expression—contributed to what has been achieved by enhancing overall levels of engagement within the game. This engagement naturally grew over time as a game refines its offerings, making them more enticing and immersive for players. As the engagement between players and the game grows stronger, it propels the game ahead of its competitors, resulting in a player community and increased revenue.

The increased revenue allows for investment in aspects that contribute to the success of the game. This includes enhancing game design, implementing strategies to attract players, and enriching out-of-game experiences while also improving profitability. In-game events play a role in maintaining and amplifying this engagement. These events act as platforms for players to interact with each other by offering captivating content and experiences that keep them engaged and invested in the game. Through these events game studios can introduce challenges, rewarding opportunities, and compelling narratives to create an appealing gaming environment (Figure 8.3).

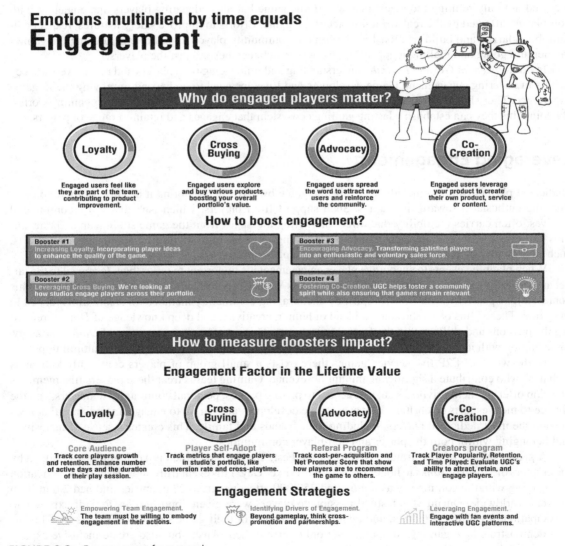

FIGURE 8.3   Engagement framework.

Monetization

9

The gaming industry has undergone a significant evolution in terms of monetization models, adapting to changing player behaviors, technological advancements, and market demands. This evolution has led to the development of diverse and sophisticated ways to monetize games, each with its own set of strategies and implications for both developers and players.

Premium Model (One-Time Purchase or Subscription): In the premium model, players pay upfront to access the full game. This could be a one-time purchase, as seen with *The Witcher 3: Wild Hunt*, where players pay once to get full access to the sprawling fantasy world and its numerous quests. Alternatively, it could involve a subscription model, such as *World of Warcraft*, which offers ongoing content updates and a massive multiplayer online experience in exchange for a monthly fee. This model is straightforward and assures a fixed revenue per sale or subscription. However, the challenge lies in convincing players to make an initial investment without first experiencing the game, which can limit the player base compared to other models.

Freemium Model (In-App Purchases or In-App Advertising): The freemium model offers the game for free, with revenue generated through in-app purchases, as seen with *Warframe*, where players can enjoy the game for free but have the option to purchase in-game items to enhance their experience. Alternatively, revenue can be generated through in-app advertising, exemplified by *Street Fighter V*, where optional ads appear during loading screens, on stages, and on costumes. This model can attract a larger player base and allows for continuous engagement and revenue generation through microtransactions. However, balancing the game's design to ensure fair play between paying and non-paying players can be challenging.

Hybrid Model: The hybrid model creatively combines elements of both premium and freemium models. It might involve an initial purchase or subscription, coupled with the option for in-game purchases or ad-supported gameplay. An example is the *EA Sports FC*, which allows players who have bought the game to further engage through in-game purchases, building their dream team. This approach allows developers to cater to a broader spectrum of players, from those willing to pay upfront for a premium experience to those maximally engaged and ready to make optional purchases for additional game content. This flexibility can maximize a game's reach and revenue potential, but it requires careful balancing to ensure that all players have a satisfying experience.

As the industry continues to innovate, these models evolve and intertwine, creating complex monetization strategies that cater to diverse player preferences and market trends. The focus of this book will be on the freemium model and its integration into hybrid models, exploring how these strategies can effectively monetize games while providing engaging and fair experiences for players.

The free-to-play model evolved from the freemium model, a concept born in the software industry of the 1980s. In this model, players are given access to a fully functional game, but the allure of additional content, features, or benefits encourages them to make in-game purchases, known as microtransactions. Sometimes, the game design incorporates significant time sinks to incentivize non-paying players to unlock additional content more quickly through payments.

The shift from premium (box games) to freemium (live services game) models has been primarily influenced by transformations in how games are distributed and consumed. Mobile devices, cloud storage services, digital distribution channels, and digital payment methods have altered the gaming landscape. Now, games can be discovered and enjoyed anytime, anywhere, without the need for physical discs.

The potential reach of freemium games is massive and unrestricted by traditional constraints, capable of engaging millions, if not billions, of players upon launch.

Fundamentally, all business models, including free to play, are flexible structures created to achieve a game's specific objectives. For the purposes of this book, the free-to-play model is defined as a business strategy in which a significant portion of a game's content is made available for free in an environment with low production and distribution costs, thereby facilitating vast scalability. Additional features, premium access, and other benefits are available for a fee. This strategy has gained traction in the gaming industry, serving as the foundation for games like *League of Legends*, *Dota 2*, and *World of Tanks*. Initially used in early massively multiplayer online games targeting casual gamers, it has since been adopted by major game publishers to promote broader player engagement.

FREE-TO-PLAY BUSINESS MODEL

The Free-to-Play (F2P) business model is designed for frictionless distribution, targeting a broad range of potential players. It's based on three main components:

- **Accessibility:** A price point of $0 makes the game accessible to the largest number of players.
- **Engagement:** The majority of players are not engaged beyond the free tier of game content.
- **Monetization:** If a game strongly appeals to a subset of players and offers opportunities for significant or repeat purchases, these players might spend more than they would have if the game had an up-front cost.

When these three components are properly balanced, they aim to generate total revenue that surpasses what could be expected from a game that requires only an up-front payment. However, certain patterns across the F2P landscape should be noted:

- **Monetization Potential:** The more universally appealing a game is, the more players it can reach, and the more widely it will be adopted.
- **Monetization Rate:** A small percentage of F2P players usually monetize, referred to as the 5% rule. This necessitates a large potential player base to achieve a respectable number of paying players.
- **Monetization Spectrum:** The total amount spent by players covers a wide range. A small minority of highly engaged players often contributes to a significant portion of the revenue.

The adoption of the Free-to-Play (F2P) model is a pivotal decision that needs to be made during the game's pre-production design phase, as it significantly impacts all subsequent development processes. Central to the success of an F2P game is not only its inherent potential but also the proficiency and experience of the development team in effectively implementing this business model. The F2P model, characterized by its scalability through low distribution and production costs, doesn't require massive scale to succeed but rather benefits from the ability to reach a broad player base.

It's important to note that a large scale is not a prerequisite for success in the F2P model. Games targeting niche enthusiasts (e.g., *World of Tanks*) can also be successful if they achieve high levels of monetization from dedicated players. The proportion of players who monetize in F2P games can vary significantly, but it's often quite low. Thus, anticipating this during the development process allows developers to build a more realistic revenue strategy. This understanding underscores the concept known as the 5% rule, which isn't an actual rule but a design decision based on the practicalities of the F2P model.

The Free-to-Play (F2P) business model, with its iterative development and operational nature, offers LiveOps teams a unique and continuous challenge. This approach demands a fine-tuned balance between adaptability and strategic foresight. Financial success in a live service game hinges not only on the initial offering but also on the team's ability to consistently excel in key areas. These include gaining deep insights into player behavior, creatively navigating monetization strategies in a free-to-play landscape, and constantly optimizing game elements for peak performance.

Insight

Insight is a crucial component of the F2P game and is gained through tracking interactions between players and the game, and leveraging data tools and procedures. This understanding allows the LiveOps team to optimize the game's performance according to specific metrics. Insight represents the game's entire data supply chain, from collection to analysis. It's a two-part process:

- **Data Collection:** This involves tracking and storing player interactions and making this information accessible. This is typically achieved by the game's developer. Further details about the technical infrastructure for data retrieval, storage, and access will be covered in Chapter 13.
- **Data Analysis:** This involves interpreting the collected data to improve the game. It can manifest as regular reporting of key metrics or analysis of specific game features to better understand their performance. This process is often known as business intelligence, a topic that will be covered in detail in Chapter 14.

Player segmentation emerges as a pivotal analysis technique, distinguishing common traits among different player archetypes. This approach is not only fundamental for understanding past player interactions (descriptive analytics) but also crucial for shaping future strategies (prescriptive analytics). In F2P models, recognizing and capitalizing on revenue optimization opportunities hinge on a deep comprehension of payment behaviors. Serving the interests of paying players—those most engaged with the core gameplay—becomes paramount. Insight here translates to a profound grasp of the reasons, timings, and conditions under which these players choose to spend.

However, insight in F2P games transcends mere record-keeping. It's about sculpting a detailed model of player needs based on their interaction history. This process is geared toward enhancing player experiences through ongoing game development. By analyzing historical data, we gain a clear picture of how players engage with the game and what drives their purchasing decisions. But more importantly, through prescriptive analytics, we start hypothesizing and testing future actions to optimize game performance. This approach is particularly vital for LiveOps teams, as it not only illuminates the path taken but also lights the way forward, suggesting what steps to take next for optimal game enhancement.

As a game's player base expands, the volume and diversity of data generated offer additional insights into player behavior. Data from non-paying players proves just as valuable in this context. It contributes significantly to optimizing revenue streams by fostering more accurate player profiles and enhancing the communication channels between players and the LiveOps team. While descriptive analytics offer a retrospective view of player interactions, it's the forward-looking, action-oriented nature of prescriptive analytics that becomes a cornerstone for LiveOps teams in continuously refining and evolving the gaming experience.

Monetization

Monetization, despite the $0 price point, remains at the core of the F2P game. While it's tempting to think that all aspects of an F2P game are constructed around monetization, the reality is more intricate. Many F2P games skillfully balance monetization with other essential elements such as player experience, community engagement, and long-term player retention.

In an F2P game, spending money doesn't simply unlock a set of features—it elevates the entire gaming experience. This model removes the initial financial barrier, thereby broadening the player base. It's an approach that is not just beneficial for those who can't afford to buy a game upfront but also for those who are initially unsure about the game's value.

Over time, F2P games reveal distinct advantages. Some players might initially lack the disposable income to make in-game purchases but could become paying players once their financial situation improves. Others might find the in-game value so compelling that they choose to invest more heavily, thereby extracting maximum enjoyment and engagement from the game.

The goal of the LiveOps team is to optimize for the latter scenario, allowing players who derive the most value from the game the freedom to enhance their experience to the fullest. This approach can unlock a revenue dynamic that outperforms traditional up-front payment models.

However, setting up such a pricing model in a F2P game requires significant effort and strategic consideration. It is crucial for LiveOps teams to understand the importance of leveraging monetization strategies in the F2P model to create a balance between player satisfaction and revenue generation.

Optimization

Optimization is the bread and butter for F2P game and is tightly interwoven with the iterative development approach. This process involves refining game elements based on player behavior data to enhance performance metrics. The goal is to make fast, informed decisions and implement improvements rapidly to reap the benefits sooner.

However, optimization in F2P game development is a balancing act. Overemphasis can divert attention from new content or features, while underemphasis might result in missed opportunities for performance enhancement. Costs are also associated with optimization, including direct costs like developer time, opportunity costs from pursuing other development goals, and hidden costs from focusing too narrowly on certain processes. Optimization takes two forms:

- **Global Optimization:** This involves enhancing the overall performance of the game and relates to monetization game design. It's more complex, requiring a broad understanding of the player experience and long-term product success, often related to revenue.
- **Local Optimization:** This focuses on improving a specific process or element within the game. It's straightforward and measurable—a process that is fully under LiveOps team control.

While local optimizations are easier to implement and measure, they could produce negative long-term results if not considered as part of a global optimization strategy. For example, making monetization mechanics highly visible might improve revenue performance in the short term, but could also alienate players, impacting the long-term success of the game.

The case of *Star Wars Battlefront II* serves as a poignant example of the delicate balance between monetization and player satisfaction. Upon its release in 2017, the game faced intense scrutiny and backlash due to its aggressive monetization strategy, particularly the implementation of a loot box system that was perceived as pay-to-win. The uproar from the community was so significant that it not only dominated gaming news headlines but also caught the attention of regulators and lawmakers around the world. Responding to the widespread criticism, the developers were compelled to temporarily disable microtransactions entirely, fundamentally reworking the game's progression and monetization system post-launch. This scenario underscores the importance of aligning monetization strategies with player expectations and the potential repercussions of prioritizing short-term revenue gains over a fair and engaging player experience. Striking the right balance between continuous improvement and ensuring net positive effects on a game level is crucial. This balance can only be achieved through insights that measure both short- and long-term impacts and can warn about negative trends.

F2P games are often designed as evolving platforms, where small, iterative process improvements over long periods allow for subtle yet impactful changes to be quickly implemented. Optimization aids the F2P model by tailoring the game to the needs and preferences of its players, but it must be done methodically. It should be viewed as a tool, not a stand-alone strategy. As such, it should not replace game development but be used to enhance already developed features with the goal of achieving long-term performance improvements.

FREE-TO-PLAY ECONOMICS

The F2P model aims for scalability and optimal monetization from the most engaged players, hence price and supply become the crucial focus points. While academic models tend to be abstract, it's beneficial to grasp the economic principles that underpin the F2P model because of its broad application.

F2P games span a wide variety of genres, making it necessary to provide a flexible and comprehensive framework for understanding and developing within the F2P model, rather than a narrow, genre-specific approach. Given the model's dynamic nature and versatility across different platforms and player demographics, it's vital to thoroughly understand the economic principles that contribute to its effectiveness.

Price Elasticity of Demand

The concept of Price Elasticity of Demand is central to understanding the economics of Free-to-Play (F2P) games. Essentially, it measures how changes in price influence the quantity demanded of a good. In general, when prices rise, demand decreases, but the rate of this decrease varies for different goods.

This idea was formally introduced by economist Alfred Marshall in his book, *Principles of Economics*, published in 1890. Marshall brought together various economic theories of his time, focusing particularly on the effects of supply and demand on prices. He suggested that price changes usually have a negative correlation with consumer demand—as the price of a good increases, consumer demand for that good decreases. This concept, known as the law of demand, describes an inverse relationship between the price of a good and the quantity demanded, assuming all other product characteristics and external market forces remain equal.

The law of demand is often represented by a demand (D) curve, where price (P) is plotted on the y-axis and quantity (Q) on the x-axis. The curve could be linear, suggesting a steady relationship between price and quantity demanded, or nonlinear, indicating a varying relationship at different price points (Figure 9.1).

Movement along this curve occurs when the price of a good changes, but overall customer sentiment and market conditions remain the same. However, when these market dynamics shift, we observe a "demand curve shift." A shift to the right, for instance, suggests an increase in demand at every price point.

In the context of Free-to-Play (F2P) games, demand curve shifts are typically driven by changes in players' capabilities or desires to make in-game purchases. This could be influenced by numerous factors such as major demographic shifts, global economic fluctuations, significant technological advancements, and other widespread or regional trends.

The 'price elasticity of demand' measures how responsive the demand for a good is to a change in its price. It is calculated as the ratio of the percentage change in quantity demanded, determined by the

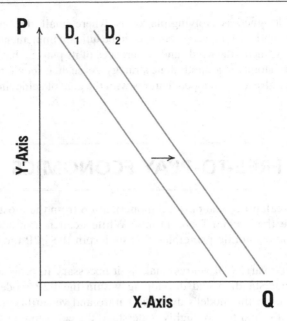

FIGURE 9.1 Shifts in demand.

difference between the new and initial quantity divided by the initial quantity, to the percentage change in price, determined by the difference between the new and initial price divided by the initial price.

In a scenario where the demand decreases by −500 in-game skins from an initial 1000 skins after a price increase of +$10 from an initial $50, the calculation of elasticity is as follows: The percentage changes in quantity demanded (−50%) and price (20%) result in a price elasticity of demand of −2.5.

If the price elasticity ratio is exactly −1, the good is described as 'unit elastic,' implying that any change in price results in an equivalent change in quantity demanded. If the price elasticity ratio falls between −1 and −∞, the good is considered 'relatively elastic.' In this case, even minor changes in price can result in significant changes in demand. This is often the case for goods with many substitutes, where players are relatively indifferent between options.

On the other hand, if the price elasticity ratio lies between −1 and 0, the good is 'relatively inelastic.' Here, even significant changes in price lead to relatively small changes in demand. This is typical of 'necessity goods,' for which few alternatives exist, and without which players' experience would be negatively impacted.

In the digital realm of games, many goods tend to exhibit unit elasticity, implying that the quantity demanded is heavily dependent on the price set. However, there are exceptions, particularly when it comes to items that offer no in-game utility or perceived value.

For instance, an in-game item that does not influence progression, has no impact on the core gameplay, and holds no cosmetic appeal is likely to exhibit perfect inelasticity at low quantities. In simpler terms, the demand for these items remains constant regardless of changes in price, primarily because they do not enhance the gameplay experience or confer status benefits to the player.

Another example is "Veblen goods," named after the economist Thorstein Veblen. These are luxury items where the perceived quality is directly related to their price. Purchasing these goods is often driven by a desire for status. This means that as the price of a Veblen good increases, so does its demand.

In the sphere of Free-to-Play games, Veblen goods could be represented by high-priced rare in-game items or exclusive features. The high price of these items enhances their perceived value and status, making them more desirable to certain players.

Price Discrimination

The concept of price elasticity of demand centers on the relationship between price sensitivity and the quantity of goods sold at various price points. However, it assumes that a single price exists for a given product. In a competitive marketplace, a supplier typically uses their production's marginal cost and the concept of price elasticity of demand to inform their pricing strategy and optimize total revenue. This happens in highly transparent markets with low entry barriers, where many suppliers produce almost identical substitute goods.

Suppliers price their goods based on the intersection of the demand (D) and supply curves (S). Like a demand curve, a supply curve is a set of points on a graph with price (P) on the y-axis and quantity (Q) on the x-axis. The supply curve has an upward slope because, all else being equal, a supplier should be willing to produce more products at a higher sale price than at a lower one (Figure 9.2).

The point where the supply and demand curves meet is the equilibrium price (EP), the price P_1 at which the entire quantity Q_1 will be sold. While Q_1 units of the product are sold at the equilibrium price, the demand curve does not originate at this price point; instead, it starts at the demand curve's intercept on the y-axis, P_0, representing a price at which no consumers would be willing to purchase the product.

Some units of the product could be sold at price levels between P_0 and Q_1; the total value of these units, known as the consumer surplus, represents savings for consumers who were prepared to purchase the product at price points between P_0 and P_1 but were offered the product at the lower price of EP. This surplus exists when a supplier sets a single price point for its product, but it can be captured by the supplier if they can identify, segment, and market to the consumers willing to pay prices on the demand curve between P_0 and P_1.

Economists began to understand that customers derive different levels of "utility" or benefit from identical goods due to their varying needs and desires. This led to the concepts of "reserve price" and

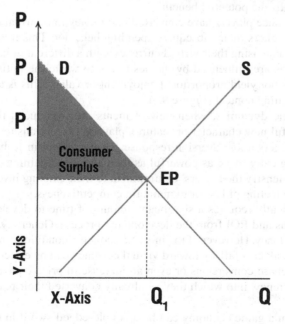

FIGURE 9.2   Diagram of consumer surplus.

"consumer surplus." Different customers may be willing to pay different prices for the same product, depending on factors like their wealth or the utility they derive from the product. For instance, a collector might pay more for a rare item to add to their collection compared to a casual player.

This strategy, known as price discrimination, involves offering different prices to different consumer segments instead of pricing a product at its equilibrium price. The price at which an individual consumer is willing to purchase a product is their reserve price. By charging consumers their individual reserve prices, down to the equilibrium price, a supplier can maximize its total potential revenue.

There's a crucial distinction to make when discussing "equilibrium price" and "price elasticity of demand" in the context of digital goods. Traditionally, these concepts assume a direct relationship between the quantity of supply and price, i.e., producers can adjust supply, which consequently affects the price. However, in the realm of video games, the supply is virtually infinite. Moreover, "profit maximization" usually depends on "marginal cost," the cost of producing and selling one more unit. But the marginal cost of digital goods like in-game assets is effectively zero.

The disruptive nature of digital replication and distribution may seem to challenge the logic of classical price economics. However, it's not necessarily the case. While certain implications are worth exploring, the effects of digital replication and distribution are often exaggerated, mainly due to a misunderstanding of economic theory. A player doesn't consume in-game items the way they would consume dairy products. Instead, we should consider the industry as a whole. There is indeed a marginal cost involved in creating a new game, vehicles, or avatar; moreover, the supply of new games is not limitless.

Sunk Cost

In the complex ecosystem of live service gaming, player engagement and investment are often deeply intertwined, particularly in the context of financial expenditures within these virtual realms. The sunk cost fallacy, a concept widely recognized in behavioral economics, plays a crucial role in shaping player behavior, especially when it comes to financial investments in games. This phenomenon, as described by Daniel Kahneman and Amos Tversky in their Prospect Theory, highlights how people tend to irrationally follow through on an endeavor once they have invested time, money, or effort into it, even if the current cost of continuing outweighs the potential benefit.

In live service games, once players have converted real money into virtual currency, they have made an initial commitment that alters their subsequent spending behavior. This initial financial commitment often leads players to continue using their virtual currency with a different mindset than they would with actual cash. Their decisions are influenced by the desire not to waste the initial investment, even if the continued investment does not yield proportional enjoyment or value. This is a direct application of the sunk cost fallacy in the gaming context (Figure 9.3).

Regarding the in-game dynamics, when new elements are introduced that overshadow previous investments (like a powerful new character or feature), players' perceptions of value and investment are challenged. This often triggers a loss aversion response, a key concept in Kahneman's work, where the pain of losing is psychologically twice as powerful as the pleasure of gaining. Thus, the introduction of such game elements can intensify the players' commitment to their existing investment, compelling them to spend more to avoid the feeling of loss or to maintain competitiveness.

Premium content typically requires a significant amount of time to develop, with the primary aim being to maximize margins and ROI from the development process. Generally, LiveOps teams prefer to sell fresh content for real money. However, if the in-game economy conditions indicate a surplus of virtual currency, leveraging the sunk cost fallacy toward virtual currency can be effective. This approach allows for potentially higher purchase conversions or even an increase in price equivalent, as players are more likely to spend virtual currency, into which they've already converted their real money, thus reinforcing the sunk cost fallacy.

The high instability in a game economy can be a double-edged sword in this context. While introducing new elements in a game can initially excite players and potentially lead to increased revenue

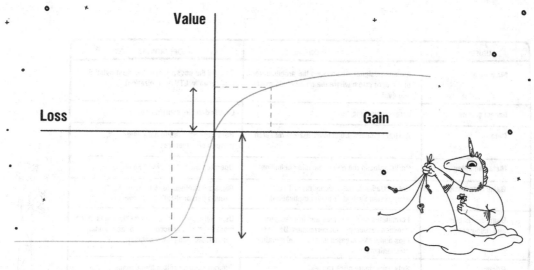

FIGURE 9.3   Value function in prospect theory.

through microtransactions, it also poses a significant risk. Over time, constant changes or imbalance can erode the perceived value of previous investments, leading to player dissatisfaction and, eventually, disengagement.

From an ethical standpoint, it is essential for game developers to consider the long-term impacts of their monetization strategies. It's not just about creating a profitable game but also about fostering a sustainable and satisfying player experience. The goal should be to design games that respect and value players' investments, offer fair challenges, and provide rewarding experiences without exploiting their inclination to honor sunk costs.

Responsible game design involves creating a stable and balanced game economy, where new content enhances rather than undermines previous investments. This approach not only respects the players' commitment but also ensures the longevity and health of the game's community. It's about building a game environment where players feel that their time and money are well-spent, leading to genuine satisfaction and a positive, long-lasting relationship with the game.

IN-GAME ECONOMY

In the dynamic world of Free-to-Play (F2P) gaming, the in-game economy stands as a crucial aspect, akin to the governance and economic systems of countries like the US or China. Just as these countries have distinct approaches to managing their economies, F2P games vary in how they structure and control their virtual economies. This variation is essential for defining the player experience and the game's financial success.

The creation and management of an in-game economy involve the expertise of two key roles: the Game Economist and the Game Monetizator. The Game Economist is responsible for designing the virtual economy, establishing a framework that dictates how players interact with and within the game world. This role involves setting up systems for player trading, establishing purchase limits, and managing virtual assets. The economist must also balance the distribution of rewards, ensure the proper funding of virtual resources, and control virtual currency inflation to maintain a stable and engaging game environment.

SUBJECT	GAME ECONOMIST	LIVEOPS MONETIZATION
Main Role	A game designer who defines the architecture of the ecosystem where the game could exist and evolve.	Operate the ecosystem in the most optimal way (usually, LTV maximization)
Impact gravity	Large-scale, long-term	Low/mid-scale, short/mid-term
Data	Abstract models, projections, market research	Hard experimentation data, forecasts, performance metrics
Meta gameplay	Participates in the meta gameplay definition	Operates with what was defined
Game progression	Creates/adjusts game economy to fit the progression system or player motivations	Adjusts incentives to reinforce progression through personalization and events
Game currencies and resources	Formulates dependencies and interactions between resources and currencies. Defines taps and sinks; creates inflation and deflation mechanisms	Uses inflation and deflation mechanisms in the most optimal way according to the roadmap, seasonality, and player segment
Pricing	Sets acceptable price ranges	Operates prices within those ranges

FIGURE 9.4 Differences between game economist and LiveOps monetizator.

Meanwhile, the Game Monetizator operates within this carefully constructed ecosystem, focusing on optimizing the game's revenue streams without disrupting the player experience. They adapt monetization strategies to the ever-changing landscape of player behaviors and market trends. This involves not only setting dynamic pricing models that respond to player demand and supply but also managing how these strategies impact the overall balance of the game's virtual assets.

The interaction between the Game Economist and the Game Monetizator is much like the interplay between government policy and business operations in the global economy. While the Game Economist sets the stage, defining the rules and structure of the game's economy, the Game Monetizator navigates this environment to maximize financial returns. They must do so in a way that retains player engagement and ensures the longevity of the game.

In practice, this involves a continuous cycle of analysis, adaptation, and implementation. For example, the Game Economist might observe trends in player trading and adjust the virtual currency's value to prevent inflation. Simultaneously, the Game Monetizator could introduce targeted promotions or special offers to encourage spending, especially in areas where there is a surplus of virtual currency (Figure 9.4). The skills required for these roles are multifaceted, blending knowledge of economic theory with a deep understanding of player psychology and game design. Just as economists and business leaders navigate the complexities of the global economy, Game Economists and Monetizators must manage the microcosm of the game's economy, ensuring it remains vibrant, balanced, and profitable.

While the in-game economy mirrors aspects of the global economy, its scope and complexity are tailored specifically to the gaming environment, making it a unique field of study within the broader economic landscape. The details of game economic design is beyond the scope of this book, but understanding the fundamentals of game economics is essential for anyone involved in F2P game development and operation.

Type of Resources

Let's use a farming game as an example to discuss the different types of resources in games. In this game, players build and expand a farm, and there are two key resources: farm buildings (like barns or mills) and coins. Farm buildings show how far a player has progressed in the game, and coins are the game's currency, used for buying things within the game.

Energy and lives represent another critical type of resource within gaming. Energy operates analogously to a player's stamina; the depletion of energy results in the loss of a life. The concept of lives encapsulates the total number of attempts a player possesses before the cessation of the game.

Intricacy can be introduced into the game by instating a delay prior to the replenishment of lives. Additionally, imposing a limit on the total number of lives a player can hold concurrently enhances the game's challenge and stimulates players to regularly return to the game.

The equilibrium between the imposed delay duration and the cap on the maximum number of lives is instrumental in fostering an enjoyable and motivating gaming experience for players. This balance ensures that the game remains neither too demanding nor too undemanding, maintaining player engagement and interest.

Soft and hard currencies emerge as two distinct types of resources in games. Soft currency is a type that players can accumulate relatively easily within the game's ecosystem, often as rewards for accomplishing certain tasks or passing challenges. For instance, the completion of levels may yield coins which can then be expended on resources such as lives or boosters. Moreover, these coins might serve as a prerequisite for accessing specific levels, thereby playing a pivotal role in the game progression.

On the other hand, hard currency, typically symbolized by high-value items such as gems or gold, represents a more premium form of resource. It grants players access to exclusive features and items. The introduction of hard currency can infuse an element of flexibility into the game, enabling players to bypass certain steps and expedite their progression. This aspect can be particularly beneficial as it accommodates players of varying skill levels, ensuring that all players remain engaged and motivated.

Notably, hard currencies typically necessitate real money for acquisition, while soft currencies can be obtained either through in-game earnings or through the expenditure of hard currency. Consequently, the interplay between soft and hard currencies can add a layer of strategic complexity to the game, enhancing its appeal and engagement factor.

As you architect the design of your game economy, it is pivotal to consider how the diverse currencies and resources will influence the progression trajectory of players. Take, for instance, a farming-themed game. In such a context, obtaining farming equipment would be an essential element of player advancement. Simultaneously, other resources, such as boosters, can serve to facilitate the gameplay, making it more accessible. By offering an array of options, you can tailor the game to cater to a range of skill levels, thereby enhancing its appeal across a diverse player base.

Resources Taps and Sinks

Following the establishment of the currencies and resources, the next critical step is the identification of the "taps" and "sinks" in your game. "Taps" might include elements such as coins earned at each level, rewards dispensed at regular intervals, or prizes bestowed upon the completion of events. Conversely, "sinks" might encompass actions like employing coins to replenish lives, purchasing boosters, or acquiring extra moves to conclude a level.

In understanding game economies, let's take the example of a farming game, where players grow crops and sell them to progress in the game. Consider this gameplay structure:

- Players begin the game with a small farm that generates produce over time, such as apples.
- They can use the revenue from selling apples to buy more farmland or different types of crops.
- Upgrading the farmland or growing higher-value crops (like grapes or olives) generates more revenue and contributes to a sense of ongoing progression.

In this example, farmland and crops, along with the game's virtual currency, play key roles. Farmland and crops are virtual goods that are bought, cultivated, and sold by players, driving their progression in the game. The virtual currency is used for in-game transactions and can also be purchased in the game's store in exchange for real money.

The game's economy is based on the flow of these resources (farmland, crops, and currency) across various game systems and loops. To understand this resource flow, we categorize these elements as either sources or sinks. Sources represent ways players can earn currency, and sinks represent ways players spend currency. In our farming game example, the source is the revenue generated from selling crops, and the sink is the investment in more farmland or different crop types.

The interaction between sources and sinks is crucial to player engagement. An imbalance can negatively impact the game's playability. If the revenue source significantly outweighs the investment sink, the game may lack challenge, potentially becoming monotonous, and players will have no incentive to purchase virtual currency from the store. Conversely, if the revenue source is significantly lower than the investment sink, the game may become excessively difficult or punishing, leading to player frustration due to excessive grinding for currency.

It's vital to balance your game's difficulty, ensuring your resources don't make the game too easy or too hard. Monitor inventory and currency over time to spot imbalances that might affect player experience, such as resource hoarding, uncontrolled growth, or severe shortages. Design your game economy with progression in mind, so no item is useless at any stage of the game, while providing high-impact goals for experienced players to pursue.

It is essential to remember that the distribution of rewards and resources across distinct "taps" profoundly impacts the player's experience. An optimally balanced game will maintain an equilibrium between the aggregate yield from "taps" and the total expenditure in "sinks." This balance is crucial in ensuring the sustainability and enjoyment of the game.

Player Purchase Journey

Most games today offer a multitude of items for purchase, featuring a wide variety of options within those item groups. Additionally, live service games frequently receive content updates and new content injections, leading to an ever-growing range of goods. These items can be broadly categorized into commodities like in-game boosters, consumables, and premium accounts, as well as more unique or premium items like skins, characters, and avatars (Figure 9.5).

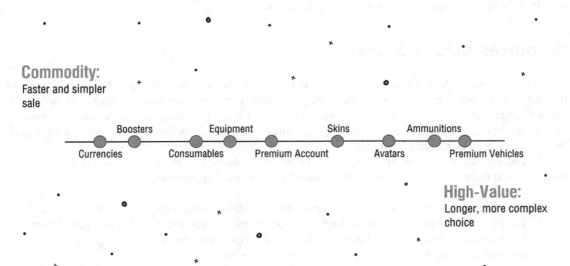

FIGURE 9.5   Content variety from commodity to high value.

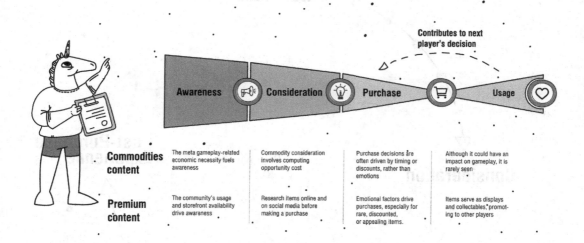

FIGURE 9.6 Awareness, consideration, purchase, usage funnel.

Commodities, such as boosters and consumables, are often driven by the game's internal economy. In contrast, premium items like unique skins or characters add a layer of exclusivity. Each category has a different purchase decision-making process, from awareness to usage, which plays a role in the player's journey through the game (Figure 9.6). Understanding the player purchase journey is critical, as it encompasses various touchpoints beyond just the in-game store.

- **Game Interfaces:** Here, players interact with the meta gameplay, encountering opportunities to make quick purchasing decisions. This can occur during regular gameplay or specific game modes where the appeal of premium content or the utility of commodities can become particularly evident.
- **Game Store:** A central hub for purchases, but it's only part of the journey. It's where players can explore and buy items, but the decision to purchase often starts elsewhere.
- **Web Portal, Launcher, or Companion App:** These touchpoints engage players when they are not actively playing the game, providing a platform for contemplation and purchase outside the immediate gaming environment.
- **Streaming Platforms:** Players watching others utilize game content can be inspired to make purchases. Seeing how premium content enhances the gaming experience can influence their decision to buy.

Each of these touchpoints contributes to a comprehensive ecosystem, influencing players at different stages of their journey (Figure 9.7):

Awareness: This is the initial stage where players first become aware of available commodities or premium content. This awareness can be sparked through various touchpoints:
  - In-game notifications or pop-ups showcasing new items.
  - Community and social media buzz about new content.
  - Observing other players using premium content during gameplay.
Consideration: At this stage, players are actively thinking about whether to purchase an item. They weigh the benefits and costs, considering how the item fits into their gameplay experience or enhances their enjoyment through various touchpoints:

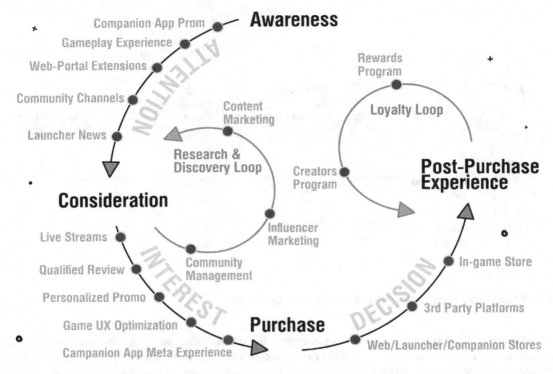

FIGURE 9.7   Awareness, consideration, purchase, usage loops.

- Detailed information within the in-game or web store about the benefits and features of items.
- Qualified reviews on third-party platforms demonstrating the use of premium content.

Purchase: This is the action stage where the player decides to buy. The ease of the purchasing process and the perceived value of the item at this point are crucial on the appropriate touchpoints:

- Store interfaces facilitating a smooth transaction.
- Special offers prompting immediate purchase.
- Third-party platform widgets or extensions providing immediate purchase options during viewing.

Usage: After purchasing, players use the item within the game. Their satisfaction with the purchase and its impact on gameplay can influence future purchasing decisions for other players:

- Recognition of player success by providing access to qualified review capabilities for premium content.
- Showcasing the player with special visuals during the game session.
- Opportunities for sharing experiences with others, encouraging word-of-mouth promotion.

In architecting your game's purchase journey, it's essential to recognize the diversity in player behaviors, skills, and preferences. While the majority of players in free-to-play games may not engage financially, catering to the minority who invest in the game is pivotal. Different levels of player engagement, from casual to deeply committed, must be considered, acknowledging that both paying and non-paying players bring value to the game's purchase journey. By strategically leveraging these touchpoints, align item types with player needs at every stage of their journey to enhance the overall experience.

Content Utilization Lifecycle

In any live service game, the absence of regular content updates can quickly diminish the game's potential for success and player engagement. Introducing new and compelling content is not just an add-on but a critical necessity for maintaining player interest.

However, it's crucial to remember that development resources are inherently limited. This makes it essential to integrate the content utilization lifecycle into the operations strategy. Without a well-thought-out approach to new content—from its initial release and permanent sale to personalized promotion and eventual elimination or rebalancing—even the most productive development team can't produce new content very frequently.

In the context of live service games, the content lifecycle represents the total time that a specific piece of in-game content is accessible and relevant to players. This lifecycle mapping can guide decisions about content release timing, pricing strategies, target audience identification, promotional activities, and more. Moreover, the content lifecycle should be closely linked with the player lifecycle. Premium content releases are significant events, but for someone who joins the game later, these events are part of the past, while the content itself is a fresh experience for them. This understanding is critical for determining the pricing and targeting.

In the content lifecycle of live service games, encompassing Development, Introduction, Growth, Saturation, and Decline stages, each phase demands distinct distribution tactics. During the Growth stage, the aim is to maximize margins and ROI from development through broad-based promotions. As the content reaches Saturation, targeted and personalized promotions become key to sustaining interest. Finally, in the Decline stage, strategies shift toward rebalancing or leveraging new audiences to extract residual value as its initial appeal diminishes (Figure 9.8).

Development: The development phase in the content lifecycle is focused on research, player analytics, and prototyping. During this stage, a significant amount of resources are spent, but no immediate revenue is generated, as the new content is still in the works. This phase's duration depends on the complexity of the content and the existing game dynamics.

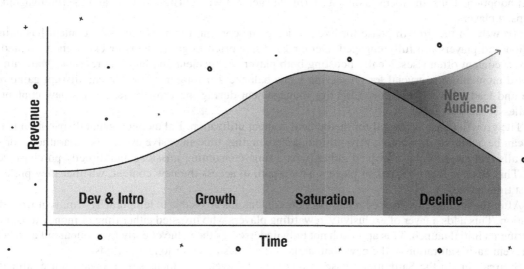

FIGURE 9.8 Content utilization lifecycle.

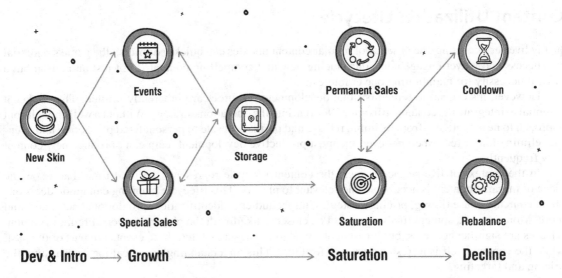

FIGURE 9.9   An example of a new skin utilization lifecycle.

Sometimes, the new content may be released to a subset of players or in a specific in-game environment for testing. This enables the LiveOps team to assess how well it is received, gather player feedback, and make necessary tweaks before a full-scale launch (Figure 9.9).

Introduction: The introduction phase is when the new content is in the final stage of development and the release date is fixed. Promotional activities ramp up during this stage, focusing on in-game promotions and external advertising. The goal is to warm up existing players and get them excited about the new content.

This phase is crucial for setting the stage for the content's future success. Early engagement with streamers or influencers can lead to positive reviews and recommendations, which can significantly impact wider adoption. Thus, the focus is on long-term engagement with existing players and the re-engagement of lapsed players.

Growth: In the growth phase for live service game content, the newly released content has gained traction and players are fully engaged. Demand for supported in-game items or experiences related to the new content often rises, ideally boosting both player engagement and in-game revenue. Maintaining upward momentum is crucial for preserving game balance. Rushing new content can disrupt game balance and lead to over-saturation. Effective management during the growth stage helps new content fit seamlessly into the game.

The growth phase is pivotal for methodical content utilization. Balancing content distribution is key and can be achieved in multiple ways: through challenging, time-intensive events like marathons, or via paywalls that cater to players who'd rather bypass time-consuming missions and directly purchase content. This ensures that all types of players have a path to access the new content, whether they prefer to invest time or money.

After the initial, time-limited release of new content, it's advisable to temporarily remove it from distribution. This adds a layer of exclusivity, rewarding players who invested either time or money to acquire it during its initial launch. This approach not only underscores the value of early investment but also helps to prevent early saturation of the new content, keeping it desirable for longer periods.

Saturation: In the Saturation phase of a content lifecycle, the focus shifts toward reuse, aimed at prolonging content relevance, maximizing player engagement, and monetization. One key consideration in this stage is the timing for content reintroduction, often influenced by financial KPIs. The ideal moment for bringing back content aligns with periods when a substantial fraction of Monthly Active Users hasn't yet engaged with it, making it essentially new and exciting for these players. For example, if new content was released during Christmas, it might be reintroduced 3–4 months later when enough of the MAU haven't played it during the initial HolidayOps release.

Alongside this, the content may transition to a state of "Permanent Sale," where it's priced in various in-game or real-world currencies to align with the game's current economic state. At this juncture, personalization becomes critical. Targeted promotions are crafted based on individual player behavior, whether that be gaming habits or financial engagement. The objective is to maintain the content's appeal, ensuring its longevity and continued relevance.

Decline: In the Decline phase of a content lifecycle, once-popular content starts to experience a reduction in player engagement and monetization. This downtrend can be attributed to a variety of factors, such as the emergence of more appealing content, shifts in player preferences, or simply the natural decline of interest over time. When content reaches this stage, the LiveOps teams face a series of strategic choices. They can opt for significant discounting to spur last-minute interest, rebalancing to make the content more competitive, or full removal from distribution to clear the field for more viable options.

However, it's crucial to remember that past premium content releases are perceived differently by newcomers to the game. For these players, past events are historical, yet the content remains a novel experience. This perspective is essential when considering pricing and targeting strategies.

MONETIZATION TECHNIQUES

In the realm of in-game economy design, achieving the desired balance and effectiveness at the first attempt is often an elusive goal. Anticipating player behaviors can be a challenging task, necessitating numerous iterations and refinements. However, the silver lining is the perpetual opportunity for optimization.

F2P economic principles aid in adeptly testing for price elasticity, ensuring your in-game items are optimally priced to maximize revenue. Implementing price discrimination strategies allows for the customization of prices according to player behaviors, striking a balance between profit maximization and fairness. Additionally, understanding the implications of the sunk cost effect on players' spending habits guides your approach in managing virtual currency and resource exchanges.

Implementing testing for different variables is critical to your game's monetization and engagement strategy, as it provides tangible evidence of what works and what needs adjustment. By systematically applying various techniques, you can iteratively fine-tune your game's economic environment to optimize player engagement and monetization.

Bundling and Discounts

Bundling and discounting techniques are rooted in the concept of price elasticity, a principle that also applies to in-game economies. The first step is to determine the intended elasticity of an item and, ideally, its actual elasticity within the live service game. Most digital goods tend to exhibit unit elasticity, meaning that the quantity demanded is directly related to the price set. However, there are exceptions. Items without any utility or perceived value in the game, such as those that neither impact progression nor possess cosmetic appeal, are likely to be perfectly inelastic at low quantities. Conversely, certain items may possess a prestige value, exhibiting reverse elasticity where higher prices actually drive demand. These items are usually cosmetics with significant emotional or brand value.

For goods with elastic demand, seasonal or event-based discounts can effectively stimulate sales. Such discounts might be introduced to meet audience expectations during specific periods like Black Friday or Summer Sales, or to correct imbalances in the game's economy. While ideally these two goals should align, they often do not. Nonetheless, it is the LiveOps team's responsibility to strive for this alignment. For example, if a game update introduces a new mode that allows players to generate soft currency, and its popularity leads to a surplus of this currency, the LiveOps team might introduce discounts on items that can be purchased with this currency to increase its "sink" effect.

Bundling is another monetization strategy that involves offering multiple items or resources together as a single package. There are commonly two types of bundling strategies employed: pure bundling and mixed bundling. Pure bundling refers to selling two or more distinct items only as part of a bundle. For example, in some games, unique skins and characters may only be available as part of a larger bundle or event. On the other hand, mixed bundling allows for the sale of individual items as well as the bundled package. These items are usually related but can also include unrelated items that appeal to a specific customer segment.

Bundles are often discounted to stimulate demand, usually at the expense of profit margins. They may also include filler items that artificially adjust the discount when the primary content of the bundle is not intended to be sold at a reduced price. In this sense, bundling serves as a discounting technique that aims to either upsell or maintain conversion value while boosting demand.

Another use case for bundling is the creation of paywalls. Unlike traditional market economies where prices are set by supply and demand, game economies may have inherent imbalances due to their legacy. For example, an overpowered or excessively popular character might be released at a price determined by its utility, making its true price higher than its "economic" price. To counteract such imbalances, a LiveOps team might bundle such characters with other items or resources, creating a paywall that reduces demand while maximizing profit.

The integration of paywalls in game economies must be approached with caution to avoid alienating the player base. A prime example of this delicate balance is Ubisoft's handling of *Rainbow Six Siege*. From its very beginning, the team was committed to a vision of the game as a long-term service, focusing on a robust online multiplayer experience rather than a single-playthrough narrative. Their pledge to support *Rainbow Six Siege* with ongoing gameplay adjustments, community events, and significant content releases was grounded in a philosophy that diverged from traditional monetization strategies. Notably, their announcement in November 2015 underscored a commitment to accessibility and community growth: *One Year, Four "Seasons" of Content. No Paywall*. This strategy not only cultivated a dedicated community but also served as a blueprint for successfully navigating the transition to a live service model. By ensuring that new content was freely available, Ubisoft demonstrated how games could thrive and evolve over time without restrictive monetization tactics, setting a standard for the industry during critical transition periods.

Currencies Exchange

In a game's economy, the flow of resources is a dynamic interplay between various systems and players. Resources can vary widely, from currencies and proxy currencies to progression points, energy, and social currencies, among others. These elements are intricately interconnected, affecting one another in complex ways, which adds an additional layer of engagement and strategy to the gameplay.

The LiveOps teams have the ability to manipulate these resource flows, employing strategies to either stabilize the game's economy or optimize existing "sinks" for maximum effectiveness. This involves a deep understanding of how different currencies and resources interact with each other and with various game mechanics.

One advanced technique at the disposal of LiveOps teams involves the use of variable exchange rates between hard and soft currencies. Unlike static, fixed rates, variable rates are designed to adapt to evolving states of the game, offering players a more dynamic and engaging experience. These variable rates can be particularly effective in responding to shifts in the game's meta-economy, thereby maintaining a balanced and enjoyable environment for players.

For instance, the game might offer players the option to convert hard currency to soft currency in varying percentage "fills," such as 10%, 50%, or 100% of their maximum storage capacity. As players advance and the game's states evolve, these exchange rates can also fluctuate. This not only introduces an additional layer of strategic complexity but also provides opportunities for players to engage in more nuanced currency management, making the game more engaging and rewarding. The variability in exchange rates encourages strategic spending among players. Higher percentage fills often offer better exchange rates, which aligns well with the core principles of free-to-play game economies by incentivizing larger transactions.

In *World of Tanks*, the concept of converting Combat Experience (XP) from Elite vehicles to Free Experience offers a strategic element for players seeking to expedite their progression through the tech tree. The standard conversion rate in the game is typically set at 25 Combat Experience for 1 gold, resulting in 25 Free Experience. However, Wargaming, the developer behind *World of Tanks*, periodically hosts events that provide players with more favorable conversion rates as part of special promotions or seasonal events.

During these events, the conversion rate might be enhanced to 25 Combat Experience → 1 gold → 35 Free Experience or even 25 Combat Experience → 1 gold → 40 Free Experience. This incentivizes players to engage more during the event period, encouraging the spending of gold (a hard currency) to gain Free Experience at a more efficient rate. These temporary discounts not only stimulate in-game spending but also provide players with an accelerated pathway to unlocking new vehicles and upgrades, enhancing their overall game experience.

LiveOps teams can also leverage this variability as a tool for fine-tuning the game's meta-economy. For example, discounted rates for converting hard to soft currency can be introduced if players accumulate a surplus of hard currency, serving as a balancing mechanism for the overall economy. For instance, the introduction of a new character line may serve as an effective "sink" for soft currency. Simultaneously, players might have accumulated a surplus of hard currency from prior sales events. In such a case, offering a discounted exchange rate from hard to soft currency could provide a strong incentive for players to "sink" their hard currency into the system initially designed to absorb soft currency.

Player's choices in currency conversion can provide valuable data on behavioral patterns. This information can be instrumental in further refining the game's economic structure and offers insights for future updates and adjustments.

Resources Exchange

Building on the concept of currency exchange in games, the next layer of sophistication comes in managing a broader range of in-game resources. Today's games don't just deal with one or two types of currency; players' inventories often include a mix of gold, silver, experience points, premium account days, boosters, customization elements like skins or avatars. To help LiveOps teams to manage this complexity, a mechanism of resources exchange offers a comprehensive solution for streamlined and flexible resource management.

The resources exchange serves as a dynamic mechanism where players can invest a diverse range of resources. This feature not only eases the necessity for developers to continuously introduce new "sinks" for these varied resources but also plays a crucial role in stabilizing the in-game economy. Importantly, it helps to increase the liquidity of currencies or resources that may be in surplus within the game's current economy. This, in turn, ensures a balanced flow of resources, contributing to a more dynamic and engaging gameplay experience.

Furthermore, the resources exchange grants players the freedom to choose not only the type but also the timing of their resource expenditure. Over an extended period, this flexibility enables players to pledge a mix of resources—such as experience points, boosters, or even days of premium accounts—to acquire new in-game assets. This approach offers them the flexibility to gather any missing elements as needed, enhancing their overall gaming experience and engagement with the game's economic system.

The feature takes resource management to another level with multicurrency spending. For example, if a player is interested in acquiring a unique avatar, vehicle, or character, they can spend a combination of gold, experience points, and other resources to make that acquisition. This diversified approach significantly enriches player engagement by providing a highly personalized spending experience.

Incorporating a multicurrency approach into the resources exchange brings an added layer of complexity but also versatility to the in-game economy. Suppose you want to sell an in-game asset that can be acquired through a combination of one hard currency, three types of soft currencies, and one booster. The first step is to determine the item's total value in a universally "Equivalent Unit" or EU. Once the total cost of the item in EUs is established, the next step is to calculate the equivalent value of 1% of the product's total cost for each type of resource involved.

For example, if the item costs 10,000 EUs, 1% of this would be 100 GUs. You'd then translate this 1% equivalent into the various currencies and the booster. So, if 100 GUs are equal to 1 piece of hard currency, 10 pieces of each type of soft currency, and 2 boosters, you'd have a baseline for constructing the item's price in a flexible manner.

The resources exchange would allow players to utilize these resources up to a certain limit, defined by the game's economic conditions and the necessity to sink particular types of resources. In this scenario, both soft and hard currencies could be used to cover up to 100% of the item's cost. However, boosters might be limited to covering only 25% of the total price, due to their higher perceived value or lesser abundance in the game ecosystem.

For instance, a player could opt to spend 50% of the item's cost in hard currency, 30% in one type of soft currency, 10% in another type of soft currency, and the remaining 10% using boosters. This flexibility not only allows players to leverage their resource pools most effectively but also provides a mechanism for LiveOps to control the flow and distribution of various game resources.

To further incentivize players, the resources exchange offers exclusive rewards for those who act quickly. Specifically, the first 30% of players to participate in a new feature or asset acquisition will receive unique identifiers for their vehicles or exclusive skins for their avatars. These exclusive rewards serve as a status symbol within the gaming community and encourage players to spend their resources more rapidly, which aids in maintaining a balanced economy.

Destiny 2's Infusion System serves as a prime example of an effective resources exchange mechanism, directly linking the game's reward structure with player engagement. Through this system, players can upgrade their favorite gear by sacrificing more powerful items, creating a dynamic market for in-game resources. This encourages players to continuously engage with various activities in search of the necessary items for infusion, effectively maintaining their interest and investment in the game. The introduction of unique identifiers or exclusive skins as rewards for early participation further incentivizes players to actively engage with new features or asset acquisitions, thus promoting a more rapid expenditure of resources and contributing to the stabilization of the game's economy.

Such a flexible pricing approach not only tailors to individual player needs but also serves the broader purpose of resource and economy management within the game. By setting upper limits on how much of a particular resource can be used in a transaction, LiveOps can effectively guide players in diversifying their spending habits, thereby achieving a more balanced and stable in-game economy.

Auctions

Auctions serve as a captivating monetization technique, drawing inspiration from real-world economics and social behaviors to add layers of complexity and engagement to games. At their core, auctions help resolve conflicts between unlimited wants and limited resources. They are a valuable tool for game balancing, particularly when introducing new content. Auctions also allow LiveOps teams to gauge the price elasticity of different in-game items, establishing an optimal price that maximizes revenue while enhancing player satisfaction.

Fundamentally, an auction involves a buyer and a seller, where the buyer places bids to acquire something offered by the seller. While player-driven markets do exist in MMORPGs, here we focus on auctions orchestrated by the LiveOps team. In this setup, auctions become an essential game mechanic, providing players with opportunities to bid on a range of resources, unique items, or other in-game assets using in-game currency. Controlled by the LiveOps team, this auction format serves dual purposes: it's a potent tool for game balancing, allowing control over the introduction of new content, and an effective strategy for monetization.

Different auction formats can be adapted to suit a variety of gameplay and economic objectives in live service games:

- **English Auction:** A familiar style where any player can raise the bid until the auction closes. This format can be emotionally charged and lead to overbidding, adding elements of excitement and unpredictability.
- **Turn-Based English Auction:** A more controlled version of the English auction where players raise bids in a turn-based manner. Once a player passes, they can't re-enter, resulting in shorter, less chaotic auction sessions.
- **Sealed Auction:** Players submit their bids secretly. This approach is useful for selling unique in-game items, as it prevents the LiveOps team from influencing player behavior by revealing ongoing bids.
- **Dutch Auctions:** The auction starts with a high asking price that decreases until a buyer steps in. This method can be effective for selling bulk in-game resources or items.
- **Buyout Auction:** The LiveOps team sets a fixed price, allowing players to bypass the auction process by making an immediate purchase at this predetermined price.

In *World of Warcraft*, Auction House stands as a bustling marketplace where players engage in the classic English Auction format. Here, adventurers can list in-game items ranging from rare artifacts to essential resources, setting a minimum bid and watching as fellow players compete to place higher offers until the auction timer expires. This dynamic system not only facilitates a vibrant economy within the game but also adds layers of strategy and social interaction. Players must gauge the market's demand, timing their bids or listings to maximize profit or secure coveted items. The Auction House has evolved into a central hub of economic activity, influencing the game's meta and fostering a community of traders and collectors.

On the other hand, EVE Online adopts a more clandestine approach with its use of Sealed Auctions for some of the most coveted contracts and items in the cosmos. In these high-stakes auctions, players submit their bids in secrecy, not knowing the amounts their competitors have placed. This format is particularly suited to the game's emphasis on espionage, strategy, and economic warfare, as it adds an intense layer of suspense and calculation. Sealed Auctions in EVE Online are a testament to the game's complex player-driven economy, where alliances and individuals vie for supremacy not just in space combat but also in the art of negotiation and resource management. These auctions underscore the game's dedication to providing a deeply immersive experience where every decision can have far-reaching consequences.

Auctions can be creatively used to generate both high engagement and revenue. For instance, a high-value auction might grant players the rights to name a street or landmark within the game world. Such personalization not only increases player engagement but also adds a layer of prestige to the in-game items.

Another intriguing option is the sale of lottery tickets for extremely rare aesthetic items like unique skins or avatars. These items become a status symbol within the community, thereby increasing their perceived value and the bids they attract.

Implementing an auction system within a game places a continual burden on the development team to provide fresh and engaging content. The success of any in-game auction is directly tied to the desirability and utility of the items or resources up for bid. This means that the LiveOps team must continually ensure that there are items worth bidding on and that these items maintain their value and relevance over time.

Loot Boxes

Loot boxes have gained considerable attention in the gaming industry, melding psychology, ethics, and business models into a complex equation. They offer more than just an extra layer to a game; they engage deeply with our human tendencies. The thrill of winning something, the excitement of receiving a gift, and the innate desire to collect items are all factors that make loot boxes so enticing. But it's not just about the thrill; it's also about responsibility. Game designers have an obligation to ensure that these features are not exploitative or predatory. The challenge lies in creating a balanced system that heightens engagement without crossing ethical boundaries.

The fair mechanics behind loot boxes can reduce the uncertainty that comes with purely random rewards; many games employ systems that increase your odds over time. For example, some use a "soft pity" system that subtly increases the likelihood of obtaining a rare item with each unsuccessful attempt. Others opt for a "hard pity" system, which guarantees a rare item after a set number of tries. These methods make players feel rewarded for their persistence, adding another layer of fairness to the game.

When it comes to the rewards themselves, it's essential to tread carefully. Cosmetic items, such as skins or unique avatars, are ideal candidates for loot box rewards. They allow players to personalize their game experience without giving them an unfair advantage. By focusing on cosmetic rewards, LiveOps can avoid the pitfalls of "pay-to-win" mechanics, which can alienate players who choose not to participate in the loot box system. In essence, cosmetic rewards maintain the competitive balance of the game while still offering a personalized experience.

Transparency is another important aspect to consider. Players should know what they're getting into when they decide to open a loot box. In some jurisdictions, it's required by law to display the odds of receiving specific items. But even where it's not a legal necessity, it's good practice to let players know what they can expect. This not only builds trust but also allows players to make informed decisions, adding an extra layer of ethical responsibility to the game's design.

In March 2009, Electronic Arts introduced a new mechanic in *FIFA 09* that would set a precedent for monetization in video games: the concept of loot boxes, then known as "Ultimate Team." These packs allowed players to assemble a dream team of association football players by opening packs acquired with in-game currency, earned through gameplay or purchased through microtransactions. This early integration of loot boxes into a mainstream sports game was more than just a novel way to enhance player engagement; it laid the foundation for a model that would become ubiquitous across the industry. By allowing players to either earn these packs through gameplay or accelerate their team-building efforts with real money, EA created a system that appealed to a wide range of players, from the casual to the competitive. This dual pathway ensured that all players had access to the thrill of opening new packs, while also opening up a significant revenue stream for EA through those who chose to purchase additional packs with real money.

Loot boxes can be a fun and exciting addition to a game, but they come with their own set of challenges and responsibilities. By focusing on a design that prioritizes fairness, offers meaningful rewards, and maintains transparency, LiveOps can ensure that loot boxes enhance the gaming experience, rather than detract from it.

Subscription

The rise of subscription models in the gaming industry owes much to the success of the Netflix subscription business model, which Google Play Pass and Apple Arcade have adapted to create bundled gaming experiences. While these services have created a new paradigm by offering an array of games under one subscription, the focus of our discussion here is on single-game subscriptions. For most games, especially those that aren't blockbuster titles, single-game subscriptions present unique challenges in convincing players to commit. However, there are strategic ways to implement such a model successfully.

Building expectations is crucial when introducing subscriptions in your game. Players need to be deeply engaged and find value in the gameplay before they'll consider subscribing. Introducing subscription options at this optimal moment sets a new baseline for in-game spending. Players who have subscribed often view their subscription fee as a sunk cost, making them more willing to continue spending within the game.

A subscription model essentially initiates a long-term relationship between the player and the developer. The player invests in a subscription with the expectation of receiving consistent and valuable benefits in return. This brings us to the concept of "Persistent Benefits," which can be categorized mainly into Access, Multipliers, and Vanity features.

- **Access:** This generally refers to unlocking levels or features inside your game that would otherwise be unavailable or require an in-game purchase.
- **Multipliers:** These could include increased experience points, better "drops," or soft currency rewards. Multipliers offer players an enticing reason to invest more to gain more.
- **Vanity Features:** These are cosmetic elements like unique skins or name tags that are visible to other players, adding a social incentive to subscriptions.

By bundling these persistent benefits into a subscription, you're offering an added layer of value beyond the basic game access. Subscriptions can include exclusive content or items that aren't available through in-game purchases, creating an additional layer of monetization that complements the free-to-play model.

In *Final Fantasy XIV*, the subscription model is designed to enhance both the access and the allure of the game through exclusive features. To maintain access beyond this initial month, players are required to subscribe. The subscription not only extends the adventure but significantly expands the player's ability to create and explore different facets of the game. Subscribers can craft up to eight characters on each server and manage a total of 40 characters across all servers. This flexibility is particularly advantageous for players keen on experimenting with diverse character builds or those looking to engage with various communities across different data centers, ensuring a rich and varied playing experience tailored to the subscriber's preferences.

Battle Passes serve as an illustrative example of a time-limited subscription model. They excel at driving both spending and engagement by providing benefits that players must actively engage with to fully realize. Such elements can also be integrated into a broader, more permanent subscription model, giving players the option to speed up the in-game grind for soft currency or character leveling.

Introducing a subscription model is a high-stakes venture, particularly because it targets the game's core audience. It also places a continual burden on the development team to provide fresh and engaging content or benefits. Hence, implementing a subscription model requires careful planning and ongoing commitment to delivering value to your subscribers.

GAME STOREFRONTS

From the players' perspective, all monetization techniques converge in the game storefront. This is not simply a combination of assets but a sophisticated system that unifies various monetization approaches to stimulate growth and revenue without altering the gameplay. For the sake of structure, we apply the time-honored marketing framework of "the Four Ps" to delve into what monetization involves, how items are sold, which storefronts are used, how offers are promoted, and at what price points (Figure 9.10).

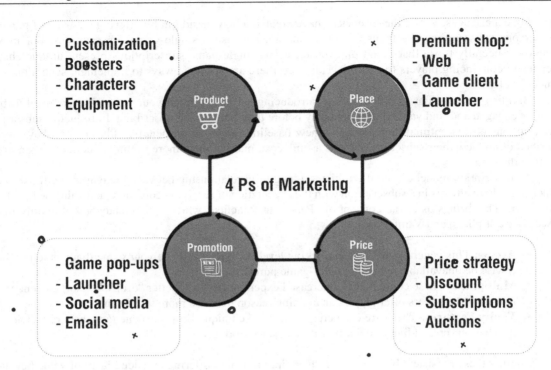

FIGURE 9.10   The four Ps of marketing with regard to game storefronts.

Product is essentially deciding what kind of items are going to be for sale permanently or occasionally. Some games focus on selling only customization options, while others offer a broader range of items such as progression boosters, premium characters, or equipment. Once this selection is established (though it can be adjusted over time), LiveOps managers set up an item library that tracks cooldowns on sales and past performance. At this stage, product bundling techniques come into play, grouping complementary items to encourage players to try new content. Furthermore, experimental products extend the player experience by offering a variety of goals and new content to explore.

The presentation of products in the storefront is influenced by both the context in the player journey and the nature of the item (be it a commodity, consumable, resource, or premium item). This context and nature affect the perceived utility of the product, thereby influencing players' willingness to pay. For instance, engaged players might need more resources during high-intensity gameplay events, making it sensible to offer a variety of resource bundles. Conversely, new players interested in discovering content may be more attracted to value items like characters and customizations.

Place is typically a premium shop, and it can be on the web, or it could be in the game client, or launcher. Players' purchase journeys may differ based on their habits, which is why storefront capabilities adjust players' experience depending on the type of content. For the commodity content with a short consideration time, the storefront is usually optimized for the fastest and easiest sales with one-click functionality embedded into the game client. For the high-value premium content with lasting awareness and consideration timeframe where players also rely on community recommendations or reviews, purchasing experience includes several touchpoints. Web storefront extension eases direct access to social media feeds and, in tandem with in-game placeholders, is optimized for comprehensive information, including comparison and extra visual effects. Moreover, once the game grows in size and complexity, the array of items extends, and the storefronts needs to allow for this—with filtering, sorting, preview, and recommendations.

With regard to the place, the player journey context, and the nature of the offer, high-value and high-price items typically require longer research and consideration than commodity items or resources. The research is usually done through community channels, so placing those items in short and trackable journey from there makes the most sense. At the same time the place for commodities is best when it's closest to the actual game loop requiring those commodities, typically, in the game client.

Promotion is all about informing players about the availability of the offers. It can be done via UX/UI elements in the game, pop-ups, banners in the launcher or portals, social media, and emails. As a rule of thumb, promotion's ad copy should be as simple as possible and convey the key message along with a call to action. Visual design should emphasize the main idea of the campaign, with attention to what the picture needs and doesn't need to depict. Optimally, the layout should include various capabilities extending products' description or adding cognitive bias like the decoy effect. A dedicated attention should be given to promotional activities of community influencers as they often have larger user base and more trust from the players than most of in-game interfaces.

At the promotion step of premium ("value") items, it's most appropriate to refer to the emotional and intangible values of the product along with functional (utility) and financial (price). The willingness to pay is most impacted by the emotional and intangible components, since price and utility are comparable and usually a feature of commodity.

Pricing in the traditional retail environment is usually quite straightforward, determined largely by the interplay between supply and demand. However, in the realm of video game monetization, pricing mechanics introduce a new layer of complexity and sometimes even serve promotional purposes. In video games, supply is often virtually infinite, shifting the focus toward a deeper understanding of price elasticity for optimization. Prices in similar or adjacent games, as well as those from competitors, also influence player expectations and set industry standards.

Within game storefronts, prices are occasionally adjusted or disguised to boost conversions, employing various monetization techniques. While these adjustments usually don't affect the intrinsic utility of gameplay, they do aim to increase players' willingness to pay. This is achieved through different strategies, such as making payments more comfortable, offering insurance, or incorporating additional gamification elements.

Operating Game Storefronts

The game storefront is not just a marketplace for virtual goods, but a finely tuned system that seeks to balance player engagement, in-game economics, and business objectives. As the epicenter of all monetization techniques, the storefront must be more than a mere inventory of purchasable items; it needs to be a dynamic experience that adapts to player behaviors, market trends, and game lifecycles.

The mastery of running a game storefront lies in a nuanced understanding of various elements—each a tool in your arsenal for driving both player engagement and revenue. Whether it's the compelling allure of "Free Offers," the subtle encouragement through "Social Proof," or the clever application of "Anchoring" to guide purchasing decisions, each mechanism serves a distinct purpose. In the following sub-chapters, we'll unpack these diverse elements, providing you with a comprehensive toolkit to make your storefront not just functional but irresistibly effective.

Store categorization

The concept of choice architecture plays a vital role here. It's essential to strike a balance between offering variety and preventing choice overload. Behavioral economics teaches us that too many options can paralyze decision-making and even reduce sales.

This phenomenon is not just theoretical; it has been validated through real-world experiments. For instance, a study in a grocery store found that consumers exposed to a wider range of options (24 types of jam, to be precise) were less likely to make a purchase compared to those who had fewer choices (only six types of jam). In gaming, this translates to the number of items you present in your store category.

To combat choice overload, consider employing the principle of "chunking," a cognitive strategy to make information processing and decision-making more manageable. Psychological research suggests that people can hold between five and nine items in their working memory. In the context of a game store, instead of overwhelming players with numerous choices of swords, shields, arrows, and loot boxes all at once, you could first offer broad categories like "Weapons," "Premium Accounts," "Boosters," and "Special Items." Once a category is selected, then you can present the more specific options within that category.

The key is to make the "chunks" meaningful. Sorting items by irrelevant criteria, like color, would not help the player find what they're looking to buy. This approach not only streamlines the shopping process but also helps players feel more confident about their choices. In addition to "chunking," affirming a player's freedom to choose—or not choose—can also enhance their confidence in their decision, adding another layer of psychological comfort.

There's no one-size-fits-all when it comes to choice architecture. Continuous testing and iteration are vital for finding what works best for your particular game, platform, and player base. This ensures that your storefront remains not just a place for transactions but an integral part of the overall gaming experience that actively contributes to both player engagement and revenue generation.

Decoy effect

Another potent strategy, deeply rooted in behavioral psychology, is the use of the decoy effect or middle action in pricing and product presentation. The decoy effect operates on the principle of asymmetric dominance, which is the phenomenon where the presence of a third, less appealing option can influence players to opt for the more expensive or profitable choice.

The core of the decoy effect lies in comparative value, not just intrinsic utility. For instance, if your game store offers two virtual items—one priced at $5 and the other at $20—introducing a third bundle priced at $50 but packed with additional items can make the $20 option seem like a relative bargain. This perceived value drives the player toward the more expensive and profitable choice, as it now appears to offer more for the money, especially when juxtaposed with the higher-priced bundle. Essentially, the player's value perception is not formed in isolation but through comparison, which can be strategically engineered through the decoy effect.

This strategy can be particularly effective when bundled with high-value virtual goods. By offering a high-priced bundle filled with numerous items and placing it beside a singular, less expensive option, the bundle suddenly appears more attractive. In this manner, the decoy effect serves as a lever, nudging players toward options that they might not have considered otherwise but now see as valuable.

Steam strategically utilizes decoy effect for the game like *Monster Hunter Rise* and its expansions. On one of the sale the target package was *Monster Hunter Rise + Sunbreak Deluxe*, which is presented alongside a slightly less expensive option *Monster Hunter Rise + Sunbreak* and a more affordable *Monster Hunter Rise Deluxe Edition*. The premium *Deluxe* combo was priced strategically to make the mid-tier option seem like a more value-for-money choice, demonstrating the decoy effect where a higher-priced option influences player preference toward a pricier but more value-perceived offer.

The key to employing the decoy effect successfully is understanding your player's journey and the nature of the offers presented in your game store. A high-priced item requiring longer consideration and research through community channels will benefit significantly from a well-placed decoy. On the other hand, commodity items that are frequently bought on impulse might not be the best candidates for this strategy.

Free offer

Within the game storefront, the power of "free" cannot be underestimated as it operates beyond just another pricing strategy. Offering something for free dramatically reduces the perceived risk for players, making it a potent tool to drive initial engagements. For example, introducing a free offer for a week or a month as a test run for a new subscription service can be an almost irresistible lure for players. The psychology of "free" taps into our natural aversion to risk and loss, prompting us to take actions we might otherwise avoid.

However, the "free" strategy comes with its own set of challenges, especially in terms of pricing. Once players associate a product with being free, shifting that perception to accommodate a price point can be a monumental task. Essentially, you risk anchoring your player's expectations at that zero-dollar mark. But despite this downside, smartly managed free offers serve as traffic generators, not just to the specific item but to the entire game store or specific sections within it.

In the competitive gaming market, savvy strategies like Epic Games Store's free game offers play a crucial role in attracting players. By periodically providing popular games at no cost, they create a surge of traffic to their platform, exposing a wide audience to their expansive game library. This approach not only boosts user acquisition but also encourages exploration and purchase within the store, as new users drawn by the free titles stay to browse additional content. This strategy highlights the effectiveness of free offers as both a promotional tool and a means to enhance store visibility and user engagement.

To optimize the utility of free offers, consider introducing progressive mechanics that encourage regular store visits. For instance, a tiered system of claiming free items could be set up to incentivize continuous engagement. Players could receive increasingly valuable free offers for each consecutive day they visit the storefront, thereby fulfilling dual objectives: keeping your store top-of-mind for players and promoting consistent engagement.

Gifting

Gifting serves as a potent yet often overlooked tool in the realm of in-game storefront optimization. The principle is simple but profound: people are more likely to take an action if they feel you've made the first move. This psychological nuance has been substantiated through various studies and tests, demonstrating that gift-receiving players often have higher conversion rates. They feel an implicit need to reciprocate the favor, thereby enriching the game's monetization strategy.

To harness the power of gifting effectively, several nuances should be considered. First, the gift should be unexpected, catching the player off-guard and making the gesture more impactful. Second, it should be personal, something that the player finds useful or meaningful within the game context. This could range from a rare in-game item to some much-needed resources. Third, it should be valuable to ensure the player perceives it as a genuine gesture rather than a throwaway offer. And importantly, the order of actions matters: present the gift first and then make your request or offer. This sequence amplifies the reciprocation impulse.

In the competitive seas of *World of Warships*, the tides of generosity can bolster a Captain's arsenal and loyalty. The game's developers regularly deploy a gifting strategy that strikes a chord with its community. A notable instance was the Premium Ship container giveaway, timed to coincide with the remembrance of Pearl Harbor. This historical event was not only commemorated through in-game activities but also paired with an opportunity for players to win prized vessels wrapped in exclusive camouflages. Participating players were propelled to engage in a marathon of naval battles, earning Portal Chips that increased their odds of winning the sought-after Japanese HYŪGA or the American CALIFORNIA, each adorned in patriotic livery. This clever use of giveaways elevates the player experience, intertwining historical education with the thrill of potential rewards, nurturing a dedicated player base inclined to sail further into the game's monetized waters.

However, it's crucial to exercise restraint and not overuse this technique, as over-reliance could make players feel manipulated rather than appreciated. For example, occasionally gifting players with a valuable in-game item can make them more inclined to consider other in-game purchases. They don't feel like they are merely being sold something; instead, they feel appreciated and are thus more likely to make a purchase.

Anchoring

Anchoring serves as another crucial instrument in shaping the player's perception of value. Anchoring happens when an initial exposure to a number, typically a price, serves as a psychological point of reference for all subsequent judgments and decisions. The number becomes an "anchor" that influences how players perceive the value of other options.

In the context of a game storefront, a high-priced package can serve as an anchor that makes all other options seem reasonably priced by comparison. For example, introducing a $100 in-game package can make a $15 package appear as a bargain, even if it's a significant investment. While few players might actually opt for the $100 package, its mere presence alters the perceived value landscape, making other options seem more palatable. This strategy is not unique to gaming; it's a common tactic in various industries, such as restaurants, where an expensive menu item like lobster makes everything else look affordable.

The *Battlefield 1* Premium Pass, introduced by EA DICE on August 24, 2016, serves as a prime example of anchoring in video game monetization. Before the game's launch on October 21, 2016, EA set an early price for the pass, creating a benchmark for value. This strategy made the Premium Pass seem like a wise investment compared to the cost of future DLCs purchased separately. As EA released more information about each DLC, their value was assessed in light of the Premium Pass's initial price, making the pass appear more bargain. This method not only spurred early purchases but also influenced player perceptions of value, showcasing the impact of psychological pricing strategies.

However, anchoring also comes with a caveat, especially when transitioning from free to paid options. If players are accustomed to receiving something for free, that zero-cost point becomes an anchor that can make even low-cost items seem expensive by comparison. This is particularly relevant when introducing new products or features in your game. If they're initially offered for free, raising the price later may be met with resistance, as players have already anchored their expectations at zero cost.

Therefore, anchoring should be strategically deployed with a keen understanding of its long-term implications. Being aware of how anchor prices can influence player perception can guide your pricing strategies and even help you reposition existing offers. Combining this with other techniques like the decoy effect can result in a more nuanced and effective storefront, driving both engagement and revenue.

Reducing friction

Another essential factor in optimizing your game storefront is reducing friction, which refers to the hurdles or blockers a player must overcome to complete a desired action, such as making a purchase. The more steps involved, the more likely the player is to abandon the process. For example, requiring players to enter an email address, create an account, and then input credit card information can lead to higher dropout rates.

You can streamline the purchase process by pre-filling information fields wherever possible, reducing the cognitive load on players. This makes the transaction smoother and increases the likelihood of its completion. Another strategy is to align new in-game purchase behaviors with existing player actions or habits. For example, if you notice that players often buy a specific type of resource just before a major in-game event, you might offer a special bundle that includes that resource, along with other relevant items, right before the event starts.

A prime example of this is the implementation of Steam Wallet across various games available on Steam. Before the integration of Steam Wallet, players often faced a multi-step process to complete transactions, requiring them to leave the game environment to add funds through the Steam platform, thus disrupting the gaming experience and increasing the likelihood of abandoned purchases. The introduction of Steam Wallet significantly streamlined this process, allowing players to preload funds into their accounts and make in-game purchases directly, without the need to exit to the Steam store. This seamless integration not only minimizes the steps required to complete a purchase but also keeps players engaged in the game, reducing the psychological and logistical barriers to spending.

Reducing friction is about understanding player behavior and making the path to purchase as straightforward as possible. This creates a win-win situation: the player has a more enjoyable, less stressful experience, and the game sees higher conversion rates and, ultimately, increased revenue.

Fear of missing out

Loss aversion is a potent psychological principle that impacts how people make decisions, particularly in the realm of purchasing behavior. Essentially, people are generally a half times more sensitive to losses than gains. When it comes to game storefronts, the power of loss aversion can be harnessed in various ways to influence player behavior and optimize sales.

Let's consider Limited Quantity Offers and Limited Time Offers, two popular mechanics in game storefronts. When these offers are framed in terms of loss aversion—emphasizing what players stand to lose by not taking action—the psychological impact can be substantial. For instance, telling players that they could miss out on an exclusive, limited time weapon could make them more likely to complete a purchase. The ticking clock or diminishing stock numbers act as additional nudges, amplifying the fear of missing out (FOMO) and the loss aversion impact.

The *Call of Duty* series by Activision effectively uses FOMO to boost sales and player activity by offering Limited Time Offers. These offers include exclusive weapon skins, character outfits, and seasonal content available for a short period. This strategy creates urgency, pushing players to acquire items quickly to avoid missing out. Activision's approach highlights the power of loss aversion, as players are more likely to make purchases when faced with the possibility of losing access to exclusive content.

Renting in-game vehicles or weapons introduces another layer to this. By allowing players to rent these items for a limited time, you tap into loss aversion twofold. Firstly, by positioning the rental items as something the players "already own" for a limited time, the desire to make the item a permanent part of their inventory becomes stronger. Secondly, players are more likely to make an outright purchase after the rental period expires to avoid the loss of an item that they have come to appreciate or rely upon in gameplay.

Coupons

Coupons and discounts hold a unique place in the realm of game monetization, but unlike straightforward price reductions, coupons not just offer a monetary incentive but also serve as a form of informational advertising. They operate on the principle of providing a "good deal," catching the attention of players who might otherwise overlook certain items or bundles in the store. This informational function amplifies the inherent price-discount effect, making coupons a powerful tool for increasing demand.

Observing coupon usage rates provides valuable insights into their effectiveness as sales drivers. When these rates cross certain empirically determined thresholds, it signals that the coupon is doing its job exceptionally well. Such data-driven insights can be invaluable for LiveOps managers, helping them decide whether a coupon should be featured more prominently in the store or integrated into other promotional activities.

On September 23, *Rocket League* launched on the Epic Games Store (EGS), offering players a new platform to download and play. To incentivize this launch, players who added *Rocket League* to their EGS library from September 23 to October 23 received a $10 EGS coupon for future purchases of $14.99 or more on games and add-ons. This promotion not only encouraged the adoption of *Rocket League* on a new platform but also drove sales within the EGS ecosystem, demonstrating an effective use of coupons to enhance player engagement and increase platform traffic.

Coupons can also be woven into broader player engagement strategies. For instance, they could serve as rewards for hitting certain in-game milestones or participating in community events. This not only incentivizes the desired behaviors but also fosters a deeper sense of achievement and connection with the game.

Despite the advancement of personalization algorithms and the input of expert opinions, predicting a player's desires remains an elusive task. Players themselves often don't know what they want until they see it. In such a complex ecosystem, coupons serve as an excellent middle-ground strategy. They frame the range of potential spending or the variety of items available yet leave the final decision-making to the players.

By providing coupons that can be applied to different categories or levels of items, LiveOps empower players to choose where they find the most value. This not only enhances the player's agency but also provides invaluable data back to LiveOps. Observing which coupons are used for what types of items can offer insights into player behavior and preferences, which can be a goldmine for future personalization strategy.

Social proof

The principle behind social proof is simple: people are influenced by the actions of others, especially those they consider similar or relevant to themselves. In the context of a game storefront, showing that other players—particularly friends or well-regarded community members—have made specific purchases can encourage similar behavior.

There are nuanced ways to integrate social proof into your storefront design and promotional strategy. For instance, instead of bluntly stating that "9 out of 10 players purchased this item," you could subtly inform players that "Most adventurers prefer this sword for their quests." The idea is to provide a form of endorsement without making it feel like a sales pitch.

Personalization is another key aspect. By tailoring the social proof to be as relatable as possible to the individual player, the impact can be significantly enhanced. For example, showing that a player's friends or teammates have benefited from a particular bundle could be a strong motivator for them to consider the same purchase.

By smartly integrating social proof into your game storefront, you can create a more compelling, socially engaging experience. This approach not only influences individual purchase decisions but also fosters a community around your game, leading to longer-term player retention and increased lifetime value.

In *Monster Hunter World* by Capcom, the Gathering Hub serves as a key location for displaying social proof, where players can directly observe the armor, weapons, and cosmetics adorned by other players. This in-game social space naturally encourages players to showcase their high-level gear and rare finds, acting as a live advertisement for the game's various items and equipment. Seeing other players with exclusive gear obtained from difficult quests or events creates a compelling form of social proof, motivating others to pursue similar achievements. Capcom's design choice to make these displays visible in the Gathering Hub capitalizes on the human tendency to emulate successful behaviors, driving player engagement and encouraging the pursuit of similar in-game status symbols.

Events

10

LiveOps event is a time-limited experience that seamlessly combines core gameplay features with new mechanics to optimize both player engagement and monetization. It offers the flexibility to tweak the game's economy or retention on the fly, all without necessitating developer involvement.

While games inherently present players with in-game goals and objectives disconnected from real-world influences, players are not confined to an isolated gaming existence. They reside within societies rich with cultural traditions, celebrations, and public holidays, all of which significantly influence game performance, audience size, and spending patterns.

The blueprint for LiveOps event creation is composed of the following:

Theme	It can be drawn from in-game elements, cultural events, media trends, or business collaborations. The theme aims to attract and retain players by offering a meaningful and immersive online experience that aligns with their gaming interests and daily lives.
Progression	This refers to the mechanics through which players gain value from the event. This could involve collective progression (where all players contribute toward a common goal), individual progression, or a mix of both. Along with the event's progression, players usually receive individual in-game rewards, which could also extend to physical rewards or game-wide content unlocks (milestones).
Promotion	This utilizes communication channels, influencers, or partners to extend the reach of the event as far as possible.
Monetization	This involves the integration of special items with the event theme, its progression, or both. For example, the more you purchased, the more rewards you would get.

Due to their time-limited and specialized progression nature, LiveOps events serve as effective mechanisms to intervene in the game economy to address or mitigate specific issues, without the need for involving development teams or requiring players to download additional patches. For example, during off-peak periods such as summer, a game team may choose to launch an event geared toward retaining casual players through special discounts or enticing rewards—incentives that may not be available during peak seasons due to balancing and other constraints.

LIVEOPS EVENT CANVAS

In order to optimize the event building process, it is strongly recommended for the event initiator to prepare an event brief. To facilitate this task, the LiveOps Event Canvas was created, based on the widely recognized visual tool, the Business Model Canvas. By using the LiveOps Event Canvas, the team can improve communication and ensure a shared understanding of the event's goals and objectives among the game studio (Figure 10.1).

This endeavor has culminated in the creation of the LiveOps Event Canvas, comprising 11 elements that collectively offer a comprehensive overview of your LiveOps event.

DOI: 10.1201/9781003427056-14

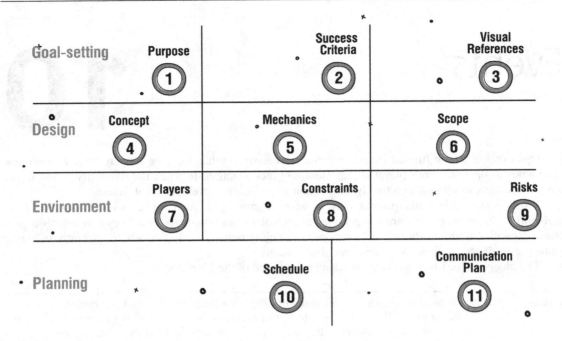

FIGURE 10.1 LiveOps Event Canvas.

The canvas is utilized by LiveOps teams to streamline communication and synchronize understanding of the LiveOps event among stakeholders—both internally and externally. The LiveOps Event Canvas can be used offline as a physical printout with Post-its, and online at vasi.uk. The tool has proven valuable for the following event's phases:

- **Initiation:** This stage serves as the foundation, where the tool is used to kickstart LiveOps events. It helps in defining the essential questions: "What are the event's goals?" "Why is it taking place?" and "How will it be rolled out?"
- **Selling and Acceptance:** This is where the tool proves instrumental as a selling resource. It helps pitch the event to the potential stakeholders in a clear and straightforward manner, presenting its benefits and enticing recipients to accept and support it.
- **Planning:** In this stage, the tool helps in developing a detailed action plan. It includes outlining strategies for event promotion, determining resources required, identifying potential risks, and devising mitigation strategies.
- **Execution and Monitoring:** As the event goes live, the tool transforms into a robust communication instrument. It aids in coordinating different activities, ensuring smooth execution, and reporting event progress regularly.
- **Closing:** Finally, after the completion of the event, the tool assists in the post-event evaluation. It helps to gather feedback, measure the event's success against the set goals, and document the learnings for future events.

Purpose

Definition: The reason for the event's execution and the aspirations of the event owner.

What is purpose?

The purpose highlights the rationale for starting the event and the expected outcomes. It acts as the primary catalyst, steering toward the final results. The purpose exemplifies the event's "benefit"—demonstrating that it delivers considerable value for not just the event owner but also for the game and its players.

The role of purpose

Suppose we initiate an event primarily to drain surplus resources and reestablish balance in the game economy after a previous event led to an excessive accumulation. Without a clearly defined purpose, this necessary adjustment may be overlooked, negatively impacting the game's economy. Alternatively, our focus might shift toward re-engaging players or winning them back after a low-activity period, such as summer vacations. Here again, a specific purpose is crucial to guide our efforts and measure our success in boosting player engagement.

How to utilize the purpose component?

The purpose, typically articulated in a couple of "broad" statements, provides the rationale for launching the LiveOps event. The subsequent questions can be valuable in determining this purpose:

- Why are we initiating this LiveOps event?
- What does the event owner aim to achieve?
- What aspects of the game will be created, modified, or improved through this event?

Tip: While establishing the Purpose, aim to express it in no more than one or two sentences.

Success Criteria

Definition: Quantifiable metrics selected to assess if the LiveOps event has accomplished its intended outcome.

What are success criteria?

Success criteria are not only set clear expectations but also guide the event management process toward the desired outcomes. These measurable indicators are crucial for assessing the performance of an event, enabling the team to understand if they have met their objectives or if adjustments are required.

The role of success criteria

If the event's goal is to extract surplus resources from the gaming economy, a successful outcome could be identified by a 10% decline in hard currency balances along with a simultaneous 5% rise in hard currency purchases.

If the focus is on re-engaging inactive players, set a specific goal, like reconnecting with 2,000 players. Define 're-engagement' clearly, whether it's just logging back in or active participation in one or more game sessions.

If you're striving to enhance player engagement, you could define success as an 18% jump in matches or games played, or a 6% spike in Daily Active Users (DAU).

How to utilize the component?

Effective success criteria are specific, quantifiable, achievable, and time bound. They should be challenging to inspire progress, yet remain within the realm of feasibility. Consider these questions when establishing success criteria for your LiveOps event:

- What specific objectives or targets need to be met to deem the LiveOps event successful?
- How will the LiveOps event contribute to the game's overall success?
- How will we track and evaluate the benefits of the event?

Tip: Incorporate a specific period during which the established criteria should be achieved.

Visual References

Definition: Visual references are illustrative materials that provide a tangible depiction of the expected aesthetic, style, atmosphere, and messaging for the LiveOps event.

What are visual references?

Visual references are a collection of images, screenshots, concept art, or even video clips that serve as a guide to the visual direction for your LiveOps event. They represent the desired look and feel for the front-end interface and gameplay of the event. These references can be derived from various sources such as other games, movies, artwork, photos, or any visuals that align with the intended atmosphere and messaging of the event.

The role of visual references

Visual references are like a visual map guiding the development and decision-making for a LiveOps event. For decision-makers, they act like a preview of the final event, helping them make informed choices about resources, timelines, and marketing. For developers, these references provide a visual guide that aids in designing the interface and gameplay elements that align with the desired atmosphere. Visual references also allow everyone to see how the event compares to or stands out from similar ones in other games.

How to utilize the visual references component?

Visual references act as a common language, bridging the gap between your vision and the tangible outcome. They ensure everyone involved in the project shares a clear and aligned understanding of the expected visual aesthetics. As you go through the following questions, remember that visual references are not rigid constraints, but guides to inspire creativity:

- What's the target atmosphere and message for your event?
- Which key features need emphasis in your visual references to showcase event mechanics?
- How will visual references be used to align the final design with your aesthetics?
- How can your visual references allow for creative flexibility during development?

Tip: Include a range of references that capture various aspects of your vision.

Concept

Definition: The Concept is a brief and clear summary of an event's main idea, easily understood by everyone involved.

What is concept?

The concept of a LiveOps event is like an elevator pitch, providing a clear and concise explanation of the event's purpose, key features, and anticipated player interaction. It is a brief summary that articulates the main idea behind the event, making it accessible to all stakeholders, irrespective of their familiarity with the current environment or available time to dive into details. Importantly, the concept should avoid any use of technical jargon or detailed explanations to maintain clarity and ease of understanding for all.

The role of concept

The concept serves as the starting point for event planning and development. By providing a clear understanding of the event's expected player journey, it helps align all stakeholders. The concept aids developers, business analysts, and even event owners in identifying the necessary features and mechanics in the early stages of development, thereby streamlining the event's creation process. It also assists in communicating the event's intent to a wider audience, including potential sponsors, partners, and even players.

How to utilize the component?

It's a guiding light that keeps everyone involved on the same page and moving in the right direction. With this in mind, consider these questions as you prepare your concept component:

- How can you outline the expected player journey with the event?
- How will the concept guide the early identification of key features and mechanics?
- How does the concept highlight your game event's unique points?

Tip: The concept is more comprehensive when it includes an anticipated player journey.

Mechanics

Definition: Mechanics are the foundational elements that drive interaction and engagement in a LiveOps event, detailing the functionality of each component and their individual use cases.

What are mechanics?

Mechanics in LiveOps events refers to the systems of interactions between the player and the event. They significantly impact the player's experience, guiding the player's actions and the game's response to these actions.

Mechanics in a LiveOps event may also influence the theme of the event. Some events might be "abstract" where mechanics don't intend to represent anything specific. In contrast, others might have a "theme" where mechanics serve to simulate a certain activity or context, providing more depth to the player's experience.

The role of mechanics

Grasping the mechanics in LiveOps events is key for developers since it forms the core of the code and guides its creation. In many events, turns are used to divide actions, and action points decide what players can do during their turns. In auction-style events, players bid to earn the right to take certain actions. In events where tokens show player strength, the aim is often to take or remove opponents' tokens. Designing LiveOps event is challenging due to the need for detailed scrutiny of all possible player scenarios, which can reveal issues requiring mechanic adjustments.

How to utilize the component?

The mechanics encompass the rules, interactions, and systems that govern how the event functions. To make the most out of this component, reflect on the following questions:

- What are the main mechanics and their purpose in the event?
- How do these mechanics interact and drive player engagement and monetization?
- Are there any repeated mechanics or mechanics that lead players to explore others?

Tip: Show how mechanics extend the concept and help define the scope.

Scope

Definition: Scope outlines what is included within the concept and mechanics of the event, and what lies outside these boundaries.

What is scope?

Scope encompasses the necessary procedures to confirm that the LiveOps event incorporates all, and only, the tasks required for its successful completion. The focus in managing the event's scope lies in clearly defining and controlling what is included and what is not part of the event.

The role of scope

The scope directly influences the overall budget of the LiveOps event. For first-time events, it may be advisable to begin with a Minimum Viable Product (MVP), consequently maintaining a modest, cost-effective scope. Conversely, if the event has previously proven successful, we might opt to expand or enhance features, which would increase complexity and associated costs.

How to utilize the scope component?

When outlining the scope of a LiveOps event, the team examines the immediate event activities, schedule, target markets, and intended outcomes. These aspects are categorized as either within or outside the scope of the event. The elements should be reassessed until a satisfactory scope is established. For the scope to serve effectively as a guideline for the event, all stakeholders should reach a mutual agreement on, and approve, the defined scope prior to developing the event. The subsequent questions can assist in defining the scope:

- Which areas of the game or player experience should this event target?
- Which areas of the game or player experience are outside the purview of this event?
- How to compromise between scope and budget to get the best possible outcome toward the set goal?

Tip: Consider the duration, scale, reusing, and complexity of the event when establishing its scope.

Players

Definition: Players who are the intended target audience, those who will benefit, or players who will experience the impact of LiveOps event mechanics.

What are players?

Players are segments who derive enjoyment, challenge, and a sense of achievement from the outcome of the LiveOps event. Therefore, players are intrinsically linked to the purpose of the event. It's crucial to understand the challenges players face and gain insight into their needs and desires, so the event addresses a real and engaging aspect of the game experience.

The role of players

Players are crucial because they validate the purpose of the LiveOps event. Without players, there is no motive nor justification for the event. Early identification of player needs increases the likelihood of achieving optimal results.

How to utilize the Players component?

When utilizing this component, it's vital to consider all potential players. Players are generally perceived as those outside the LiveOps team; however, team members can also be influenced by or involved in the outcomes of the LiveOps event. The following questions can be useful when identifying these players:

- Who is the target audience? To optimize the impact of a LiveOps event, it's advisable to tailor the event's mechanics to be easily accessible for your primary target audience, which may be a specific segment like newbies or casual players, while ensuring the event appeals broadly and doesn't solely depend on this group for success.
- What player's problems do we solve? Once we've differentiated between segments, we need to determine a unique value proposition for each one in the areas of engagement, onboarding, winback, and monetization.
- What exactly is offered? Upon identifying the value, we should establish the product and price. However, price isn't confined to monetary terms; it could be the player's time or any form of advocacy.

Tip: When characterizing players segments, focus on data-driven insights and avoid speculative thinking.

Constraints

Definition: Limiting factors such as specific game features, regional legal particularities, or other complexities could potentially interfere with the delivery of a LiveOps event.

What are constraints?

Every LiveOps event comes with boundaries dictated by its environment. This could include gameplay interactions, community guidelines, or game design standards. It might also be influenced by factors such as event duration, budget, technological capabilities, or game lore and mechanics.

The role of constraints

Being conscious of the constraints is key for all parties involved in the event, particularly the LiveOps team. This team needs to factor in these constraints for effective planning and adjustment of the event. The constraints essentially determine who will participate in your event. Game may manage several regions, each with varying relevance to their games. For example, Belgium has strict regulations against the use of loot boxes, viewing them as a form of gambling. Similarly, in China, there are stringent time regulations for players under 18, limiting their gameplay to 3 hours per week.

How to utilize the constraints component?

When preparing to launch a LiveOps event, the team should identify the gaming-specific constraints and understand how they might affect each of the other elements in the canvas. Here are some useful questions to consider:

- What current in-game or player community limitations are there?
- Which restrictions might impact the event development?

Remember, in the realm of game design, constraints are not barriers, but rather springboards for creativity and innovation. By integrating these constraints into your planning process, you can design LiveOps events that are not only within game limitations but also culturally relevant and engaging to players across various regions.

Consider a St. Patrick's Day-themed LiveOps event. Usually, this event would involve wearing green. However, in Chinese culture, when a man "wears a green hat," it signifies that his partner is cheating on him, leading to mockery.

When aiming for a global launch, an understanding of such cultural nuances is crucial. Instead of using the green hat symbol, adjustments to visuals and messaging could help resonate with Chinese players without causing offense. Alternatives like changing the hat color or using a different accessory altogether can maintain the St. Patrick's Day spirit while respecting cultural sensitivities.

Tip: Remember to balance the three key constraints—Time, Resources, and Quality.

Risks

Definition: The probability of certain circumstances or occurrences that can either positively or negatively influence an event.

What are risks?

In the context of LiveOps event, risks differ from constraints in that they are potential events rather than current realities. They can manifest as both challenges and opportunities, bringing uncertainties that can impact events both positively and negatively.

For instance, launching an event around a local sports team might excite fans and offer the chance to scale up during the World Cup. However, this could pose risks. In regions where gambling is banned, it may meet regulatory challenges. Also, integrating real-time scores could require significant development time, potentially causing delays.

The role of risks

Risks are inherent in all aspects of LiveOps events. Therefore, it's crucial to identify and keep them in mind, but not to shy away from them. Understanding potential risks can bolster the chances of meeting the objectives of your LiveOps event. Furthermore, efficient risk management can keep the LiveOps event on track and aligned with the original design and player expectations. It allows you to plan for potential player reactions, server issues, or balancing challenges, ensuring the event runs smoothly and successfully.

How to utilize the component?

When charting out your LiveOps event, it's crucial to identify potential risks and understand how they could impact various aspects of the event. Remember, in game LiveOps events, risk assessment is not just about averting threats but also capitalizing on opportunities. Here are some guiding questions tailored for game LiveOps event planning:

- What are potential in-game events or conditions that could influence the LiveOps event?
- What threats, such as technical glitches or player backlash, could jeopardize the success of the event?
- What opportunities, like sudden surges in player activity or trending game mechanics, could boost the event's success?
- How might these risks impact the event's engagement, retention, or monetization?
- What strategies can be implemented to minimize negative risks or enhance positive ones, such as thorough testing or leveraging popular game features?

Tip: It's essential to qualitatively and quantitatively assess each risk identified.

Schedule

Definition: Schedule represents crucial points in an event, effectively breaking it down into manageable parts.

What is schedule?

In the context of a game's roadmap, the schedule takes into account slot availability, connections to real-world events or holidays, and ensures sufficient player engagement. It may also include various milestones such as Decision Points for key decisions, Coordination Points for event alignment, Approval Points for securing permissions, and Liability Transfers for task shifts within the LiveOps team.

The role of schedule

The event duration should be carefully planned to ensure maximum participation, even from those who may discover it later in its course. A well-thought-out schedule can take into account the sequential launch of an event, encompassing the teaser, pre-launch, and launch phases.

There may be instances when the event is dependent on multiple components, each having their own unique launch dates. An example of this could be a time-limited mission, offering points upon completion, which can be used in a dedicated shop.

A balanced schedule ensures that players have sufficient time not only to complete the mission but also to utilize their earned points. The points spending period could even extend beyond the event's conclusion unless these rewards are intricately linked to the progression of the event itself.

How to utilize the schedule component?

Schedule is designed to guide the execution of various event phases, providing a clear roadmap to follow. Generally, it's beneficial to establish a schedule that encompasses the entire lifecycle of the event. Here are some key questions to consider when defining a schedule:

- When are the critical milestones expected to occur?
- How can late-joining players still benefit from the event?
- What metrics will we use to confirm a milestone has been successfully achieved?

Tip: Make sure your schedule has room for adjustments in case of unexpected changes.

Communication Plan

Definition: Communication plan maximizes event awareness, participation, and engagement through targeted messages and consistent promotion across channels.

What is communication plan?

The communication plan includes details on how, when, and where to disseminate information about the event, thus ensuring players are well-informed and can participate in a timely manner. It addresses a common issue in event participation: players often miss out on events simply because they didn't hear about them or learned about them too late.

The role of communication plan

Promoting events involves a variety of communication channels, each serving a unique purpose and reach. You need to identify which channels are most effective, considering any potential restrictions due to other game features or events.

Promotion consistency is key. Visual identity and messaging need to align across all channels so players can easily associate all promotions with the specific event.

Another crucial element is targeted communications, based on specific actions players achieve within the event. These communications could be active, triggered by a player's action, or passive, based on data tracked from the player's account at a particular time.

How to utilize the communication plan component?

The communication plan is a roadmap that outlines how you will disseminate key messages to your target audience effectively. It includes communication channels, targeted messages, timeline, frequency, and feedback mechanisms. Below are some questions that will help guide the utilization of the communication plan component:

- What are the key messages about the event?
- Which communication channels are most effective for reaching your target audience?
- When should you start promoting your event, and how often should updates be sent?

Tip: Each communication should include a clear call to action and be timed strategically to re-energize your event as needed.

Use Case

Celebrate the biggest football event of the year with your favorite online tank game! Pick your team and predict the winner of each match to score brand-new mission and leaderboard rewards! (Figure 10.2)

Activate a bonus code each game to unlock special in-game combat missions for an epic 2D style. Bag leaderboard points for correct guesses or draws, and climb the table for two extra 2D styles and themed decals. This year's Matchday will give you the opportunity to compete with your friends in private leaderboard rooms for the title of most accurate predictor. Join us, predict match winners, and get rewards for your talent as football oracles!

FIGURE 10.2   An example of LiveOps event in *World of Tanks*.

How does it work?

- Make a prediction before the start of each match. Click the team and activate the special bonus code.
- You will get 2 leaderboard points for a correct prediction, 1 point for a draw (regardless of which team you have chosen), and 0 points for an incorrect prediction.
- You will be granted access to a special battle mission once the first bonus code has been activated with a prediction. Complete the Matchday 2022 #1 mission 10 times to get an additional event reward.
- The leaderboard will be updated once per day after players' results have been calculated.
- The match schedule will be updated on the game event page.
- By activating the bonus code, you consent to your results being displayed on the public leaderboard Figure 10.3.

How to Use LiveOps Event Canvas

The LiveOps Event Canvas is a flexible tool that can be adapted to fit the unique needs of your game event. While flexibility is one of its key strengths, it's recommended to follow the suggested sequence outlined in this guide.

The components of the LiveOps Event Canvas are divided into four groups: GOAL SETTING, DESIGN, PLANNING, and ENVIRONMENT. Each group signifies a specific stage in the facilitation process. The diagram provided demonstrates the arrangement of these components and the order in which they should be addressed. The corresponding questions for each element aid team members in identifying areas of focus, streamlining the decision-making process.

A facilitator, be it an individual or a group, is required to use the LiveOps Event Canvas. This could be a team lead, or a group of developers assigned with the task. Prior knowledge of the Canvas is essential for the facilitator, whether acquired through a workshop or by independently studying the explanation of elements given in Chapter 2. Each element should be clearly explained by the facilitator(s) to the team before any information is added to the canvas.

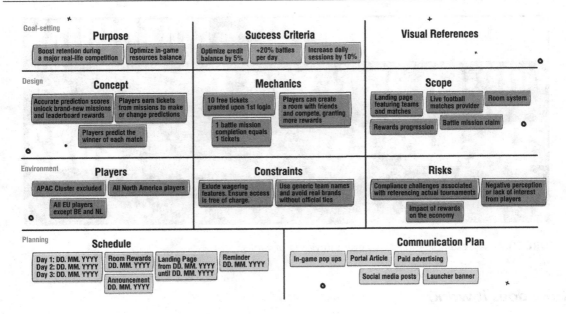

FIGURE 10.3   An example of LiveOps Event Canvas for *Matchday*.

It's important to foster a sense of collective agreement when adding new information to the canvas. Using "sticky notes" or a similar method can facilitate this process, allowing all members to contribute. The canvas is designed for continuous refinement and doesn't need to be perfect from the get-go. The goal is to ensure everyone is on the same page as you iterate and evolve your LiveOps event.

Tip: Establish an "Idea Incubator" to nurture promising concepts that don't have an immediate place in your current event.

Facilitation in Four Steps

Step 1: goal setting

Firstly, define the Purpose of the event: What is the primary objective of the LiveOps event? Once the Purpose is clarified, it's essential to agree on quantifiable Success Criteria. These are the targets that must be met for the event to be considered successful. The Success Criteria will enable you to evaluate whether the event is aligning with the predetermined goals. Lastly, during this goal-setting phase, detail the Visual References for the event: What should the event visually represent?

Step 2: define design

To start the process, ask yourself about the Concept: What is the central idea of this LiveOps event? It should be brief, clear, and easily understood by everyone involved. Next, consider the Mechanics of your event: What are the key elements that will drive interaction and engagement during this event? You need to describe the functionality of each component and their individual use cases.

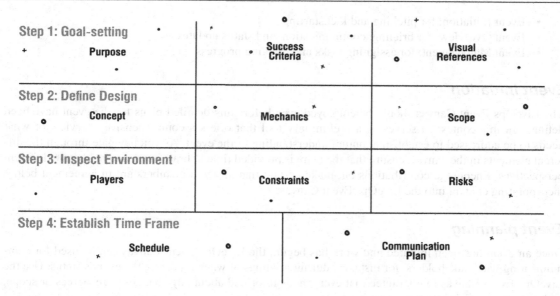

FIGURE 10.4   Four steps of using LiveOps Event Canvas.

Lastly, define the Scope: What elements are included within the concept and mechanics of the LiveOps event? What aspects are outside these boundaries? It's crucial to clearly identify the boundaries of the LiveOps event to ensure all parties involved understand the extent and limitations of the event.

Step 3: inspect environment

Now it's time to assess the environment of the LiveOps event. Initially, focus on the Players, the intended target audience of the event: Who are the beneficiaries, or who will experience the impact of the LiveOps event mechanics? Secondly, identify the Constraints of the event. What are the known limitations that could impede the event's success? While recognizing these constraints aids in establishing clear parameters and expectations, gauging the Risks enables your team to prepare for any unforeseen circumstances. Therefore, question your team: What unexpected scenarios could potentially influence the LiveOps event in a negative way?

Step 4: establish time frame

The final step involves crafting the timeline for the LiveOps event. Begin by determining the Schedule which represents significant points in the event, effectively breaking it down into manageable segments. When will the event start, and when is the end? What are the key checkpoints and when do they take place?

Post outlining the Schedule, it's time to devise the Communication Plan. The Communication Plan is critical to maximizing event awareness, participation, and engagement through targeted messaging and consistent promotion across multiple channels. Correspond each communication activity with its relevant checkpoint in the Schedule (Figure 10.4).

Where to Implement the LiveOps Event Canvas

The LiveOps Event Canvas is a dynamic tool that can be utilized in various contexts depending on the scale and intricacy of the event, the team's requirements, and the event's current stage. The use of the LiveOps Events Canvas falls into three contexts:

- Event Initiation: for pitching and kickstarting
- Event Overview: for briefing, communication, and status updates
- Event Management: for assigning tasks and tracking progress

Event initiation

The LiveOps Event Canvas should be employed even before any detailed plans for the event have been defined. In this context, it serves as a preliminary tool that offers a comprehensive overview of what needs to be addressed to establish a mutual understanding of the event. As you navigate through the different elements in the canvas, ensure that the team is provided time to brainstorm and deliberate different perspectives. Encourage contributions but make certain that all team members are in agreement before incorporating content into the LiveOps Event Canvas.

Event planning

Once an event has been initiated and work has begun, the LiveOps Event Canvas can be used for communicating with stakeholders, for instance, during briefings or when reporting the event's status. Use the LiveOps Event Canvas to guarantee that everyone is informed about any changes to resources or scope, and how present risks are being managed.

Event execution

When a LiveOps event is already in progress and the team needs a simple management tool, the LiveOps Event Canvas proves useful for assigning tasks and charting progress. In this context, the tool allows all members of the team to gain insight into the event's status on a daily or weekly basis.

CONTEXT OF USE	EVENT INITIATION	EVENT PLANNING	EVENT EXECUTION
Conditions	Preliminary planning tool, Idea generation, Conceptualization	Engagement with Stakeholders, Briefing, Scope Outlining	Event management, Tracking progress
Guidelines	Initiate with the query, "What is the LiveOps event all about?" Traverse through all the elements on the Canvas (this task can be performed by an individual or multiple team members). When working collaboratively: stimulate brainstorming and open discussions, respect diverse viewpoints and ideas. Retain simplicity: refrain from overcrowding with excessive details, only incorporate what is relevant and beneficial.	Keep track of event parts that may change over time, especially during mechanics discussions. Pay attention to any changes in player segments, resources, or mechanics, and make sure any changes still fit the event's original concept. Monitor changes in constraints, which could be influenced by community guidelines, design standards, event duration, budget, technology, or game mechanics.	Start by highlighting completed schedule or communication plan stages and then illustrate the advancement toward success criteria (status). Concentrate on elements that evolve over the course of the event. Track alterations in the target audience and pinpoint any deviations in scope to retain focus. Understand the current risks and strategize their management.
Average time frame[a]	2–4 hours	1–2 hours	Ongoing

[a] The event duration depends on its complexity and team size, which is usually between 4 and 12 people.

LIVEOPS EVENT FEATURES

After going through the planning process facilitated by the LiveOps Event Canvas, the important step in creating an engaging LiveOps event is to implement key features. These features are an extension for the blueprint for LiveOps event creation that consists of themes, progression, promotion, and monetization.

The features of a LiveOps event play a role in shaping player interaction and determine how the event flows its appeal and ultimately its success. These features include challenges, quests, interactive activities, and special offers, among others. They act as gears that transform the LiveOps Event Canvas into a reality. Through these features the LiveOps team can engage players, enhance their gaming experience, and strengthen their connection to the game (Figure 10.5).

Themes

The thematic essence of LiveOps events is their ability to merge in-game elements with cultural, media trends, or business collaborations, crafting themes that resonate deeply with players. Such themes serve as the cornerstone of LiveOps events, aiming to captivate and retain players by offering experiences that align with their gaming preferences and mirror aspects of their everyday lives. As players navigate through these themed events, they find themselves interacting with the event's core feature that sets the tone and forms an enduring bond with the theme design and implementation.

Tournament

Leaderboards have always been a component of gaming, seamlessly blending the social aspects of gameplay with the desire for accomplishment. LiveOps events can revolve around leaderboards, which not just enhance the atmosphere but also allow players to gauge their progress against others, fostering a sense of community through shared challenges and achievements.

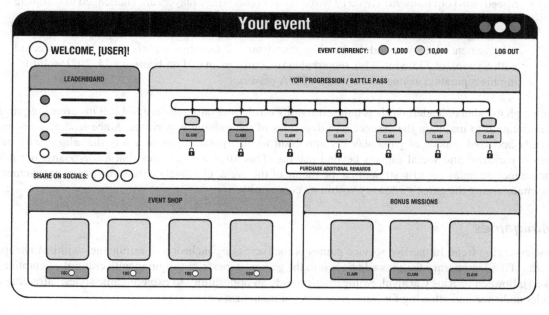

FIGURE 10.5 LiveOps event features.

In the past leaderboards were systems where players vied for scores. However, in live service games these systems have evolved into intricate rankings that serve as a multiplayer extension of the classic high-score chase. They not just motivate players to surpass their bests but also to outperform their peers in an ongoing cycle of competition and improvement.

Leaderboards can give additional depth to your regular missions and additional incentives to play through competition. The way you calculate points in a leaderboard should be carefully planned as well; it can either be straightforward, with calculations based on a single mission condition, or more complex with the addition of a secondary condition. For example, a simple leaderboard could just summarize total damage dealt for each player, while a more complex leaderboard may count points based on total damage dealt and amount of enemies destroyed. Additionally, you can choose between summing up the points or using averages depending on the desired gameplay experience.

Integrating social elements elevates leaderboards from being a ranking tool to becoming a dynamic social feature. In games bustling with players personalizing leaderboards to reflect a player's circle can significantly enhance engagement. Look for solutions that seamlessly integrate with social networks providing players with a competitive environment among friends. Do not forget to utilize notifications as a tool to re-engage players and motivate them to regain their positions in the rankings.

Time-sensitive leaderboards introduce a fresh dynamic, transforming the leaderboard experience into a competition with accolades such as "high score of the week" or "most improved player." These scheduled events encourage engagement and effectively turn a standard leaderboard into an exhilarating weekly or monthly challenge that keeps players invested and coming back for more.

Geolocation and friend-based leaderboards add a personal touch. By aligning players' standings on leaderboards, with their locations or social connections you create an intimate competitive atmosphere. Leaderboards play a role in driving player competition and serve as a theme. Among the types of tournaments there are some that gained prominence, each presenting challenges and rewarding players' commitment in distinct ways:

- **Collection Tournament:** In *Division 2* players' positions on the Global Events leaderboards are determined by their hour of gameplay during a Global Event. The rank is calculated based on the number of GE Credits earned in a 60-minute period selecting the players' performance while the event is active.
- **Speedrun Tournament:** *Gears of War 5* hosts events where players are challenged to complete campaign missions or multiplayer maps quickly as possible.
- **Winning Streak Tournament:** *FIFA 21*s Ultimate Team Weekend League witnessed an achievement by 15-year-old Anders Vejrgang from RB Leipzigs esports team. He set a record with a streak of 535 wins. This remarkable run came to an end on February 14, 2021, solidifying his reputation as one of the world's FIFA players.

Although the idea of leaderboards is quite straightforward, integrating them into LiveOps events requires consideration to maintain the essence and dynamics of the gaming experience. Since leaderboards are usually accessed outside of gameplay it's important to incorporate them in a way that aligns with the game's narrative and social aspects beyond playing. This alignment ensures that leaderboards not just encourage gameplay but also strengthen the theme of the event, ultimately enhancing player engagement and maintaining the game's vibrancy within its community.

Minigames

One emerging trend in the live service games is the increasing inclusion of minigames within LiveOps events. These temporary features add a twist to the gameplay perfectly aligning with cultural celebrations like Halloween or Rios Carnival. Minigames provide an opportunity to explore game styles, attracting a wider audience and allowing for innovative ways of monetization.

Let's take *The Division 2* as an example. They introduced ECHOs, which are augmented reality experiences through Messenger and Facebook pages. These ECHOs allowed players to delve into narratives and earn in-game rewards seamlessly blending the apocalyptic theme with innovative AR features. Such initiatives demonstrate how minigames can enhance LiveOps events by providing players with an extension of the game world.

Integrating minigames into LiveOps events goes beyond novelty; it aims to diversify the gameplay experience. For instance, *League of Legends; Wild Rift* introduced a themed minigame during their winter holiday event while *Genshin Impact* celebrated Lunar New Year with engaging minigames. These events not only offered players challenges but also fostered a sense of community participation in broader cultural celebrations.

In some cases, popular LiveOps minigames have successfully transitioned into gameplay modes. This evolution showcases how minigames have the potential to deeply resonate with players, making them an important addition to the game experience. It's fascinating how minigames can start as elements in LiveOps events and then evolve into parts of the game contributing to long-term player retention and engagement.

Integrating minigames into LiveOps events offers advantages:

- **Increased Player Engagement:** Minigames provide exciting experiences that can re-engage existing players and attract new ones breathing new life into the game.
- **Appeal to a Wider Audience:** By incorporating gameplay elements from genres minigames can cater to a range of player motivations and preferences.
- **Flexible Gameplay:** Minigames offer developers a testing ground for mechanics, offering insights into player preferences and potential future gameplay elements.
- **Monetization Opportunities:** Designed minigames can introduce new avenues for monetization either through in-game purchases related to the minigame or by boosting overall player engagement indirectly.

Minigames not just add depth to these events, they also serve as tools for increasing player engagement, diversifying gameplay experiences, and exploring innovative monetization strategies. As the world of live service games continues to progress, the significance of minigames in LiveOps events is expected to expand, presenting captivating opportunities for both players and developers.

Self-challenging

By giving players the freedom to determine their challenges, LiveOps events tap into an area of personal investment. When players set their goals, they become personally involved in the outcome. This engagement typically leads to a desire to play as players are driven to accomplish what they have set out for themselves. Achieving self-determined goals creates a sense of fulfillment. This is because these goals are often tailored to the player's interests and abilities, making the accomplishment more meaningful.

The ability to set their goals allows players to tailor challenges according to their skill level. This customization helps maintain a level of difficulty keeping the game engaging without becoming overly frustrating. Players who establish their objectives experience a sense of autonomy and control over their gaming experience. This autonomy is a factor that drives engagement since players feel more connected and responsible for their in-game actions and outcomes.

Need for Speed Unbound serves as an example of self-imposed challenges, allowing players to place side bets at the beginning of each race. Players aren't just focused on winning place; they're also strategizing to outperform rivals they've bet against. This adds a layer of depth to the races, encouraging players to take on high-stakes challenges against competitors who are expected to outperform them.

For LiveOps teams this self-challenging system provides a way to manage the fun and engagement levels. For instance, in *Need for Speed Unbound* the game predicts each racer's finish before the race, which adds an element of strategic planning. Players can use these insights to customize their bets, bringing an aspect of decision-making into the racing experience. Moreover, this system gives less flashy in game content a chance to shine. Players who prefer vehicles like VW Beetles or Mini Coopers can still participate effectively and potentially earn rewards by making smart bets. This approach broadens the game's appeal and makes it enjoyable for a range of players.

The implementation of this self-challenging theme in LiveOps Events represents a shift from the focus on "finishing first" and introduces a more realistic inclusive approach to competition and success. By incorporating self-challenging mechanism, LiveOps can introduce more diverse in-game vehicles or persona selections and richer, more varied gameplay experiences. This not just increases player involvement but also makes the game more accessible to casual gamers.

Temporary collections

The joy of gathering items, whether it's weapons or sleek digital cars, seems to tap into a fundamental human instinct. Although experts aren't entirely sure why we find collecting so appealing, many believe it could be an adaptation of our ancestor's instinct to gather resources. In today's world, where we no longer have to hunt or gather for survival, collecting things in games satisfies this urge. Some even argue that building collections helps us find solace and meaning in life by creating a sense of permanence through the things we accumulate.

Within the realm of gaming, establishing a collection can be as simple as wanting to impress friends or experiencing a sense of accomplishment from completing a set. Another intriguing concept is known as the "endowment effect," which suggests that people often attribute value to items they possess simply because they are theirs. When players collect items within a game, they tend to feel an increased sense of pride and connection toward the game itself.

Temporary collections can be likened to exhilarating treasure hunts that occur during time-limited LiveOps events. For instance, during the Overwatch Summer Games event, players have the opportunity to amass limited-time items, like skins or emotes. These special items related to summer sports are specifically available during the event period.

To make these collection events truly enjoyable it is essential to include items that players crave including some that are extremely rare and difficult to obtain. Additionally providing opportunities for players to display and showcase their collected items is crucial. The thrill of hunting down these treasures adds excitement for players. It's also important to have a space within the event where players can view their accumulated items and track what they still need to find. This encourages players to revisit the event page and strive toward completing their collections. If players receive a reward upon completing their collections, such as an exclusive bonus, it adds an extra layer of satisfaction. Incorporating a feature that allows players to share or view players' collections fosters a sense of camaraderie and transforms collecting into a competition while creating a sense of community. Ultimately, crafting a collection event in a game revolves around constructing a realm filled with unique items that entice players to pursue them, proudly display them, and enjoy the experience together.

Real world

Integrating real-world data into LiveOps events brings a layer of depth and relevance, capturing players' attention beyond the gaming environment. For instance, imagine an event centered around the Olympic Games where live data feeds are incorporated to enhance the event design. This would provide players with up-to-date information on sports matches, player statistics, and team rankings. Through this integration, a dynamic and captivating experience is created by bridging the virtual gaming world with real-world sports events. Additionally, integrating traffic data or news feeds can introduce a sense of realism and timeliness to events that are set in open-world environments or city-building themes.

An example of integration can be seen in *World of Tanks: Matchday*. They introduced a football World Cup event that allowed players to select teams and make predictions about match winners. Accurate predictions and draws earned players missions, leaderboard points, as well as unique in-game rewards like 2D styles and decals. The leaderboard was updated in real time following match outcomes, adding a fresh element to the event that encouraged player participation.

Progression

Keeping track of progression is important in a LiveOps event since missions or challenges usually form the gameplay experience. This allows for individual (player progression) or collective (cluster progression) milestones to be triggered when certain objectives are met. The concept of a Battle Pass is an example of this approach, which has gained popularity in live service games. In games without defined seasons, experiences with Battle Pass mechanics can also be highly effective in keeping players engaged.

Creating a timeline, including start and end dates along, with weekly goals can naturally guide players in their gaming experience. In games where resources may be limited, strategically reserving this feature for LiveOps events can be an approach to maximize its impact and keep players engaged.

The concept of the Battle Pass often faces misunderstandings related to its monetization aspect. While it's easy to focus solely on the rewards offered, the true value of a Battle Pass lies in its role as a monetized engagement mechanic. In F2P games, where only a small percentage of the player base makes purchases, the Battle Pass becomes more about retention and engagement rather than direct monetization.

Originally popularized in games like *Dota 2* and *Fortnite*, their success lies in the way they cater to a wide array of players. Battle Passes incentivize both non-payers and payers to play consistently. They come with a free track of rewards that encourages all players to stay active and earn rewards. For those who purchase the Battle Pass, the desire to maximize their investment keeps them coming back. Moreover, Battle Pass-related quests encourage players to explore different aspects of the game, from engaging with specific modes to experimenting with various characters. These missions, often released progressively, provide ongoing reasons for players to return to the game.

Battle Passes often present such compelling value for their cost that they become a straightforward purchase decision for a wide range of players. Many players view the Battle Pass as their sole repeatable purchase, establishing a regular and sustainable spending pattern. This approach is crucial for long-term engagement and transforms gaming into a manageable hobby.

It's worth noting that BPs may not be well-suited to user-generated content (UGC)-centric environments like *Roblox* or *Fortnite Creative*. In these spaces, the diversity and constant evolution of player-created content present significant challenges in developing coherent and consistent BP tasks.

Free Track: It's a powerful tool to keep both new and existing players engaged with your game. Offer attainable goals and rewards on this track to maintain a welcoming environment for all players. This approach respects the free-to-play model and creates a natural pathway for players to transition from free to paying players.

Ensure that the rewards on the free track are balanced. While they should be less lucrative than those on the paid track, they still need to be compelling enough to keep players interested. Moreover, incorporating in-game currencies as part of the free track rewards can be a strategic move. It allows players who regularly engage with the game to eventually access premium content without direct monetary investment. This not only rewards their dedication but also encourages them to make in-game purchases down the line.

Challenges: Crafting an effective Battle Pass requires a thoughtful balance between quests, tasks, and their duration. It should offer a diverse array of quests that cater to different player types and encourage exploration of all game modes and features. For instance, in first-person shooter games, you might want to include quests that appeal to both snipers and objective-focused players.

Equally important is how you manage quests across different game modes. Consider games with strong competitive element, where players can complete tasks in both competitive and casual play. This flexibility allows players to explore all facets of the game without feeling confined to a single mode. However, be mindful of the challenges in team-based games. Avoid quests that might disrupt team dynamics, such as tasks that force everyone to play the same class. Instead, better to stick to the design where team objectives contribute to individual player's quest progress.

The duration of your Battle Pass should reflect your game's content depth. Games with rich story-telling might benefit from a longer Battle Pass, giving players more time to immerse themselves in the world. But it's not just about length; it's also about content variety. Remember to avoid pushing players into repetitive gameplay. A game like *Destiny 2*, which offers a mix of PvE and PvP activities in its Battle Pass, can be a good model to follow. You want to ensure that players feel rewarded for both immediate engagement and long-term commitment.

A well-designed Battle Pass should weave into the fabric of your game, enhancing the overall player experience by encouraging exploration, offering variety, and rewarding both short-term and long-term engagement.

Catch-Up: This approach ensures that players who join late or take a break mid-season can still enjoy the full experience without feeling left behind. Consider introducing tasks that cleverly overlap in objectives. For example, a week 1 task might involve securing a specific district, while a later task requires players to collect items from the same location. This design allows latecomers to efficiently complete multiple tasks in a single session, fostering a sense of accomplishment and progress.

While offering the option to purchase Battle Pass levels can be a revenue stream, it's important not to lean on this as the primary catch-up mechanism. It's more about offering a shortcut for those willing to pay, rather than a necessity for progression. However, as the season nears its end, discounting these level purchases can be a smart move. It not only boosts revenue but also allows players to use their accumulated in-game currency to unlock levels they may have missed, adding an extra layer of player engagement and satisfaction.

End-of-Season: As the season draws to a close, players who have achieved tasks may start to feel tired, while others might feel the pressure to finish the Battle Pass before time runs out. Halo Infinite tackles this issue by allowing Battle Passes that are not confined to a season. They don't expire, giving players the freedom to progress at their pace and tackle them in any order they prefer. This flexibility reduces the burden on players who can't dedicate time and alleviates the frustration of rushing against a ticking clock. Moreover, it maximizes the value of content, although it does raise questions about diminishing the fear of missing out (FOMO) effect, which usually plays a role in initial Battle Pass purchases.

To address challenges with player engagement toward the end of a season, developers can introduce recurring season challenges or rewards once players reach the final levels. This provides incentives for those who have completed most of the content. Additionally, for games with competitive elements, guiding players toward those modes and offer separate rewards can prove to be an effective strategy. For games without big varieties of modes, utilizing tools like story developments or enticing content additions (such as teasing new characters, weapons, or gameplay mechanics) can keep players engaged as they anticipate future seasons.

Teamwork: Design quests and challenges within the Battle Pass that encourage players to work together. Consider mechanics where players share the rewards or objectives, thus avoiding repetitive tasks and encouraging group formation. Moreover, shape the Battle Pass tasks to be inclusive of different player roles and abilities. Instead of singular, character-specific achievements, opt for team-wide objectives that players can contribute to irrespective of their chosen role. For example, rather than requiring individual accomplishments like headshots or kills, consider objectives that the entire team can work toward, like collective points or team victories. This approach not only fosters a sense of unity but also respects the diverse playstyles within your game.

While it's important not to force players into team play, offering incentives for spontaneous collaboration can enhance the social experience. Create tasks that solo players can easily join in with others, facilitating on-the-spot team-ups. Ensure that solo players don't feel penalized or left out. While encouraging social play, also offer a range of activities that can be completed independently. This balance is crucial for catering to your entire player base and keeping all segments engaged.

Leveraging the Battle Pass as a tool for enhancing social play requires thoughtful design that promotes team collaboration, rewards group efforts, and respects individual play styles. By doing so, you can create a more engaging and inclusive gaming experience that strengthens your game's community and encourages players to connect and play together.

Rewards: The initial and final rewards in a Battle Pass are particularly significant. They serve as key motivators for purchase and completion. The first few rewards should offer immediate value to justify the purchase, while the final rewards should be highly desirable, giving players a strong incentive to complete the Pass. A well-balanced Battle Pass should have a mix of smaller, frequent rewards and larger, milestone rewards. This creates a satisfying rhythm to the progression, where players regularly receive minor items and currencies, punctuated by significant, high-value rewards at key intervals.

The rewards should cater to different player preferences, including cosmetics, in-game currencies, exclusive items, and perhaps even unique gameplay mods; moreover, some rewards should be exclusive to the Battle Pass. This variety ensures that there's something appealing for every type of player and exclusivity creates a sense of urgency to acquire these rewards before the season ends.

The way you distribute hard currency can have an impact on how players perceive the value of the Pass and their spending behavior. There are two points: if you don't include hard currency in the Pass it might seem less valuable; if players can earn hard currency with one Pass to afford the next one they might keep renewing their Passes for free, which could pose challenges for you monetization model.

To tackle this issue, developers have some options. One straightforward solution is to price the Pass as a purchase of using fiat currency. This would break the possibility of players renewing their Passes for free. Another way to handle this is by mixing up the rewards in the Pass. You can set it up so players can save up the game's hard currency, but you have to be careful not to let them save so much that they can keep getting new Passes for free forever. Also, you can make a rule where players need to collect a certain amount of hard currency to buy the Pass. This amount should be just enough so that, when they add it to the hard currency they get from playing the game, they can buy another Pass, but not keep buying them without end. You have to think about all the different ways players can get hard currency in the game. Some games try different things, like making it easier to earn hard currency when players first buy the Pass. This way, players might get the next chapter for free, but they won't be able to get the whole season without paying.

Aligning rewards with progression through gameplay ensures that players are actively participating in the game to advance through the Pass. Remember, while rewards should be attainable, they shouldn't feel unachievable. Balancing the difficulty and time investment needed to obtain rewards is key to keeping players motivated without feeling overwhelmed or frustrated.

Even on the free track of the Battle Pass, include rewards that are enticing enough to keep non-paying players engaged and returning to the game. By offering high-value rewards, especially at the start and end of the Pass, players are more likely to perceive their purchase as worthwhile, encouraging them to continue investing time (and potentially more money) in the game.

Drivers: Players often have two reasons for purchasing the Battle Pass: the fear of missing out (FOMO) and the perception of opportunity. They worry about losing out on rewards they've already worked hard to earn if they don't buy the Battle Pass before it expires. This urgency creates a motivation to make the purchase.

Efficiency is also a factor that comes into play. Players feel like they're not maximizing their rewards during gameplay without the Battle Pass. Moreover, the appeal of content adds to their motivation. The fear of missing out on items or experiences can be highly motivating for players. Players see value in buying the Battle Pass when they realize how much content can be obtained at a price. Game developers design this well by offering a great amount of content through their Battle Pass, emphasizing its value for money.

To reinforce these motivations, game designers implement various mechanics. They introduce progression systems like XP boosts or exclusive tasks tied to the Battle Pass. Instant exclusive rewards are also used strategically to provide unique items, which helps alleviate any regrets after making the purchase.

Some games even offer rewards available only to premium players. This means that once players reach a point, they realize that they won't get any rewards unless they have the pass. These passes not just provide content but also encourage monetization efforts.

Fortnite also uses a strategy by linking LiveOps events with Battle Pass content. They introduce time-limited events that require players to have the content available in the Pass. This approach ensures that Battle Pass holders not just receive rewards but gain access to significant expansions of their game-play experience. On the other hand, non-paying players are consistently reminded of what they're missing on in terms of actual playable experiences. For example, *Fortnite* had time-limited Deadpool Challenges where exclusive rewards were given. To participate, players needed to own the Deadpool skin, which was only available through the Pass.

Upsell: When it comes to upselling techniques, one popular method is offering tier skips. This allows players to skip levels and progress faster. For instance, in *Call of Duty: Warzone* players can buy Tier skips at any time without missing out on any content. Even if players decide to purchase the Battle Pass after progressing through tiers there's no issue; they will immediately receive all the rewards from those tiers they have already unlocked through gameplay.

Sometimes players have the choice to reroll missions that don't align with their preferences, giving them control over their Battle Pass experience. Certain games have even introduced Battle Passes that cater to events or different game modes.

To enhance the Battle Pass experience, some games offer subscription systems where players auto-matically receive Battle Passes and exclusive bonuses like skins and in-game currency. Moreover, gift-ing Battle Passes to friends has become a way to connect within gaming communities. It often leads to increased sales as players enjoy sharing the experience with others.

Cannibalization: Developers must strike a balance when implementing Battle Pass systems to avoid consequences. They should ensure that the Pass adds value without overshadowing monetization methods or negatively impacting the game's economy. The key is to provide incentives that encourage players to pur-chase and engage with the Pass while also maintaining an appealing monetization strategy for the game.

To assess any impacts, game developers should closely monitor performance indicators (KPIs) such as Average Revenue per User (ARPU) and Average Revenue per Paying User (ARPPU), conversion ratios, and how players distribute their spending across in-game purchases. If these metrics start to decline, it could suggest that the Battle Pass is giving too much value over other sources.

Another important aspect to consider is the game's economy. If the Battle Pass becomes too gen-erous in its offerings it might discourage players from making purchases. Keeping track of how many non-paying players transition into paying players for the first time and analyzing the lifetime value (LTV) of player groups can provide insights into this matter.

Moreover, developers should be mindful of how resources are managed within the game. Having an overflow of resources or a lack of depth in spending options could indicate cannibalization. This can be evaluated by studying how resources flow in and out of the game, examining player inventories and analyzing player progression patterns.

Promotion

We have discussed promotion in detail in Chapter 5 but there is one feature that has paramount impor-tance within LiveOps event, which is social media integration. Using authentication tokens from social media platforms, you can let users share anything from your event on their social media account. It goes from generic sharing leading to the main page of the event to specific aspects of the event (for example, if you make a quiz, players could share their result while prompting their friends to participate as well). In order to incentivize sharing, you can even reward players with LiveOps event's currency or in-game rewards whenever they share something.

Monetization

LiveOps teams have a lot of monetization techniques in their disposal to launch LiveOps events, focus-ing on optimizing the game's revenue streams without disrupting the player experience. This involves managing the overall balance of the game's virtual assets or support of game's revenue KPIs. We have discussed monetization in detail in the previous chapter but there are two core monetization features related to LiveOps events.

Event currency

A LiveOps event's currency is a type of game currency that is specifically created for an event. To keep things simple, we'll refer to this currency as "points," although it can be represented in any form that you choose, such as coins, tickets, or stardust.

The use of a point system allows players to have more flexibility in choosing their rewards, compared to a fixed progression system. The concept is straightforward: as players complete missions, they earn points instead of receiving direct rewards. These points can be accumulated and spent in a special event shop, which can be located on a landing page or within the game itself if the feature is implemented.

While it may be more convenient for players to spend their points on the same page where they can interact with the event, it may be more beneficial for your game to direct players in-game to spend their points. This is because entering the game client increases their likelihood of playing, which can ultimately improve your game's performance.

Event shop

While directing players to your official storefront for any transactions may seem like a simple solution for monetization, it's important to acknowledge that the player journey from the event platform to finalizing a purchase can be cumbersome and discourage conversions. This process typically involves clicking a button, logging in to the store, selecting a package, viewing its description, clicking to buy, choosing a payment method, entering payment details, and finally confirming the purchase.

To improve the player experience and boost conversion rates, it may be worth considering allowing players to purchase directly from your event page, using an integration similar to what your shop provides. However, this approach can be costly and require significant development efforts, which means that it should be thoughtfully planned and evaluated based on the event's size and objectives.

LiveOps event missions' rewards can be distributed differently; they can be sent automatically to the player's account after reaching certain milestones (passive) or be claimed (active). Each of these mechanics needs to be planned carefully, as they require a specific solution to be implemented and might serve different purposes. As much as you can invoice rewards, it is also possible to grant exclusive packages or discounts based on achievements or simply to a specific target audience. Event shop can also include a possibility to claim a mission via the click of a button. This may be used, for example, in events proposing paid missions of various difficulties, each worth a specific number of points, with a limited number of tries.

Personalization

11

Personalization is customization of player experience and/or communication based on information a game has learned about the player—data collected, experiments conducted, and research done. In massive multiplayer games, personalization is usually applied to the communication channels. This is done in order not to create discrepancies in complexity of the gameplay for different cohorts, in other ways, so that your friend doesn't have a simpler game than yourself. However, over time the game universe grows and expands into an array of activities that, naturally, couldn't interest every player. At this point personalization gets to the deeper level of customizing customer experience.

Predictive Modeling: Segmenting is crucial to building an adequate approach to different players, but that's not quite enough for an ultimate success. To reach it, you need to be proactive, forward looking, anticipating outcomes and behaviors based upon the data and not on a hunch of assumptions, and here is where predictive modeling comes handy. Speaking scientifically, predictive analytics is the branch of advanced analytics used to make predictions about unknown future events. It uses several data mining, predictive modeling, and analytical techniques to bring together the management, information technology, and modeling business process to make predictions about the future. The patterns found in historical and transactional data can be used to identify risks and opportunities for the future (Figure 11.1).

Personalization Engine: When it comes to the execution, a rule engine enables game teams to create logic that would adjust experience (send offer, activate discount, give a gift, set a challenge) to a specific segment of players at a specific trigger at a specific timeframe. Triggers are usually disregarded

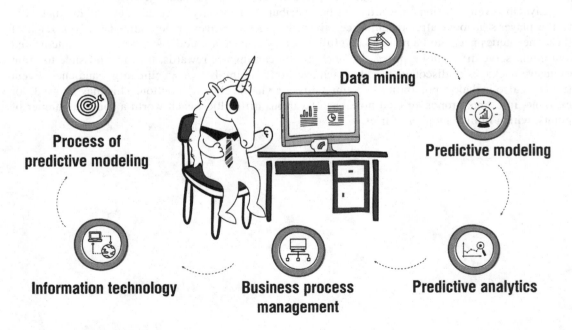

FIGURE 11.1 How to make prediction.

DOI: 10.1201/9781003427056-15

Target group   **Control group**

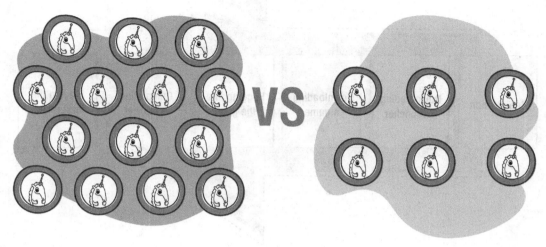

FIGURE 11.2   Target vs. control groups.

as personalization component; however, in video games industry it all boils down to emotions. In many cases, a powerful emotional moment, such as well-deserved victory or an achievement, impacts more the offer performance than segmentation or discount or bonus.

Personalized Placement: Personalization is only powerful if it has interfaces. Mapping player experience from the registration page, to email confirmation, to launcher, to game client helps to identify players where customized messages or offers may be relevant.

Personalization is the most robust area of LiveOps from the analytical perspective. Unlike most game activities or events, LiveOps teams may create a special control group and a target group for personalization campaigns to accurately track the impact of those on player monetization, retention, social behavior, etc. LiveOps activities rely on different predictive models based mainly on the engagement level of the players, which chases several needs like gaining revenue by upselling or cross-selling, increasing engagement, and preventing churning (Figure 11.2).

ONBOARDING

When the marketing machine works well and a game gets newly registered players, LiveOps's job is to make them stay for long, become engaged, and well acquainted with the game as soon as possible. That includes setting up everything related to the game if needed, finishing in-game tutorials, and acquaintance with the main mechanics or interfaces. A new player must not feel abandoned right after signing up, instead, they must feel well guided with care through their first steps.

In the onboarding case, it's difficult and not even very necessary to apply any predictive analytics. First, you don't have any historical data and predict anything, and second, at this stage, players are mostly new to the game (yeah before they could watch some steams or their friends playing, but that could hardly make them experienced), and should be treated with maximum care. Therefore, the answer to the question **"Who is the target audience?"** from the 3LAP framework is seemingly apparent—all newcomers.

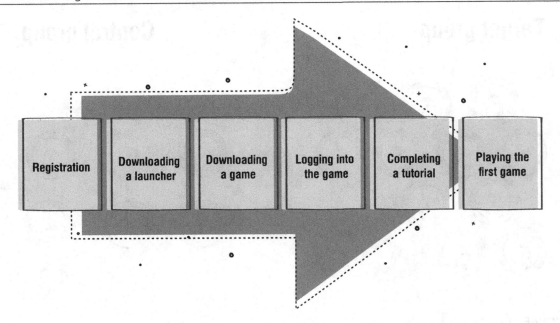

FIGURE 11.3   An example of a PC game player onboarding journey.

If a game is mobile or console, the first touch is embedded into the platforms (Apple Store, Google Play, Xbox, or PlayStation), and a player waits for the game to be downloaded and installed, afterward goes through the onboarding process. If a game is on PC, this may include a few steps to take along the player's initial journey, and on each of them, they can drop and thus need to be contacted (Figure 11.3).

For PC games, an account creation may take place on the game website before a gamer actually downloads anything, and, in this case, only the next step could be downloading a launcher or a game. It is not uncommon that a gamer may see an advertisement or get a recommendation from a friend, then quickly sign up in order not to forget, but do not immediately set up everything. For example, a gamer can register from a mobile device, from a corporate laptop, or can simply be in a hurry and have no time for the rest. That's why LiveOps shouldn't leave it like this and, in a day or a couple, push a gentle reminder that some important affairs are still waiting. Be persistent here because the longer your potential player does nothing, the higher the chances of losing them.

Onboarding steps may depend on a game or a distribution platform but in general has the following order: registration, downloading a launcher, downloading a game, launching and logging to a game, completing a tutorial, playing first game, or start real action. Understanding the onboarding journey helps tackling the question from the 3LAP framework "**What exactly is offered?**" and guiding the player at the beginning of his experience.

General Advice: PC games take some time to download as they are huge, so players can banally need to be reminded that the installation is over. Don't stop by sending just one message till you reach the goal. A chain of messages is totally acceptable here, and if you see that plain messages don't work, try giving some rewards for completing the target action. Remember, a player is not at all familiar with the game and rewards should be something commonly understandable and valuable.

Personal Advice: The tracking system can tell how exactly players have joined the game. For example, if they were brought to the game by their friends with a referral link, feel free to personalize the communication and rewards, making an accent on the team spirit or platoon benefits. If they came with an invite code from an influencer that a game partners with, LiveOps can please the newcomers with a personalized welcome letter sort of "written on behalf of that influencer," give a skin with their face or anything. The tracking system also knows from which country players came, which gives the ability to suggest them something thematic related to their country (vehicles, customization, or local streamers).

When a player has successfully completed the primary part of the onboarding journey and gets into the game client, it does not make a player an expert, and he still needs context guidance depending on the situation because there is a lot to explore. Bringing a gamer inside the game opens more doors toward finding treatment by answering the last question from the 3LAP framework, **"What should the offer look like?"**.

Hints: imagine a player doing something for the first time. For example, navigates to a new interface, plays on a new character class, fights against a new enemy, this is the right moment to give a useful hint on how to do it right. Alternatively, if a player keeps losing to some specific enemy, or has issues with a certain type of character or map, it's time to throw a guide to cheer them up and give useful tips to increase survivability and efficiency.

Tasks: provide a player with a set of educational tasks to master multiple aspects of the game, for instance, character classes, usage of equipment, consumables, or customization, and, of course, do not forget with a useful reward as a recognition of players' efforts and acquired skills.

With the first part of the onboarding, where the goal is to make a player start playing ASAP, there's no actual trigger, we should try making this happen as soon as possible since the risks of losing a potential player are high. Feel free to use all the means at your disposal: operating system notifications, emails, or advertisement networks. With the second part, when your player is already in action, in-game pop-ups, promo screens, tool-tips/hints, and messages in a launcher are increased conversions in target actions.

RETENTION

It's hard to embrace but players' activity tends to decrease—they just get tired, less interested, annoyed with the current mechanics, have insufficient hardware, or for any other reason. These players need different treatment, something that would elevate their motivation to play further. That is why it's so challenging to find appropriate hints or offers that help to retain the players, keep them interested, and incentivize them to login stably. It is important to catch these players while we still can, while they are still active, because first, it is simpler to retain than to win someone back, and second, in-game communication channels have the highest efficiency.

We're going back to the 3LAP framework and answer the question **"Who is the target audience?"** by extending our player's profile with churn-related attributes which help to enhance personalization.

Churn Prediction: When it comes to retention, we must be proactive and detect those who have a high probability of churning in the nearest future to adjust players' experience. A more advanced version of the churn model can even tell a bit more precisely how or even why your players decrease their activity. Of course, most factors influencing players' likeliness to play lie outside of the game, and it's hardly possible to impact them with campaigns; however, it still increases your chances of giving the proper "medication" for a player's "disease,"

Overall churn scoring is key to understanding the results of the machine learning but together with the weight of each model's parameter it's easier to pick an appropriate action.

- **Premium:** Players who didn't play, for instance, last week and are running out of premium subscription are more likely to churn, and the impact of this feature increases the more time a player has spent playing during an active premium subscription.
- **Own Activity (Not Average):** Players decreasing their own activity are more likely to churn; on the other hand, veteran players with decreasing activity are more likely to cycle out and come back than to churn permanently.
- **Own Content Consumption (Not Average).** Players who haven't unlocked a level/vehicle/personage "on time" are more likely to quit. It's hard to assume if becoming more likely to

quit reduces unlocking or if reduced unlocking increases quitting, but each game has designed breakpoints for unlocking in-game content (e.g., 10–20 days since the last vehicle unlock). Depending on the game, we can add the buffer up to 5%–10% and use this parameter to clarify the likelihood of churn better and apply it for weekly active players.

- **Hardware:** Players with personal computers that underperform are more likely to quit and sometimes the impact of this feature increases for newbies with less than certain hours or battles played.
- **Gap Patterns:** Gaps are periods when players go inactive. These patterns differ by battles or hours played, with shorter-term gaps being more problematic for the less experienced players and longer-term gaps being more problematic for the more experienced players. It is recommended to define the personal pattern of inactive days or weeks to avoid false actions.

With the personal churn score at our disposal, decreasing activity trend, and desire to maintain player engagement and time spent in the game, we're moving to the next question from the 3LAP framework **"What exactly is offered?"** and each of the segments with the different weight of churn parameters has a set of personalized offers depending on their playing behavior.

Self-Expiring Content: It is not being collected on the account balance and given for free as a bonus. For example, a premium subscription has a limited number of days and starts immediately. If a player uses it, we reached our goal and made them stay longer with us, but if not, we didn't hurt the game economy, because the subscription will be over and will not be stocked as a resource on the player's balance.

Achievable Mission: Tasks should be challenging enough to make players spend some time and effort on them but at the same time achievable enough in order not to frustrate lapsing players with something they cannot complete.

Personal Outlet: The sense of uniqueness stimulates curiosity; moreover, the sense of achievement drives intrinsic motivation. In the reality of content deficit, you can utilize imaginary proxy currency in the personal outlet with handy goods that can be bought by playing. In a way, you let your players work to earn "money" and then purchase the same content of their choice. Keep in mind that we're trying to retain players so the exchange rate of proxy currency could be extremely appealing, while not causing negative community feedback.

Personal Daily Rewards: That could be logging in to the game, playing a match, etc. As rewards you may use a limited number of consumables, progression boosters, customization, or anything less that would not harm the economy too much if given for free. Bonuses can be equal by value from day to day or have it increasing with every day to enhance the motivation. You can let the players know beforehand what's the maximum they can get or make it secret and stir up interest and curiosity of what can they get tomorrow and in the very end.

Discount: Players who invest their fiat money in the game are less likely to abandon it just like that, a simple regret of the spent money. Note that here you are dealing with someone who is going to churn, so standard upselling monetization offers may be a bit toxic, and would be good to consider something more juicy than usual, stimulating motivation (like some days of Premium subscription), maybe with more affordable prices.

Once the audience is extended with churn-related scores, assumed decreasing activity reason and relevant proposition, it's time to answer the last question from the 3LAP framework, **"What should the offer look like?"** and come up with a way to communicate this to the players in the most proper manner.

When it comes to retention campaigns that include more complicated mechanics like battle missions, series of consecutive actions, rewards with conditions, etc., a player should have a clear understanding of what we want from them, how exactly it should be done, and what the final result they will get is. For those who are still active in the game, the best communication will be through in-game channels like pop-up windows or promo screens. They have the highest probability of being noticed and read as well as can be thrown at the best suitable moment.

Also, it is worth trying to reach out to those who are likely to churn but had their last battle a couple of days ago. Since they played just recently it means that they are still interested in the game, and you can try to win them back quickly or "make iron while it's hot." Out-of-game communication channels may not be that efficient in terms of open rate; however, generally, cover the larger chunk of your audience via push notifications or operating system tray messages in the launcher. The message should be catchy, comprehensive, and calling to action, with the main goal being to make players open your game again.

It's worth to mention that for someone who is about to leave us, giving a good treat on an unsuccessful moment could work (match loss, defeat in the game, etc.); low moments of motivation are not bad to give a consolatory bonus like your retention campaign. For freshly lapsed players you cannot track their activity outside of the game, so here your triggers are pretty much generic. However, you can still play with the timing when you can contact your players, for example, lunchtime, evenings, and weekends may work better depending on the platform of your game.

WINBACK

Regardless of our efforts on retention, it is sad but true that players do churn. As mentioned, this may happen due to plenty of reasons: they get bored, lifetime changes and they have no longer time to play, new device, all progression is achieved, or they simply didn't like the game from the first steps. But the good news is that it is possible to influence all this, and such behavior is often not irrevocable.

Predictive analytics may help you to determine the behavioral patterns of players and predict their probability to get back in action in a certain amount of days, but at the same time, it may be worth targeting all your lapsed players regardless of what the model says, after all, an extra reminder about yourself will not be that extra.

Engagement here is the key factor that matters what winback strategy you're going to apply, and it's closely related to the question from the 3LAP framework **"Who is the target audience?"** The more engaged a player is, the less likely they are going to lapse forever and the more likely they are going to return organically in some time.

Churned Newbies: Considerable efforts should be concentrated on recently churned newbies (each game should determine its own definition of newbies by the number of specific actions, amount of time spent in the game, etc.) since they have the highest probability of being gone for good. Contact them as soon as possible by using all the channels at your disposal. Finding the juiciest and the most exciting piece of content is the key goal here and not letting them lapse. On the other hand, newbies may not be tempted by something with a value they cannot understand, and the content must be as comprehensive as it can. For example, soft currency, premium subscription, ability to play for some hyped character/vehicle—valuable, understandable; booster on third perk on second ability restoring your HP under unknown circumstances, which only works if you have a certain spell enabled on a certain weapon while playing for a certain character—useless, incomprehensible.

Engaged Churners: Engaged players know what a game has and how it works, that is why quite often, they may just have some sort of a pattern. For instance, playing a couple of weekends every month, so it is totally fine if they disappear for a month and then come back organically. So maybe it does not make too much sense to spam them just a couple of days after their last session, especially if there isn't anything interesting for them to suggest. On the contrary, if a considerable amount of time has passed (a game determines this amount depending on the design, platform, segment, or engagement level of their players), it may be worth reminding about yourself. For example, hit the right target at the right moment with a message and a player will see it and think, "hm, a chilly evening, really, why don't I log in to my favorite game," especially if there's something juicy.

The Winback strategy should focus on retaining lapsed players, offering something valuable, creating a feeling of loyalty, and making players feel important. Although there are plenty of positive researches confirming the value of a robust winback campaign, it's crucial your game, regardless of size, takes the essential steps to protect the active audience when brainstorming the question from the 3LAP framework **"What exactly is offered?"** and do not offer more value to your lapsed base.

TYPE OF WINBACK	*WHAT TO DO?*
Recent or highly engaged churners. Retention—players who are involved in the game and come back to the game on a regular basis. Re-engagement—players who don't have regular pattern of coming back, but seasonality and in-game changes make them return to the game.	Automated winback chain in direct channels like email, social media, messengers, or launcher. Monthly or quarterly ad hoc winback campaigns with border media usage in addition to direct channels.
Re-acquisition—players who were not active for a long time and haven't played enough time recently to be considered as engaged player.	Big occasions or updates using broad media with acquisition focus.

Reminders: the safest tool possible. Players may have some premium subscription left that is going to expire, which is the perfect occasion to remind or some hard currency that can be invested in valuable goods. Reminders can be used regardless of the engagement level.

"Did You Know?": a message highlighting not the most obvious, yet useful parts of the game. Some tutorials, game modes, character features, benefits of in-game equipment/consumables, tactics. Also mentioning a big community your game has where players share their feedback and find answers to their questions. "Did you know?" may be mostly useful for new players.

Announcements: a very nice occasion to contact a player. If your game has an update, new gaming modes, characters, events, or any other new content, it's a crime not to let players know about it. It may be more efficient for more engaged players who churn because there was nothing interesting for a while in the game. Newbies may be not that interested in new stuff if they are not yet familiar with the basics.

Test-drives: let players try something not normally easily available. Short-term premium subscription, possibility to play premium rare character/vehicle (note: it should be really good, hardly playable characters would only cause frustration), or any other content which could bring new experience will work good. It works regardless of the engagement level, and still may be better for newbies since the engaged players have less things to be surprised with.

Rewards for Target Actions: you ask your players to perform certain action (log in to the game, play a match, connect their account with our partners, bring a friend back, etc.) promising a reward for that. You are free to choose your rewards from the pool which would not harm your economy—cost of such a retention should be lower than LTV. Operate with self-expiring resources like premium subscription or time-limited test-drives, or consumable content like soft currency, progression boosters, consumable game equipment, and customization. Premium subscription is a good choice since first, it makes players come back, and second, it makes them play the duration of this subscription. Rewards for target actions work well regardless of the engagement level.

Challenges: giving rewards is nice and simple, but earning rewards is interesting at the same time. Announce a juicy reward worth little sweating and explain how to get it, put a special and exclusive mission to a player. A small challenge may make it less boring for a lapsed player to earn it compared to a general gameplay, and the reward itself should make the player stay with us longer.

Winback capabilities are a bit limited here since a player has already left the game, and we cannot send in-game notifications or promo screens. In spite of potential low conversion rate of communication, there is still some promising power in reflections around the last question from the 3LAP framework **"What should the offer look like?"**

Launcher: if your game has a launcher working on a background of the operating system, it can be the most efficient type of a notification when a player is in front of their PC and has high chances to be noticed and read.

Emails: the easiest and the most guaranteed way of communication where you are free to experiment with wording and visuals. However, due to lots of spam people receive nowadays, the open rate of emails is expectedly not very high.

Push Notifications (if your game is mobile or has a mobile companion app): quite efficient to remind about yourself, a mobile phone is something almost always in your hand. Still, with the amount of notifications we receive it may be also lost.

Ads in Social Media: paid posts in Instagram or Facebook feed, banners on different websites distributed through partner networks.

If you ever worked with "cold" sales, you probably know that contacting a lead just once and immediately forgetting it is not something that works. Always admit that your message can be lost, got to spam, just missed. It is very important to respect the balance of being persistent and too pushy/spammy and build your message chains in the way to be eye-catchy, interesting, offering something relevant and valuable for your player; between reach outs choose a wise timing (for example, if you contact someone on all 7 days and you fall on, for example, Wednesday 15h00 when your player has a weekly meeting with a team, it's very unlikely that any of your messages will be opened).

You may have different messaging, different rewards or missions depending on the number of a reach out, and then depending on if you achieved your goal (depends on login or playing a match), personalize in-game experience further. Briefly, you are free to create a range of scenarios using different ways of communication and different content to create your winback chains.

Winback activities do not have possibility to tie a message trigger to any in-game actions and have to use generic conditions. Depending on the message you're trying to communicate, this can be: how many hours/days passed since the last gaming session, or since the last reach out or how many hours/days or quantity of the resource left on the balance you're trying to remind about or release of a new update you want to announce.

Don't forget to play with the timing of your messages. It may not be too much strict with mobile projects because a phone is always in hand and players often procrastinate in transport, queues, cafés, or even at work; however, if it's a PC game, it may make more sense to reach out when people are more likely at home not far from their computer, moreover, the conversion increases in the evenings and on weekends. Feel free to experiment with the different timing and intervals within your chains; this way, you have more chances to catch a player in different moments of their daily and weekly routine and cover more potentially suitable situations.

MONETIZATION

The goal of such campaigns is the upgrading of owned products and current experience. Existing players are offered a better and more profitable product than the one they already own. Hence, these campaigns aim at switching players to "premium" products, and they can be supported by corresponding classification models which estimate the "upgrade" propensities.

Let's go back to the 3LAP framework and answer the question **"Who is the target audience?"** by extending our player's profile with more monetization-related attributes which help to enhance personalization.

Purchase Probability: In the beginning, it's necessary to forecast the probability to buy something in the indicated period based on historical data of purchases of the game's characters or vehicles, non-bundle fiat or virtual currency, premium subscription, or any purchase. Simply saying it can answer whether a player is going to pay or not ("yes/no" probability score). Depending on the game, all scores can be provided for active players with at least 1+ active day during the last week/month as of the snapshot date, and each game defines its definition of an active payer.

Revenue Forecasting: Talking about such a model, in a way, we can consider it as an ideological evolution of the purchase probability model. In addition to "yes/no" probability, revenue forecasting is able to tell how much a player is going to spend for a given period of time (1/2/3/4 days/weeks or whatever). The revenue forecasting model forecasts an approximate amount of fiat or virtual currency to be spent by each player in the following period. The bin (range "from $ to $$$") we predict these players to pay is calculated dynamically using the modal daily/weekly bin of the previous days/weeks as of the snapshot date.

These two models help to better monetize players, which more deeply can be split roughly on the following levels:

- **Non-payers:** we must find something which would "break the ice" and show a player that paying for our game is a socially normal behavior and nothing bad happens if you spend a couple of bucks on a thing that gives you joy.
- **Not Active Payers:** speaking about players who had their last payment a while ago, most likely we're dealing with someone who is only ready to spend on some special offers, exclusive content not available on a regular basis, discounted content, bonus for purchase, etc. With these players we need to make efforts to make them pay regularly.
- **Active Payers:** we don't need to convince those players to pay, we're already there. What we need is to make them pay more than they would usually do.

PLAYER SEGMENTS	GOAL	KEEP IN MIND
New Non-payer: These players have not made any payments and have less experience, meaning they are not yet acquainted with the game's economy and gameplay mechanics. It's important to tailor your game metrics to new non-payers, which could be fewer than 100 battles, 50 active sessions, or 10 hours of playtime.	To convert into consistent payers while maintaining or improving their retention in the game.	**The Earlier We Engage, the Better:** Our objective is to determine the average number of days before 50% of players churn and to ascertain the average number of sessions, battles, or total hours spent before 50% of players conduct their first transaction. Identifying these critical opportunity windows allows us to engage players promptly and effectively, maximizing monetization potential.
Regular Non-payer: These players have also never made a payment but possess at least a basic understanding of the game's economy and gameplay mechanics. For this segment, you can introduce more appealing offers, possibly at discounted rates.		**New Players Do Not Know Your Game:** Newbies are not yet familiar with your game's mechanics and may not recognize the value of premium content or be ready for high-level experiences. Offer content that is clearly valuable to beginners and avoid targeting them with offers designed for high-skilled players.
Recent Ex-payers Likely to Pay: X days without purchases but have high probability to pay.	To boost ARPU through increasing share of payers among ex-payers.	**Be Careful with ARPPU**: Big discounts may significantly decrease users' ARPPU. Consequently, even an increase in the share of paying users might not lead to a rise in ARPU.

(Continued)

(Continued)

PLAYER SEGMENTS	GOAL	KEEP IN MIND
Recent Ex-payers Not Likely to Pay: X days without purchases and have low probability to pay. **Middle Ex-payers:** from X to Y days without purchases. **Old Ex-payers:** more than Y days without purchases. You can experiment to find X and Y for your game or analyze your historical data.		**The Longer Gap, the Higher Discounts:** If players haven't paid for a long time, they probably won't start paying on their own. So, we can risk giving bigger discounts as it might only affect ARPPU of a few players. **Take Care of Winbackers.** One reason for a player's non-payment could be their absence from the game. Dealing with returning players requires a special approach, as the primary goal is to retain them in the game.
Active Payers Likely to Pay: these are players who have had payment for the last Z days and have high probability to pay. **Active Payers Not Likely to Pay:** these are players who have had payment for the last Z days and have low probability to pay. You can experiment to find Z for your game or analyze your historical data.	To boost ARPU through increasing payers' ARPPU	**Avoid Discounts:** It's not recommended to offer discounts to active payers, especially on resource bundles, as it may decrease their ARPPU (especially in the long term). **New Players are Still New:** Even if new players have made a payment, you should be careful about offering them content designed for high-skilled players. **Recent Payment Doesn't Mean Regular Payments:** Just because a player made a payment recently, it doesn't necessarily mean they will be likely to pay again in the near future.

The hardest part of game operations is to come up with new monetization offers from month to month, develop seasonal events and sales, creating packages with delicious content. On the other hand, that is a beautiful practice which can offer a new experience for sophisticated, stably paying players and a seductive reason to spend first monies for non-payers. The next question from the 3LAP framework is **"What exactly is offered?"** and each of the segments has a set of personalized offers depending on their payment behavior—from "starter packs" and non-restricted coupons for a non-paying player to strictly restricted coupons and expensive supreme bundles for stably paying audience.

Discount: It may look like a direct discount—coupon with %, or like a bonus (buy anything and get free premium—also a discount in fact, but not that direct), or like a package with lots of goods, which costs cheaper than buying all of them separately. *Warning*: watch who your discount is targeted to, it may work suitably for conversion of non-payers or non-active payers; however, it may damage active stably paying audience (instead of paying the full price they would have paid anyway, you allow them paying less).

Exclusive Content: Something not available on a regular basis. Rare characters, skins/customization, boosters, consumables, equipment. *Warning*: make sure that the stuff you promote is not used in other special events. If the game community is strong, someone may get pissed when they find out that something they had to fight for with endless marathons, missions, battles pass, etc., you received just like a regular daily offer.

Personal Challenges: Not a simple purchase, but an opportunity to challenge yourself with unique missions or quests, with an opportunity to get some rare or useful goods.

Retargeting Offers: These are tailored promotions directed at players based on their browsing history within the game's storefront. If a player has shown interest in an item but hasn't completed the purchase, a retargeting offer can be the nudge they need. This could involve a slight discount, an additional bonus item, or exclusive access for a limited time. This personalization makes the offer more relevant and can effectively convert interest into sales.

Action Points: These are strategic incentives linked to specific in-game actions. For instance, purchasing a new vehicle might come with an exclusive skin or specialized equipment. These action points act as immediate rewards for engaging in the desired behavior—making a purchase. They can be particularly effective if the bonus content enhances the utility or aesthetics of the purchased item, adding immediate value to the transaction and encouraging further investment in the game.

Indirect Monetization: Quite often the most frequently bought item in F2P games is the hard currency. This currency usually allows you to buy premium content in-game, accelerate your progression, skip the wait, convert to the soft currency. In a word, a valuable resource for your comfort playing. Flushing this important currency resource with the corresponding offers is a nice way to make players purchase it again for real money. Moreover, psychologically it's easier to spend something you've already paid for, rather than open your real wallet.

Once the audience is extended with monetization-related scores along with types of value proposition, it's time to answer the last question from the 3LAP framework **"What should the offer look like?"** and come with the way to communicate this to the players in the most appropriate manner.

There is primarily one group of players to target with the monetization offers, and they are the active audience. The rest is questionable, it is not a good practice to bombard full newbies with monetization when they don't understand the game, what is valuable or not, or if they will continue playing at all. Offering fiat money deals for those who are tired of the game and is about to leave also is not the best—will you donate to something you're going to abandon? With lapsed players it's even more obvious.

Since the target audience is actively playing, the most efficient and obvious way to do this would be through in-game channels. Depending on the game and platform this could be in-game pop-up window, promo screen, or embedded operating system notifications.

The message you give there should be short and comprehensive, ideally with a Call-to-Action link or button. The less clicks a player must do in their journey to purchase, the higher conversions you have, so ideally a player should be able to purchase stuff directly from your pop-up window. Or at least, try to lead them to the item directly in the in-game storefront.

PART IV

Competing through Operations

The ability to consistently deliver exceptional value to players is what distinguishes a successful game from the rest. Echoing the wisdom of Eric Schmidt (CEO of Google from 2001 to 2011) in the book *Trillion Dollar Coach*, inspired by his relationship with Bill Campbell: "To Bill, being an executive of a successful company is all about creating operational excellence. As a manager and CEO, Bill was very good at making sure his teams delivered." This part of the book explores how strategic operations management can be your ultimate tool in creating and sustaining this value. The core of thriving LiveOps lies in its independence; envision a system robust enough to run smoothly without constant intervention from the game development team.

This independence ensures that operational agility is never compromised by the need for frequent updates. Within this framework, it is crucial that LiveOps and Game Development teams are creatively aligned yet operationally autonomous. This dual approach allows game developers to focus on crafting outstanding games while LiveOps manages the business aspects, ensuring that both domains excel in their respective roles and collaborate effectively to enhance the overall game experience and financial success.

Operations management is not just a support function; it is the driving force behind a studio's competitive edge. By focusing on operations, studios can ensure that player experiences are delivered quickly, affordably, and with the variety and quality that keep players coming back. From the strategic alignment of daily activities to the utilization of cutting-edge tools and analytics, every aspect of operations is a step toward more efficient and effective game operations.

This section is divided into three critical chapters—Operations Management, Toolset, and Analytics—that together build a comprehensive framework for enhancing studio efficiency. By delving into these areas, you will learn how to match your operational processes with your game's needs and translate your players' value propositions into robust operational strategies. Remember, if you can't measure it, you can't manage it. Through the strategic use of analytics, you will unlock the power to manage and enhance your operations, ensuring that your game not only survives but thrives in the competitive landscape of live service gaming.

It's important to acknowledge that the landscape of PC, console, and mobile games is significantly influenced by major platforms like Steam, PlayStation, and Apple. Each of these platforms comes with its own integration points and constraints, which necessitate adjusted operational processes. This part focuses primarily on PC games as they exist within a more open ecosystem, allowing for broader operational flexibility. However, the principles and recommendations provided can serve as a general guide for establishing effective operations management across different gaming platforms. This foundational knowledge equips you to adapt and innovate within the specific requirements and opportunities of each platform.

Operations Management

12

Before going deeper into any new areas like live game operations management, it's always good to have a well-known reference from ordinary life. As was mentioned, LiveOps as a discipline is based on the underlying principles of marketing and business development, plus modern gaming specifics related to digital distribution, free-to-play business model, or micro-transactions. A similar analogy could be used for a game operations management that utilized fundamental principles from supply chain, inventory, or order fulfillment management.

Zara: In general, apparel retailers worldwide have similar supply chain beginning with fabric, cut and dye, and ending with sew, distribution, and stores. Roughly 50% of Zara's products are manufactured in factories located in Spain, Portugal, or Morocco and the other 50% of production comes from outside suppliers, with 30% located in Eastern European countries and 70% in the Middle East. Just think of how huge and complicated their procurement and production processes as well as warehousing management must be to fulfill customers' demands; however, these same complexities can also constrain designers' creativity. A live service game has a comparable chain, but for digital apparel it begins with assets models or templates (fabric), followed by image resize or resolution alignment (cut), bundle composition (sew), and ends with organizing digital distribution via a content delivery network (CDN) and store operations on various platforms like Steam or Epic Store. Now imagine a live service game with 100M+ players operating in all countries, and their digital warehouse, which supplies hundreds of designers in different locations, storing thousands of assets and at the same time ensuring quick response to the players' feedback and smooth functioning (Figure 12.1).

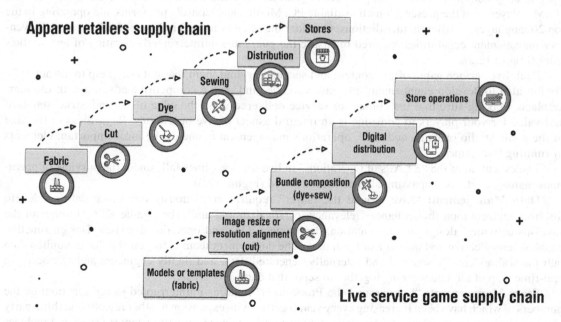

FIGURE 12.1 Comparison between apparel retailer supply chain and live service game supply chain.

DOI: 10.1201/9781003427056-17

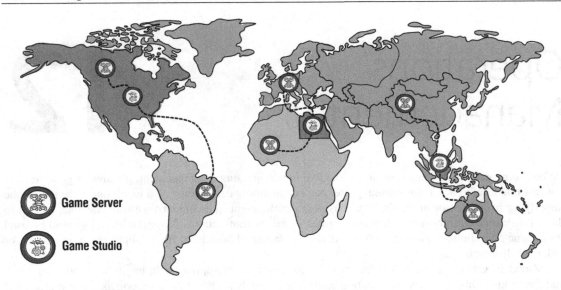

FIGURE 12.2   Game's assets distribution system.

Amazon: Fulfillment by Amazon (FBA) is a service that allows businesses to outsource order fulfillment to Amazon. Businesses send products to Amazon fulfillment centers and when a customer makes a purchase, Amazon picks, packs, and ships the order. Amazon can also provide customer service and process returns for those orders. It is not difficult to imagine the scale of FBA and what sophisticated processes are behind the scene. Similar happens in live service game operations when a game product team sends weekly or monthly plan including digital products, a game operational team orders, customizes or reuses game-related assets (pick), localizes and creates bundles or missions (pack), and uploads digital products to game servers and third-party digital stores (ship). If for any reason, a player faces an issue with a purchase or wants to return the order, the operational team helps to process the issue in conjunction with player support. And again, let's pretend that there is a live service game with 100M+ players and the presence on all available PC, Mobile, and Console platforms and operating in the top 20 languages in different jurisdictions. Consider the scale of its multi-channel fulfillment and inventory management capabilities required to ensure the guarantee uninterrupted operation of any studio's titles (Figure 12.2).

Each live service game offers content and services around them that not only help to attract players but also to develop engagement, increase revenue, and give a competitive advantage in the marketplace. Making sure that the content or service delivered is on the edge of the industrial standard and value for your players to consume is an integral aspect of live operations. Regardless of the size of the game studio or game audience, operations management is one of the most important elements of running live game.

The execution of the "3 LAPs of Operations" in live service games falls under the purview of operations management, encompassing all activities involved (Figure 12.3):

Data Management: "Live around the Player" requires continuously delivering data needed to discover segmentation that enhances relevance, personalization, and drives game KPIs throughout the LiveOps activities' design, implementation, deployment, QA, and operational phases. Design function enables the collection and delivery of fresh data. The deployment team is responsible for the united data hub for both externally sourced and internally generated data; and finally engineers and QA access a real-time map of all data working together to serve that data.

Store Management: "Live around the Proposition" requires uninterrupted stores functioning, the numbers of which have been increasing every year together with expansion to other regions and third-party gaming platform integrations. As a game's store expands, the need for extra support arises and includes

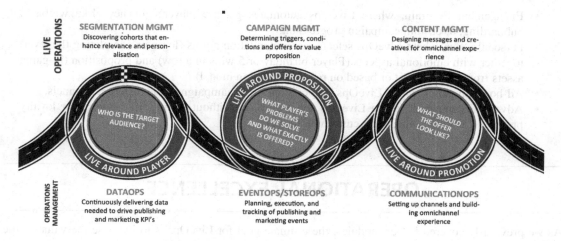

FIGURE 12.3   The 3LAPs of operations framework.

monitoring sales plans, ordering necessary content, creating bundles and related items, and setting up supportive materials such as coupons or bonus codes.

Content Management; "Live around the Promotion" comprises comprehensive processes that involve creating, organizing, publishing, and withdrawing content. Moreover, the implementation of an omnichannel strategy and regional relevance increases the complexity of templates creation and in-game assets relevance. Also, conducting a pre-launch check, setting up different channels, and monitoring the performance become more challenging.

The 3LAPs framework unites segments from data management, products from store management, and promotions from content management, which allows LiveOps team to organize campaigns or events. This framework enables the following typical campaign types (Figure 12.4):

- Storefront Promotion, where LiveOps matches available products with the most appropriate segments for the ongoing promotion.

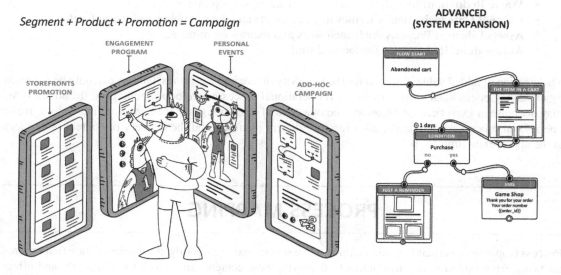

FIGURE 12.4   Campaign types.

- Engagement Program, where LiveOps automates generic player's journeys like winback, onboarding, or custom campaign progression.
- Personal Offer, where LiveOps selects recommendation points (login or completing the level) together with emotional aspects (Player birthday or 5 wins in a row) and proposition (in-game assets from the wish list or based on recommendation model).
- Ad-hoc Campaign, where LiveOps supports one-time campaign in the different channels.
- Advanced campaign, where LiveOps sets up events without coding, like referral or loyalty programs, players' surveys, or custom battle pass.

OPERATIONAL EXCELLENCE

As we previously covered in our modules, the ultimate goal for LiveOps is to increase the value of the game, and this goal is achieved by offering fascinating events, emotional propositions, and personalized experience. Players spend their time with a game if it's delivered quickly, with a suitable variety of content and appropriate quality. LiveOps team ensures that the business processes involved in designing, producing, and delivering content or services are optimized to meet these player expectations.

Unlike traditional physical products, digital products like video games do not require costs for materials or physical manufacturing. The virtual goods within the game are just lines of code that materialize when a player purchases them, but it doesn't mean that we should forget to take operational cost into account. The equation to calculate the added value brought by any LiveOps activities should not only consider the additional revenue or engaged players or any KPI's uplift, but also consider the operational cost of running such activities (workforce payroll, acquiring technology, or tools development).

Added Value = KPI uplift − operational cost

In this way, **operations drive value creation** by focusing on the following areas:

- **Processes Mapping:** Visual representation of the steps involved in delivering a content.
- **Waste Reduction:** Identifies and eliminates waste to keep things lean.
- **Content Categorization:** Clarifies in-game assets and defines policies of usage for them.
- **Assets Library:** Prevents duplicated work and focuses on re-using.
- **Automation:** Reduces production lead time.

The creation of added value is crucial for the longevity of live service games, but this can only be achieved by managing operational costs effectively. If operational processes are poor or complex, the added value may decrease or even become negative. The objective of operations management is to find ways to make operational processes more agile, allowing for efficient planning and the delivery of content or services at the appropriate time.

PROCESS MAPPING

Process mapping is a crucial tool for running a live service game smoothly. It's the foundation that ensures all tasks, from updating in-game stores to deploying new content, are completed efficiently and effectively, without overburdening any one team. A process is a collection of tasks connected by a flow of

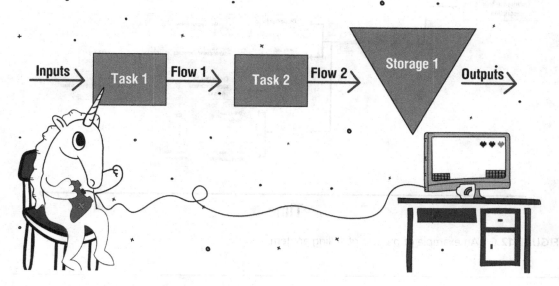

FIGURE 12.5   Process components and flows.

content and information that transforms inputs to outputs. It's a simple way to show how different parts of the game operations work together (Figure 12.5).

- **Inputs:** These are the things you need to get the job done, like the time your team puts in, the creatives you use, or the technology at your disposal.
- **Outputs:** This is what you're working toward, like new event in your game for your players.
- **Tasks:** Each box represents a job that needs to be done, which takes your inputs and gets them closer to becoming the final product.
- **Flow:** The arrows show how everything moves along in the process, from one task to the next.
- **Storage:** The triangle shows a point where things might be on hold, waiting to move on to the next step.

Process mapping is important to understand your operational costs and brainstorm about potential optimizations. It is important to have a deep understanding of all the necessary steps to go from an idea to a valuable product. This map will help you to acknowledge what are the important and time-consuming steps and will allow you to distinguish between tasks having high value for business and the ones having a very low value. Sometimes, the correlation between time spent on a task and the value for a game is negative: this is probably a task you want to consider for future optimization.

Process mapping is not about designing the perfect process; it's about **matching your process with your game**. You want to start mapping the current way things are working to reflect the current reality and create discussions about potential perk-ups. It is also important to not map only the steps but also to consider the amount of time spent on them and how they are organized through time: maybe you have some "waiting" time between two steps during which nothing is done.

Figure 12.6 provides a theoretical example of a process mapping and depicts the process of selling an item in the in-game store, starting from the writing of the bundle description, then moving to the bundle validation, followed by the creation of several tasks and the different steps to deliver them.

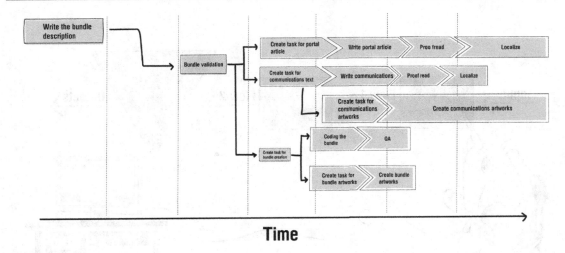

Time

FIGURE 12.6   An example of process of selling an item.

WASTE REDUCTION

When we think about lean management, the first company we can think of is usually Toyota. Through its history, Toyota faced several challenges that pushed the management to rethink their production system. Among these challenges, we can mention the fact that in the 1930s Toyota had only one production line to manufacture several car models for the Japanese domestic market, which was emerging at this time, while Ford had one assembly line per model for a booming domestic market. Another challenge: in the 1980s, the US government adopted some taxation for car imports. Automotive parts were not impacted by the new taxes. To stay competitive on the US market, Toyota decided to export automotive parts to the US and opened a production unit to assemble the cars on the American territory; this strategic decision significantly complexified the production process by bringing some new logistic challenges.

The managerial output of all these challenges is the Toyota Production System. This section is not about presenting the entire system and its application for gaming industry (the full Toyota Production System is not only about waste chasing but also embraces the organization's vision and philosophy). We will only focus on the eight types of wastes Figure 12.7 the system lists and adapt the definitions to the gaming industry. Then we will apply this framework to the process example from the previous section (Figure 12.8).

Transportation: Waste in transportation includes movement of people, tools, inventory, equipment, or products further than necessary. It is easy to understand how it can be a waste when we are talking about physical goods: unnecessary transportation consumes more energy, takes time, and increase the risk of having the goods damaged by accident.

In the realm of live service game operations, the concept of transportation waste translates into the digital movement of information. When launching an in-game event, the marketing team might create promotional content, while the development team handles the technical implementation. If the event details are scattered across multiple emails, chat messages, and document formats, valuable information could get lost or outdated. A centralized system where all departments access and update a single source of truth could save hours of cross-checking and prevent the launch of mismatched event details.

Inventory: Having too much inventory means having more products, raw materials than needed. In a live service game, a too big inventory can be a list of events or campaigns. Having too many of them will eventually create a queue to process them. If you accept this queue, it means that you must prepare and plan your events way before they are needed. In the end, it means you will probably create

Skills
Underutilizing people's talents, skills & knowledge

Inventory
Excess products and materials not being processed

Motion
Unnecessary movements by people

Waiting
Wasted time waiting for the next step in a process

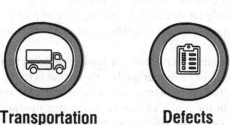

Transportation
Unnecessary movements of products & materials

Defects
Efforts caused by rework, scrap and incorrect information

Overproduction
Production that is more than needed or before it is needed

Overprocessing
More work or higher quality than is required by the customer

FIGURE 12.7   The eight wastes from the Toyota Production System.

events which will be no longer needed at the time of release. Let's imagine you plan an event A to be launched at the beginning of the month, immediately followed by an event B. Both events have a revenue objective. Because you know there's a queue for the events to be developed, you plan the two of them way in advance.

When event A is released, you notice an important overperformance with way more players making a purchase than you expected. You know that if you run event B immediately after, this one will most likely underperform because only few players will open their wallet twice in such less amount of time. You have two choices: running the event and underperform or cancel it. In both cases, you wasted some time to work on something which is not needed.

Motion: in the sphere of live service game operations, "motion" waste doesn't involve physical movement but is rather about the unnecessary digital "steps" team members must take to complete a task. This type of waste often goes unnoticed but can significantly hamper efficiency. For instance, if an operations manager needs to compile a new in-game bundle, they might have to toggle between a pricing database, a digital asset management tool, and a separate content schedule. Each transition between these tools not only consumes time but also increases the risk of errors and can lead to mental fatigue.

To address motion waste in live service game operations, teams should aim to consolidate and integrate tools and platforms. Unified systems that aggregate necessary functionalities can significantly reduce the digital back-and-forth, creating a more streamlined workflow and allowing teams to focus more on content creation and service improvement, rather than on navigating a labyrinth of tools and documents.

Waiting: In an office setting, waiting waste can occur when employees are waiting for a response to an email, waiting for a file to be reviewed, or participating in ineffective meetings. In the video game industry, this type of waiting can be similar to inventory waste, but there are other factors that contribute to waiting such as people working in different time zones, a multi-step process involving multiple teams or individuals, and the need for approvals.

Reducing "waiting" in live service game operations can be achieved by implementing more asynchronous work processes where possible, so that teams can progress with other tasks while awaiting responses. Additionally, overlapping work hours for teams in different time zones and streamlining approval processes—perhaps through an automated system that alerts the next approver when it's their turn—can cut down on these wasteful periods of inactivity, keeping projects moving and improving overall operational efficiency.

Overproduction: It occurs when content or part of content is manufactured before it is actually needed or requested. In live service game operations, "overproduction" can take shape as an excess of in-game bundles, an overcrowded calendar of events, or specialized features targeting only a handful of players. These missteps lead to player overwhelm, unused content, and a dilution of development resources. Balancing the quantity and timing of content releases with player demand is crucial.

To prevent overproduction, LiveOps should focus on understanding player behavior and demand through data analytics. This ensures that the development of content, features, and events is aligned with what players are genuinely interested in and when they're ready for it. Careful planning can help LiveOps prioritize and schedule production to meet actual player demand without overwhelming their audience or misallocating resources.

Over-processing: Refers to doing more work, adding more components, or having more steps in a product or service than what is required. It can also refer to having a higher quality than what is required: for instance, if you manufacture a water-proof watch to dive up to 30 m deep, a component designed to resist up until 100 m deep is over-processed. Similarly, in the realm of live service game operations, "over-processing" is the act of adding more features, steps, or complexities to an event or campaign than what players actually need or value. It's essentially putting in more effort than what the situation calls for, which can waste time and resources.

Take the example of creating marketing content for an in-game event. If the team invests in high-quality cinematic trailers, extensive social media campaigns, and elaborate press releases for a minor update or a small event, they might be over-processing. This is especially true if simpler communications in the past have proven effective. To combat over-processing, LiveOps should strive for simplicity and clarity in both event or campaign design and player communication.

Defects: These are shortcomings or errors that undermine a game's functionality or the player's experience. These can range from technical bugs to poorly executed game events that don't align with the game's goals or player expectations. Imagine two events are launched simultaneously in a game. One event encourages players to spend their accumulated in-game currency to receive rare items, aiming to balance the game's economy. However, the other event rewards players with an abundance of that same currency, which negates the purpose of the first event. Such contradictory goals can confuse players and lead to an imbalance in the game economy.

To prevent defects, it's essential to maintain clear and consistent communication across teams, and ensure that all events and campaigns align with the game's overall strategy. Moreover, having robust rollback plans and responsive support teams ready can mitigate the impact of any defects that do slip through.

Skills: This is the waste of human potential, talent, and ingenuity. This waste occurs when organizations separate the role of management from employees. In some organizations, management's responsibility is planning, organizing, controlling, and innovating the production process. The employee's role is to simply follow orders and execute the work as planned. By not engaging the frontline worker's knowledge and expertise, it is difficult to improve processes. This is due to the fact that the people doing the work are the ones who are most capable of identifying problems and developing solutions for them. This waste can also be the result of too much split between tasks when a process is distributed among more services or people than needed. To make it simple, it occurs when talents are not fully utilized.

PROCESSES MAPPING V2.0

As you can see, these eight types of wastes are interconnected: overproduction can lead to waiting and inventory wastes for instance. Skill wastes can lead to defects, if you do not train your people and under-utilize their skills, it can generate some stress ("I feel my job is really basic, will I be able to find a work in any other company in the future?") that will be transformed to errors or absence due to burnout or depression.

Now, having them in mind, we can discuss about the process from the previous section:

- We notice we have two waiting times between bundle description (first step) and bundle validation and between bundle validation and task creations. Are these waiting times really needed? Why do we have them? Can we remove them? These are the questions you should always be in mind to adopt a continuous improvement mindset.
- We notice bundle description is transformed into several tasks. It can be interesting to check what these tasks contain. Maybe they are simply duplicating the info already provided on the bundle description document, in which case we have an over-processing problem: we are wasting time to do twice the same job.
- We notice we have different tasks for things requiring the same skillset: the portal article and communication tasks are separated while they are both about copywriting. Maybe it is a good idea to consider having both tasks done by the same person, to ensure consistency between portal article and communication.
- We can notice the same thing for assets creation: one team is responsible for creating the bundle artworks and another team will create the communication artworks. Having the same team or person in charge of doing both will not only help to ensure consistency, but it will also allow to save time and ensure smoother communication by having one task instead of two (Figure 12.8).

The updated process results in fewer tasks, reducing the risk of errors. The elimination of waiting times also allows for faster release of bundles, resulting in increased agility. Of course, this second version can be perked up (this is the essence of continuous improvement): the longest step is the copywriting. Maybe the team in charge of localization does not need to wait for the English copywriting version to be finalized to start localizing it, maybe they can work in parallel by using a tool to highlight the changes between two versions of the English document. Maybe localization team has the necessary skills to create their own documents for each language, being not only localizers but becoming copywriters on their own (again, this is just an idea to think about and it should be discussed: maybe the localization team is not in-house and will not be able to do copywriting or promoting localization team to copywriters would involve salary increases that will affect the operational cost).

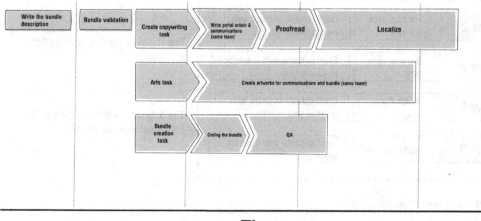

Time

FIGURE 12.8 The same process revisited; less tasks reduce the risk of errors. By removing waiting time, we reduced the time needed to deliver the product, allowing the process to be more agile.

With our improved processes, we can now explore the possibility of content categorization and establishing an assets library. Our current process is designed for creating a store bundle from scratch. However, if we need to pause sales and use the same bundle later, repeating the entire process would be inefficient. Instead, a simpler process utilizing the asset library could be implemented.

CONTENT CATEGORIZATION

Effectively organizing your content is crucial to defining the scope of each LiveOps activity. This encompasses different projects with distinct goals, such as player retention, monetization, or reengagement of churned players. Additionally, similar activities may have varying effects depending on their environment, for instance, an in-game event compared to an event outside the game. To have a better understanding on the impact on operations, let's take one way to organize the content (Figure 12.9):

The organization of content will help to keep your operations costs under control because of the following impact:

- **Clarity:** The operational team will have a clear list of approved in-game assets for various activities, reducing the need for multiple discussions and meetings to determine the suitability of specific content for a given event.
- **Visibility:** Limiting the use of in-game assets during parallel events can prevent the need to revisit already planned events. For example, if the same content is used for both a previously planned event and a more important event happening at the same time, the first event may need to be altered, leading to an increase in operational costs.

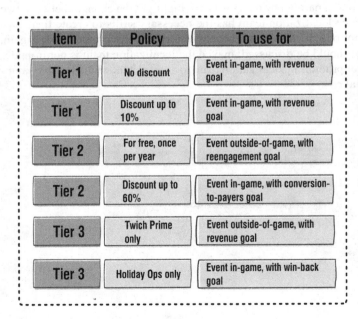

Item	Policy	To use for
Tier 1	No discount	Event in-game, with revenue goal
Tier 1	Discount up to 10%	Event in-game, with revenue goal
Tier 2	For free, once per year	Event outside-of-game, with reengagement goal
Tier 2	Discount up to 60%	Event in-game, with conversion-to-payers goal
Tier 3	Twich Prime only	Event outside-of-game, with revenue goal
Tier 3	Holiday Ops only	Event in-game, with win-back goal

Tire 1: Available for distribution for a limited timeline with a recommended cooldown of 3 months. Not recommended as a permanent offer.

Tire 2: Can be used as reward after approval

Tire 3: Strictly prohibited for distribution. Additional approval needed.

FIGURE 12.9　Content categorization.

ASSET LIBRARY

Creating an asset library is crucial in reducing operational expenses, as it helps prevent duplicating efforts. Here are some important guidelines to keep in mind.

Create Smart, Reuse Wisely: When creating something new, all team members should keep in mind the potential for reuse. This means that the developers should ensure the code necessary for operating the event is easily updatable for future repeats of the event. Copywriters will also need to keep that in mind. While it may seem more attractive to have articles written specifically for a launched asset, it is sometimes better to opt for generic texts that can be easily altered. For example, in creating a bundle, the bundle description should be considered in the same manner (Figure 12.10):

This bundle description is fine, but not ideal for building an asset library. The description may become outdated in 6 months and require additional copywriting and localization, resulting in increased costs. A better option would be to use a generic description that can be reused for future:

Connect Everything: An effective event library should be easy to use and accessible. It should provide seamless access to all relevant information without the need to switch between various tools or pages. Consider utilizing a well-structured wiki folder with sub-folders and pages to store technical information and link to issue tracking tickets. BAD STORAGE scatters asset elements across various locations, making retrieval difficult, while GOOD STORAGE connects all asset components in a unified way, facilitating easy retrieval (Figure 12.11).

Do Not Overload: Start with a minimal version, identify low complexity for repetitive tasks. A low-complexity library is easier to design, and its efficiency can be tested quickly.

Adopt Habits: Creating an asset library requires changing habits. Event design should focus on the option to reuse them in the future. People managing events need to document each one for easier reuse. Big changes to tools may not be the best way forward. This could slow down the process or increase the risk of mistakes, leading to resistance to change.

FIGURE 12.10   An example of two different ways of creating content description.

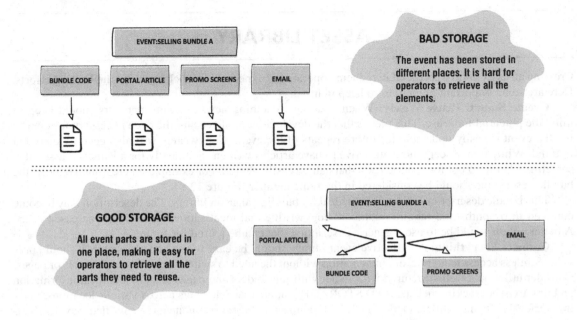

FIGURE 12.11   Bad vs. good storage.

AUTOMATION

Computers are useful to make complex calculation and automate repetitive tasks. If we go back to the history of Toyota Production System, Toyota went into a period where the management was considering automating everything that can be automated (if this automation was supposed to gain on efficiency of course). They rapidly observed that such strategy was not the best: production lines were blocked by automated procedures that stopped working, automation brought some high level of complexity when management wanted to improve processes, thus having a negative effect on agility. Toyota now limits the development of new technologies when it comes to automation and came up with the principle that any automation must rely on well-known and well-established technologies and processes.

In light of Toyota's experiences with automation, there's a valuable principle that live service game operations teams can adopt: Before turning to automation, prioritize the optimization of internal processes, everyday interactions, and even the organizational structure. Simplification should be the first step in enhancing operational efficiency. Only once all aspects of a process have been streamlined and are functioning optimally in a manual setting should automation be considered.

This approach ensures that the operations team focuses first on making each process as efficient and straightforward as possible. Simplify first, then elevate with automation. This means examining and refining each step of a process to ensure it's not just automated but optimized. It's crucial that all stakeholders are involved in this optimization and are satisfied with the manual processes, perceiving them as efficient and effective, before they are automated.

Streamlining your automation efforts with standardization is another key step. Standardizing source information and processes not only supports the successful implementation of automation technologies but also reduces the likelihood of errors and inefficiencies. Without standardization, automation efforts can actually increase complexity and restrict the potential benefits of the technology. By ensuring that every process follows a consistent pattern and format, automation tools can be more effectively applied, leading to better control over outcomes and more predictable improvements in productivity and quality.

In the context of selling a Tiger bundle across three different regions, let's explore the implications of automation and the challenges that might arise due to regional variations and a lack of standardization.

Firstly, consider the complexity introduced by having different item and token IDs for each region. This variation complicates the automation process, as each region would require specific scripts to fetch the correct local pricing and tokens. Automating this without a standardized process could lead to errors and inefficiencies, such as the need for manual checks or adjustments in each region (Figure 12.12).

Secondly, discrepancies in how tasks for bundle creation are allocated and the tools used across regions can further complicate automation. If one region uses a different system or method for bundle setup than another, the automation tool must accommodate these differences, potentially leading to a bloated and less efficient system (Figure 12.13).

The key to successful automation in this scenario is standardization. By standardizing item IDs, token types, and the tools used for setting up bundles, you can streamline the automation process. This reduces the need for manual interventions and ensures a smoother, more reliable setup across all regions. Standardization minimizes the number of integrations and adaptations required by the automation tool, making the entire process more manageable and less prone to error (Figure 12.14).

In summary, before embarking on automating any processes, it is crucial to first optimize and standardize the manual process. This involves making sure the process runs smoothly and efficiently on a manual level, and all stakeholders are satisfied with the workflow. It's also important to remain flexible and open to making further adjustments to the process map and organizational structure as you integrate automated solutions. This approach ensures that automation enhances the operation without introducing new complexities or inefficiencies.

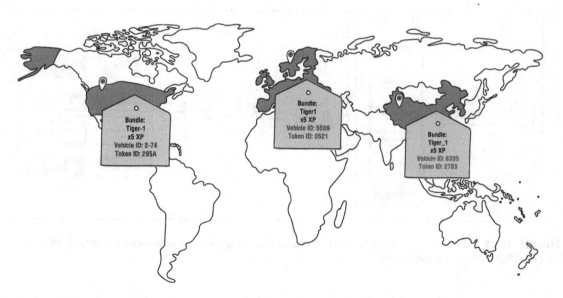

FIGURE 12.12   Non-standardized and not common databases bring complexity.

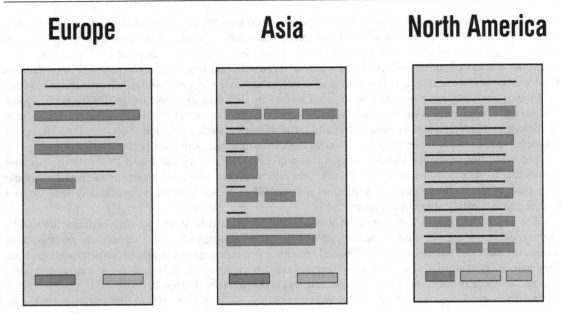

FIGURE 12.13   Different ticketing system layouts for copywriting tasks for each region.

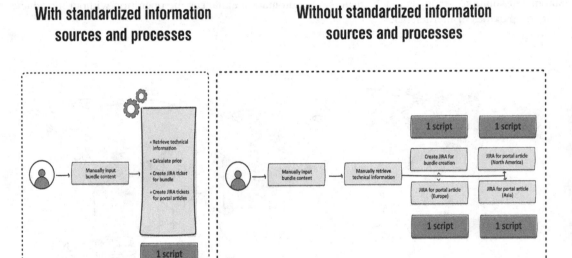

FIGURE 12.14   The lack of standardization increases the complexity of automation scription. Plus, all the process steps cannot be automated.

Toolset

13

As you venture into the development or enhancement of a live service game, a fundamental decision awaits: not just whether to build your own tools or buy existing ones, but also determining the sequence in which to develop or integrate these toolset features. This decision, while framed around the "build or buy" dilemma, extends to prioritizing which features to implement based on your game's current and future goals. This approach acknowledges that there is no universal right or wrong strategy, but rather a tailored response to each game's unique circumstances, including internal processes, team expertise, and specific game objectives.

Strategic alignment of your toolset with your game's goals is essential, whether those goals involve boosting player engagement, enhancing monetization efforts, or extending your game's lifecycle. Each goal might prioritize different features from a LiveOps toolset, such as sophisticated analytics for understanding player behavior or robust content management systems for keeping the game fresh and engaging.

The capabilities of your studio significantly shape this decision-making process. Factors such as your budget, team size, and their technical expertise are pivotal in determining whether an off-the-shelf solution is adequate or if a custom-built toolset is essential. Moreover, these choices are also driven by the necessity for tools that either integrate seamlessly with existing workflows or are capable of introducing new efficiencies.

Importantly, the legacy of your studio or game adds another layer of complexity to this equation. Integrating any solution, no matter how promising, into an ecosystem that has been developed over decades can be exceptionally challenging. The existing architecture and established systems often have deeply ingrained processes and dependencies that may not easily accommodate new technologies. Therefore, when considering the integration or development of new toolset features, it's crucial to evaluate how they will coexist with and potentially enhance the mature frameworks already in place.

In the context of operations management processes discussed in the previous chapter, the integration of new tools into your game's ecosystem is a critical consideration. These tools should not only enhance or seamlessly fit into existing workflows but also match your team's current technical skills and support their ongoing development. It's essential to ensure that any new toolset can scale with your game and refine or redefine current operational methods without disrupting the established ecosystem. This approach aids in long-term planning, helps prevent future operational disruptions, and maintains player satisfaction by supporting the growth and evolution of your game within its existing framework. This chapter will explore the key features of Live Service Game Toolsets, focusing on how they integrate and sequence to create a cohesive system that supports effective game operations and growth.

KEY FEATURES OF A LIVEOPS TOOLSET

Operations management focuses on the efficient functioning of business processes designed to maximize outputs and outcomes within the game. Each gaming studio has systems and frameworks in place to make sure the title continues to operate, but the extent to which they run those frameworks varies greatly depending on the toolset they use to collect data, set up assets, launch events, and monitor the effectiveness. In fact, game operations itself can come in a variety of forms; nevertheless, there are main components of the overall operations infrastructure that help to encounter numerous challenges (Figure 13.1).

DOI: 10.1201/9781003427056-18

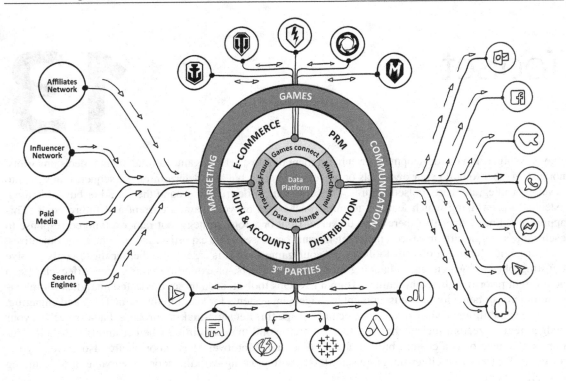

FIGURE 13.1   LiveOps toolset architecture.

Data integration and management can be cumbersome without a dedicated data platform. Teams may struggle to efficiently exchange and analyze data from various sources, hindering their ability to make informed decisions or set up personalized player experience based on accurate and timely data insights.

- Without an **attribution solution**, it becomes difficult to track user acquisition effectively and protect against fraud. This can lead to inefficient spending on marketing and a poor understanding of where players are coming from, as well as increased vulnerability to fraudulent activities.
- **Omnichannel communication** is crucial for engaging players outside the gaming environment. Without it, teams face challenges in managing consistent and effective communication across various channels, potentially leading to a disjointed player experience and decreased engagement.
- In terms of **commerce**, the absence of a robust system to manage payment gateways, order fulfillment, and organize game stores can complicate revenue streams and player experience. This often results in frustrated players and lost revenue opportunities.
- The lack of a **Player Relationship Management** (PRM) system can prevent teams from utilizing data to improve player interactions and personalize gaming experiences. This can lead to generic and less engaging player experiences that fail to retain players.
- Without efficient **distribution** mechanisms, keeping games updated and delivering fresh content to players becomes a logistical nightmare, potentially leading to outdated game versions lingering among players.
- **Security** in player accounts, crucial for maintaining trust and compliance, is compromised without strong systems for authentication and authorization. This exposes both the players and the platform to security risks and breaches.

Comprehensive LiveOps toolset is designed to overcome these challenges and enhance the operational efficiency of managing a live service game. By providing integrated tools for data management, user acquisition tracking, omnichannel communication, commerce, player relationship management, content distribution, and account security, LiveOps platforms empower teams to streamline processes, engage players more effectively, and ensure secure and enjoyable gaming experiences.

DATA PLATFORM

This component allows the exchange of data, events, messages, etc., and collects real-time data from a variety of sources, starting from clicks of you future players and finishing with combat behavior (Figure 13.2). Data Platform is the centerpiece and integration point of the LiveOps toolset, which, in addition to basic real-time data collection, storage, and processing, serves as a bridge between all other components. Robust data platform solution helps with the following areas:

- **Player Segmentation:** To send a relevant tip to the player's game client or messenger, as well as a special offer or additional promotion for a unique bundle in the store—the data hub should provide the overall player's progress history.
- **Retargeting:** To organize winback activities for lapsed players outside of the game universe, the Data Platform should identify player's attributes and when he is gone, as well as be able to send data to external platforms like Google or Facebook, where their algorithms start looking for our players inside third-party platforms.
- **Data Enrichment:** To launch BizDev collaboration or bring offline context into LiveOps events, it's crucial to collect third-party data in real time. For instance, the football World Cup is the most significant event with a huge audience and for sure, lots of games have overlapping interests among their own audience. In order not to compete for attention during football matches, it's better to integrate the match results service and extend LiveOps event mechanic based on the final game score.

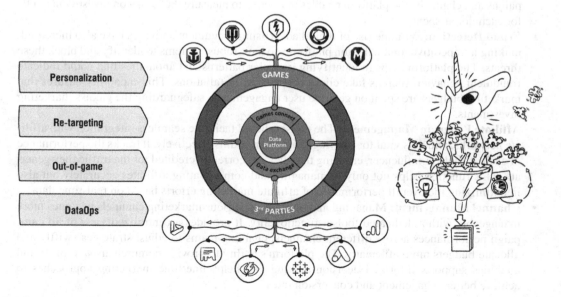

FIGURE 13.2 Data platform.

For this kind of task, the Data Platform organizes a quick and convenient connection for games with the data hub and, together with the data enrichment module from the external sources, instantly gives the games the ability to communicate with players inside and outside the game using first- and third-party data. With that capability, for instance, the marketing team gets the ability to optimize traffic based on the player's in-game behavior.

However, the data hub itself helps only to organize the data flow, which is only half the battle. The second half is to organize the data management of this flow, formation of metrics in the player's profile, event monitoring, processing of prefabricated metrics, monitoring of the corresponding rules, etc. This is the point where operations management and development teams have to make a decision on the particular technological solutions and establish a holistic DataOps function. In an ideal world, it should come to the point where the operations management team can set up and launch LiveOps event without running to the development team for each metric or data sources integrations, as well as carrying out real-time monitoring without developers' support.

PERFORMANCE MARKETING

Player acquisition function attracts users and transforms them into future players, tracks acquisition channels, fights fraud, and analyzes traffic based on game metrics (Figure 13.3). But what exactly helps to organize performance marketing? For the sake of simplicity, performance marketing is the act of purchasing traffic with the payment for the target action (registration, first login, first battle, first payment, etc.) and when it's impossible to tie a dollar spent to an event in a game, media buying is optimized, for instance, to maximum coverage in the social networks or video platforms. A robust attribution platform is essential for effectively managing player acquisition and it supports several critical areas:

- **Traffic Attribution:** The platform should offer tools to track and analyze where traffic is coming from, which allows teams to understand which channels are most effective at converting users into players. By attributing new registrations, logins, and purchases back to specific campaigns and channels, the platform enables marketers to measure the return on investment (ROI) for each dollar spent.
- **Fraud Detection:** With the rise of digital advertising, fraudulent activities have also increased, making it imperative for attribution platforms to have robust systems to identify and block these threats. The platform helps in identifying irregular patterns and anomalies that could indicate fraudulent behavior, such as fake clicks or artificial installations. This capability ensures that marketing budgets are spent on genuine user engagements, safeguarding the game's marketing investments.
- **Affiliate Program Management:** The toolset should facilitate seamless integration with affiliate networks, which is vital for running affiliate programs effectively. It tracks the performance of each affiliate or influencer, ensuring that they are correctly credited for the traffic they generate. This function helps not only in managing and compensating affiliates accurately but also in optimizing the overall performance of affiliate marketing efforts based on real-time data.
- **Channel Management:** Managing and optimizing various marketing channels becomes more manageable with a dedicated toolset functionality. It provides a centralized view of all campaign performances across different channels, enabling teams to adjust strategies swiftly and allocate budgets more efficiently. The platform's ability to provide comprehensive reports and analytics supports informed decision-making and helps fine-tune marketing approaches to achieve better engagement and conversion rates.

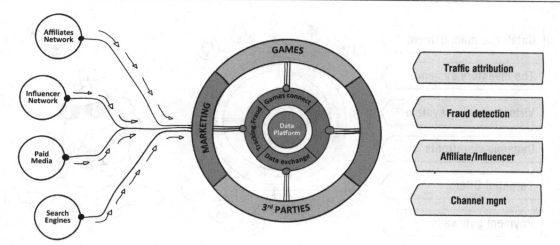

FIGURE 13.3   Performance marketing.

Imagine any game in the early stage of the launching process reaches an advertising agency to arrange media buying. Advertising agency managers very professionally prepare a plan, distribute the budget via different channels, conduct campaigns, and even provide reports from the advertising platforms, as well as audience responses to surveys. Moreover, to a certain extent, a game would even be satisfied with results, but as you can see, it has nothing to do with controlling every dollar of the marketing budget spent.

There is a great opportunity for operations management and development teams to help the title and switch it to the track of performance marketing. With that being said, Data Platform provides a quick and convenient way to connect a game to the data hub, which enables additional functionality to attribute traffic, marketing budget and product internal metrics (e.g., registration, first login, first battle, first payment, etc.), block fraudulent spending and data-driven integration with affiliate networks.

COMMERCE

Managing a virtual economy is crucial for driving player progression, engagement, and monetization. The virtual economy goes beyond mere transactions of in-game items; it encompasses the strategic balancing of what players can earn versus what they must purchase, catering to both highly active players and those who engage more casually (Figure 13.4).

To support such dynamic economies, commerce tools help in managing scalable backend systems, content, and marketplace interactions efficiently. The core functionalities refer to providing a payment gateway to accept settlement in any methods and in any currencies, organizing fulfillment by helping to receive, process, and deliver orders from players and arranging a virtual warehouse by managing all items and bundles in the game stores. It provides a comprehensive set of functionalities that ensure your game's economy remains vibrant and responsive to both LiveOps inputs and player activities by supporting several critical areas:

- **Catalogue management** is crucial for maintaining a structured and detailed inventory of all virtual items available within the game. This system allows LiveOps to effortlessly manage and update the game's catalogue, adding new items or adjusting existing ones. The ability to manage these items seamlessly ensures that the game can adapt to new trends and player demands without disruption.

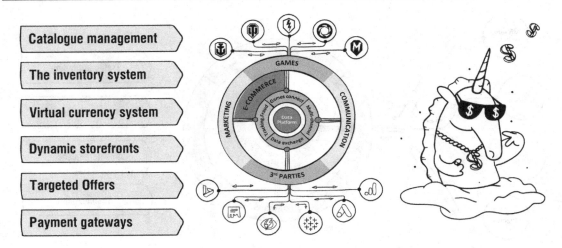

FIGURE 13.4   Commerce.

- **The inventory system** in a LiveOps tool provides comprehensive tracking of every item a player owns, ensuring clarity in asset management, which is vital for both gameplay balance and enhancing the personalization of the player experience. Furthermore, it supports multiple inventory configurations, enabling players to have specialized storage options like seasonal or event-specific inventories. This feature not only helps in keeping the player's assets organized but also enriches the gameplay by aligning storage options with game dynamics.

- **Virtual currency system** typically involves a dual-currency model, which includes a "soft" currency earned through regular gameplay and a "hard" currency that can be purchased with real money. This structure allows for a clear distinction between basic in-game content accessible through gameplay and premium content available for purchase, thereby catering to different player engagement levels and spending behaviors. The flexibility in how these currencies are used within the game enables a dynamic economic environment that can be finely tuned to encourage fair play and engagement.

- **Dynamic storefronts** are essential for tailoring the shopping experience to different segments of the player base. Game storefront UX/UI is the essential part of a player experience and the toolset should enable LiveOps to adjust shop layout, categories columns, and product details according to their needs and preferences. These storefronts can offer items at alternative prices or under special conditions, effectively managing how different goods are marketed to various player groups.

- **Targeted Offers:** As we remember, our game has already been connected to the data. By adding a few more events related to the player's gaming or financial behavior we unfold the opportunity to make personalized offers and utilize the core functionality of commerce (coupons, free products, special offers from payment partners, etc.) in a more targeted way. This capability not only enhances the purchasing experience by making it more relevant to individual players but also maximizes the revenue potential of the game by strategically adjusting offers based on player behavior and market trends.

- **Payment Gateways** are essential for facilitating secure and versatile transactions within the game, allowing acceptance of various payment methods and currencies from any location globally. These integrations ensure that players can easily make purchases using their preferred payment options, whether credit cards, digital wallets, or bank transfers.

This toolset not only enhances the overall gaming experience by providing seamless interactions and diverse functionalities, but it also ensures operational efficiency and economic stability. By facilitating smooth and secure transactions, personalized player interactions, and dynamic content management, this system supports the continuous evolution and sustainability of the game's environment. It allows LiveOps to adapt to player needs and market demands swiftly, maintaining engagement and satisfaction.

COMMUNICATION

A communication component helps communicate with players outside of the game universe through the most convenient player's channels: social networks, messengers, email, operating system notifications, etc., as well as a content management tool (Figure 13.5). This tool not only facilitates direct interaction with players but also integrates seamlessly with Data Platform to leverage enriched player data for targeted and personalized messaging.

- **Email:** Automating email communications is crucial for maintaining consistent contact with players. This can include sending notifications about game updates or personalized offers based on player behavior. The ability to trigger these emails based on specific player actions or milestones ensures timely and relevant communication, enhancing player satisfaction and retention.
- **Push Notifications:** These are brief messages pushed to a player's mobile or desktop device to re-engage them or prompt an action. Integrating push notifications within the LiveOps tool allows for real-time interaction and keeps the game top-of-mind. By segmenting players based on behavior, location, or engagement level, these notifications can be personalized and tested (A/B testing) to optimize their effectiveness.
- **In-game Promo:** The most contextual, as by definition all target audience are active players, therefore it typically provides the best conversion for monetization and retention activities.
- **Messengers:** With the widespread use of mobile phones, messenger is a direct and immediate channel to reach players anywhere. Automated messages can be set up as reminders for upcoming events, alerts about new content, or exclusive offers, ensuring high visibility and response rates.

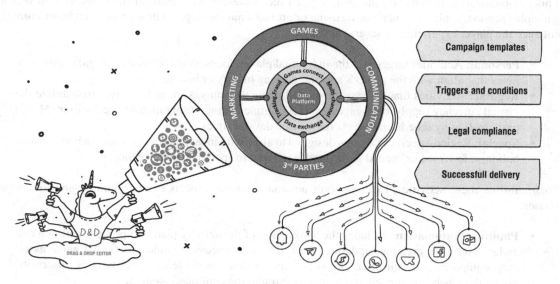

FIGURE 13.5 Omnichannel communications and content management.

By integrating additional metrics from a player's journey, such as the last login, into the data hub, we can strategically address long-term absences or issues new players face during the onboarding process. This enriched data allows for tailored communication strategies:

- **Automated Winback:** Depending on the player's activity profile, we can set up a sequence of communications across multiple channels. This might include emails, social media posts, SMS messages, or system notifications, all aimed at re-engaging the player.
- **Automated Onboarding:** For new players at various stages of the installation funnel—from downloading the game to completing the tutorial—we can initiate targeted retargeting campaigns within third-party advertising platforms to draw them further into the game.

Content management enables LiveOps managers to craft localized campaign templates for various platforms, including email, messengers, and social media posts. The Player Relationship Management (PRM) system then dispatches this content based on specific triggers and conditions. Essential functionalities also include selecting language localization, ensuring GDPR compliance, and interfacing with external platforms to guarantee message delivery. This comprehensive approach ensures that each player receives relevant, engaging content tailored to their specific interactions and status within the game.

PLAYER RELATIONSHIP MANAGEMENT

Player Relationship Management (PRM) systems are integral to managing interactions with players by utilizing metrics and events collected from various sources such as the game's website, client, emails, marketing integrations, and social media (Figure 13.6). These systems enable game titles to gain deeper insights into their player base and tailor the gaming experience to individual needs, thereby enhancing player loyalty and driving audience growth. PRM strategies encompass the guidelines and policies a game employs to engage with its lapsed, active, and prospective players.

PRM utilizes vast amounts of events from Data Platform to personalize interactions with players. This personalization is achieved through targeted recommendations based on the player's most recent gameplay session, avoiding generic advertising or promotional messages. These recommendations aim to enhance the player experience in several key areas:

- **Personal:** Activities targeted at the individual player, focusing on promoting in-game events or items that align with the player's specific gaming history or inventory.
- **Regular:** Activities that address the overall game economy, such as initiatives to stabilize the virtual currency supply, or engagement tactics aimed at increasing monthly active user (MAU) participation by scheduling events on specific days or times.
- **Special:** Region-specific activities designed to align with local market interests, such as regional holidays, festivals, or special game modes tailored to specific demographics.

To streamline these activities, LiveOps tools automate various aspects of the planning and execution phases:

- **Planning Automation:** Includes the automation of the activity planning process within a calendar system for creating, updating, verifying, and approving game events. All game assets (e.g., equipment, consumables, skins) and economic elements (e.g., currency rates, discounts) are meticulously catalogued and managed through the commerce system.

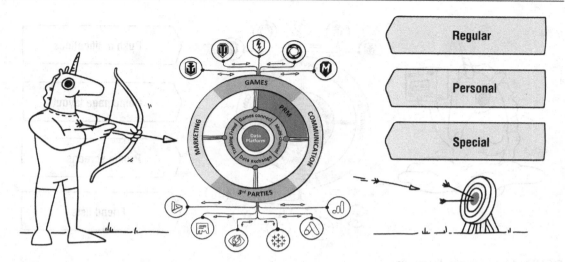

FIGURE 13.6   Player relationship management.

- **Launching Automation:** Ensures that activities transition smoothly from the planning stage to live deployment, minimizing friction during quality assurance and rollout phases.
- **Forecasting Automation:** Utilizes historical data and current market or product needs to recommend activities that promote new features, address issues within the game economy, or enhance the impact of special events.

Overall, PRM is a sophisticated framework that not only responds to immediate player behaviors but also anticipates future engagement opportunities, ensuring a dynamic and responsive gaming experience.

DISTRIBUTION

Digital distribution is a complex solution typically accessible only to very large gaming studios or publishers that can afford the necessary investments. Moreover, distribution solutions within consoles, such as the Xbox Games Store or PlayStation Store, generally operate within nearly closed ecosystems with limited features for LiveOps. It's no surprise that there are not many PC game launchers apart from Battle.net, Ubisoft Connect, or Wargaming Game Center. However, game distribution is a critical aspect of live service game operations and should be considered carefully when planning LiveOps activities. Leveraging your own game launcher capabilities or using Steam's features is crucial for optimizing player engagement, facilitating seamless updates, and implementing monetization strategies effectively.

The main benefit of a game launcher is that it helps players always have fresh versions of the games and provide easy access to them. This is a very important part of the infrastructure because imagine that your performance marketing campaigns chase a player on external platforms and call him to play (or) commerce campaigns prepare a special offer in the store and invite him to pick it up (or) communication campaigns send a message to his phone inviting the special game mode. The player turns on the PC, and then the 50GB+ upgrade begins. Therefore, it is very important for the operations management that the player always has everything ready for the game (Figure 13.7).

Continuing from the established benefits of game launchers in live service operations, leveraging their capabilities can significantly enhance the operational efficiency and player engagement in PC live service games:

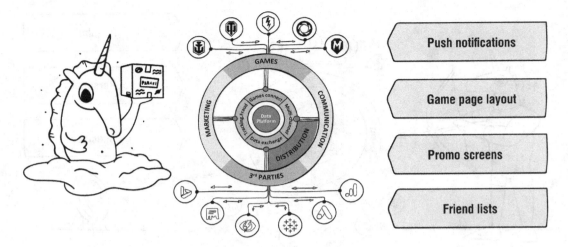

FIGURE 13.7   Digital distribution.

- Customized game page layout and tailored news. Adapt the launcher interface to player preferences, highlighting favorite games and providing curated news and updates.
- Promotional tools. Use the launcher to showcase promotions, such as free weekends and exclusive discounts, tailored to player interests. Send targeted notifications about new events, updates, or promotions to enhance player engagement.
- Social activities based on friend list. Integrate social functionalities for challenges, progress sharing, and direct friend invites, fostering a vibrant community.

Overall, a game launcher can provide a range of features that enhance the player experience, increase engagement, and improve communication between the game and its players. By providing a central hub for managing and launching games, a game launcher can help players to discover new games, stay updated on game events, and connect with other gamers.

ACCOUNTS AND PRIVACY

A component that holds the keys to all the doors and is responsible for authentication and authorization with the main task is ensuring security. However, even with such a straightforward functionality, LiveOps can leverage the capability of this component (Figure 13.8).

- **One-Click Registration:** It is important for acquisition that the future player can quickly create an account in a convenient way via social networks, messengers, etc.
- **Integration:** It is important for engagement that the player could bind the account of other services, for example, the military ID or student ID services enable tailored treatment for military veterans or provide discounts for concrete university.
- **Compliance:** It is important to comply with regulations such as the General Data Protection Regulation (GDPR) or the California Consumer Privacy Act (CCPA) and to ensure that communication and data storage are secure.

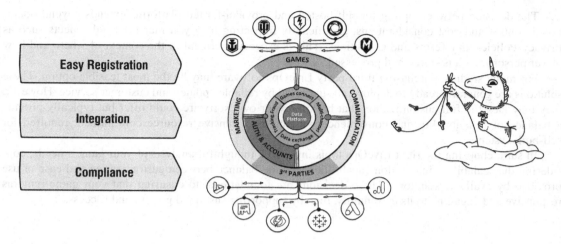

FIGURE 13.8 Accounts and privacy.

CHOOSING LIVEOPS TOOLS

Selecting the right LiveOps toolset is a critical step in managing your live service game effectively. The decision impacts not only your game's current operations but also its future scalability and adaptability. It's essential to ensure that the tool offers the necessary functionality to meet your LiveOps needs. This includes supporting real-time analytics to understand player behaviors, robust player relationship management systems to maintain engagement, and content management system to keep the game fresh and engaging. An intuitive, user-friendly interface is crucial, as even the most feature-rich tool will hinder your operations if it's too complex for your team to use efficiently.

Cost is another important factor—looking beyond the initial purchase to the long-term implications of maintenance, upgrades, and any additional features your game might require as it evolves.

Toolset scalability is essential as your game grows; the tool must handle increased loads related to more data and players. Integration plays a key role here, as the toolset should seamlessly meld with your existing systems and tools, enhancing rather than complicating your workflow. Reliable customer support from the software provider can be a game-changer, especially when issues arise unexpectedly. Additionally, customization is crucial as every game has unique needs, and your LiveOps toolset should allow you to tailor its features to better fit your specific requirements.

The ideal time to integrate LiveOps toolset is during the game development phase, allowing you to build your game with these operations in mind from the very beginning. This integration ensures that the software functions seamlessly within your game's architecture and allows for the early testing and adjustment of LiveOps strategies. If integration during development isn't possible, incorporating the software before the game's launch is crucial. This enables you to begin collecting and analyzing player data right from the start, allowing for quick adaptations based on initial player feedback.

The choice between self-hosted and provider-hosted platforms depends significantly on your team's capacity and needs. Self-hosting offers control over your data and operations, allowing for significant customization and potentially enhanced performance tailored to your specific needs. However, this option requires a high level of technical expertise and can be resource-intensive. Conversely, provider-hosted solutions offer ease of use and reliability, with the provider handling all technical aspects, though they may come with higher long-term costs and less control over your operations.

The decision between opting for self-hosted and provider-hosted platforms extends beyond operational control and cost considerations, significantly impacting how you manage legal aspects such as Privacy Policies and Terms and Conditions. This is especially crucial in the context of where and how player personal data is stored and processed.

For many studios, purchasing third-party LiveOps software may be the most feasible option. These solutions are generally ready to deploy and supported by reliable updates and customer service. However, they may lack the full customization that building your own software could offer but typically provide a balance of functionality and convenience without the extensive resource commitment required for self-built systems.

In sum, choosing the right LiveOps tools involves a thoughtful analysis of your game's needs, considering the scalability, integration capabilities, and the balance between customization and ease of use provided by available solutions. These decisions are foundational to ensuring that your game remains responsive and engaging to its community, thereby supporting sustained growth and success.

Analytics

14

Data is a lifeblood of Live Operations. Since a big part of the premise of live service games is constant optimization, this is of critical importance to set up the analytics function in the best possible way for the organization. Failure of building the right foundation for analytics and developing a productive data culture undermines the rest of the efforts of running live service games.

This may not come naturally in every organization. Historically in the pre-LiveOps days of the industry, game development was driven by the creative inspiration and in best scenarios by player feedback. This is still true in many cases, and the creative part is something that makes this industry so exciting at the end of the day. However, digital distribution, online connectivity, growing population of games added a third source of inspiration for game makers—the data describing player behavior online, out of games, and across games.

The rise of data and analytics added a sense of scale to player feedback, an understanding of importance of certain features and a clear intention, or common language, to seek an alignment on the purpose inside the teams.

In the most straightforward way data functions in game teams need to answer two types of questions: a descriptive "did it work?" and a forward-looking "why are we doing this?" Before we start any event or campaign, asking "Why are we doing this?" is important. It makes us think about our goals and challenges our assumptions. It helps us understand what we're aiming for. After we've done something, asking "Did it work?" is important too. It helps us see if our changes are helping us move closer to our goals. This way, we can make sure we're always using the best strategies to reach our overall plan. In this chapter we will try to add colors to these questions and offer a nuanced approach to structuring and running the analytics function in LiveOps.

"If you don't measure it, you can't manage it" is a famous mantra attributed to Peter Drucker, a management guru. While it's certainly true in most cases and it lays a foundation of reporting analytics, the complexity of game ecosystems requires us to add a few more:

- "If you can't measure it (yet), it doesn't mean it's bad." Often, projects and ideas are shut down because there is no trackable impact. Think about community initiatives such as streaming—they may not have direct effect on revenue or audience metrics; however, they are certainly not bad. The need to approach analysis of ideas that are new and haven't been implemented before often results in experiments and creates an important type of analytics in LiveOps: experiment analytics.
- "There are known knowns. These are things we know that we know. There are known unknowns. That is to say, there are things that we know we don't know. But there are also unknown unknowns. There are things we don't know we don't know." Attributed to Donald Rumsfeld, this phrase focuses on the need to stay open to insights and frequently generate all sorts of hypothesis that could result in experiments. For instance, it's possible that your audience also over-indexes as fans of Jean-Claude Van Damme, which is a surprising yet impactful information if you're building a marketing campaign (think Volvo case with "The Epic Split feat. Van Damme"). This analytics function is sometimes called data insights or research.
- "Data is a tool for enhancing intuition." With the appearance of big data and predictive analytics, game teams observe that the predictions done by machines often outperform the experts' opinions. And in some cases, such as when dealing with user level data, it's impossible to solve

DOI: 10.1201/9781003427056-19

prediction with expertise only. That opens up a field of machine learning and predictive analytics that operate in deep connection with personalization.

- "Torture the data and it will confess to everything." When the complexity of data and the subject matter is too high, the analytics is often abused to either please stakeholders or make a point that doesn't hold the critics. In these circumstances it's vitally important to have a reflex of peer reviews, a validation of methodology, and findings by a peer analyst. This can be referred to as data culture.

Ultimately, the goal of analytics in live services games is to turn data into insights that could turn into business improvements. In the following parts we'll give a brief introduction in each of the components of an analytics powerhouse of free-to-play games.

REPORTING

The reporting analytics is crucial to understand the overall and high-level performance of the game. It often indicates potential opportunities or issues related to the game and provokes business users to ask additional questions. Reporting is needed to understand the health of the audience, the product, and key functions, as well as see the impact of recent events and changes.

A good practice is to organize reporting into a hierarchy leading up to the financial performance and revenue. This kind of structure enables stakeholders to drill down a few layers below the target metrics to better understand causalities or correlations within the game. This structure is rather game-agnostic and can be applied to any live service. It aims to provide consistency and common language in reporting, as well as build a habit for stakeholders. As you may already know, there are many component parts and pieces that offer a holistic view of live service game operations. However, there are three main areas that encompass all metrics: acquisition, retention, and monetization (Figure 14.1).

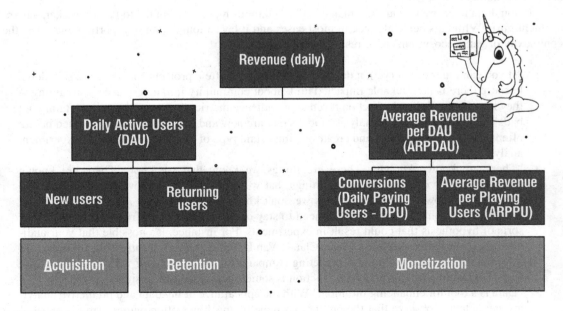

FIGURE 14.1   Three main areas that encompass key metrics.

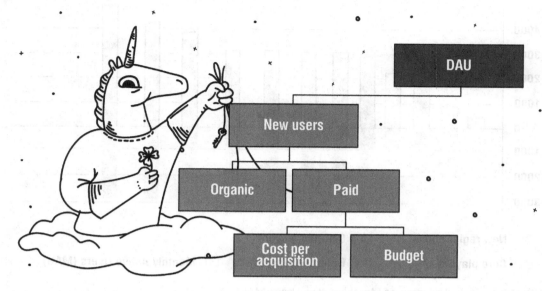

FIGURE 14.2 Decomposition of Daily Active Users (DAU) from user acquisition perspective.

The left part under Daily Active Users is focused on Audience. How many players registered in the game, how many play actively, how many churn? (Figure 14.3) It can be split into Acquisition and Retention or Engagement to cover corresponding business functions withing the organization.

Acquisition answers the question "How successful are we at getting new users?" (Figure 14.2) Depending on the specifics of the game it can cover the following categories:

- **Platforms:** Analyze the platforms where the game is available (e.g., PC, consoles, mobile) and assess user acquisition metrics specific to each platform.
- **Marketing Campaigns:** Evaluate the effectiveness of various marketing campaigns deployed to acquire users, including their reach, engagement, and conversion rates. Ultimately understand return on advertising spend (ROAS) by analyzing LTV vs. budget.
- **Marketing Mix:** Break down the different components of the marketing mix used, such as paid media (advertising), branding efforts, public relations activities, etc., and assess their impact on user acquisition.
- **Campaign Optimization:** Explore strategies for optimizing marketing campaigns to enhance user acquisition, including A/B testing, adjusting targeting parameters, and refining messaging.
- **Funnel Analysis:** Examine the user acquisition funnel from top to conversion and analyze the drop-off rates at each stage to identify potential optimization opportunities.
- **Attribution:** Determine the contribution of each marketing channel or touchpoint to user acquisition, using attribution models.
- **Funnel Optimization:** Implement strategies to improve the efficiency of the user acquisition funnel, focusing on friction points and the user experience at each stage.
- **FTUE (First-Time User Experience):** Assess the initial experience of new users with the game, areas for improvement to increase user retention and engagement.
- **Re-targeting:** Evaluate re-targeting efforts aimed at re-engaging users who have shown interest but haven't yet converted, and analyze their impact on user acquisition and retention.

The Engagement or Retention sections focus on "How successful are we at getting users to come back?" (Figure 14.4). What is the number of active days per month (week, day) and number of games per active day?

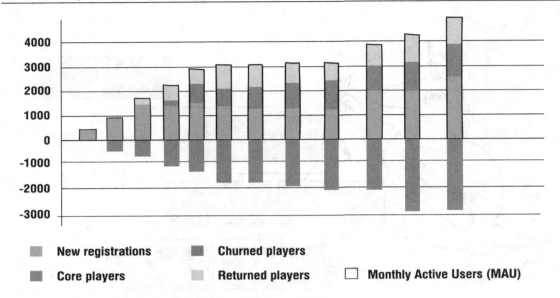

FIGURE 14.3   Overall dynamic of Monthly Active Users (MAU).

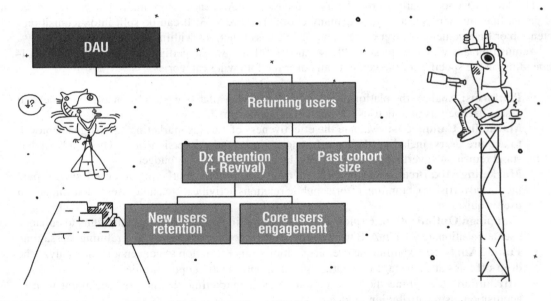

FIGURE 14.4   Decomposition of Daily Active Users (DAU) from player retention perspective.

- **Retention Rate:** Calculating the percentage of users who continue to play the game over a specific period.
- **Churn Analysis:** Investigating the reasons why users stop playing the game and developing strategies to reduce churn.
- **Event Participation:** Measuring the participation rates in various in-game events, tournaments, and challenges to gauge user interest and engagement.
- **Player Schedule:** Examining the timing of user activity and the impact of in-game events on engagement.

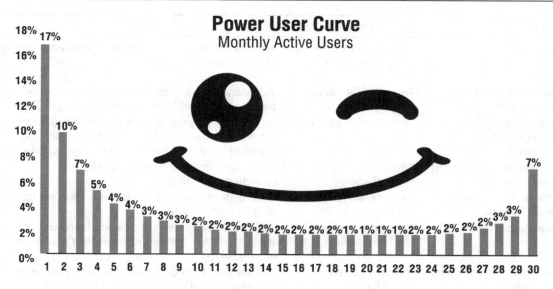

FIGURE 14.5   Power user curve.

- **Winback:** How many players return to the game after long periods of inactivity, how long do they stay after that? This is essentially a part of retention of audience group that is often presented separately for older games.
- **Playtime:** Analyzing user activity data to understand how much time users spend playing the game.
- **Lifetime:** Estimating how long the game will remain popular and retain its user base per cohort, country, and other dimensions. How long on average does a player stay in the game?
- **Power User Curves:** A great way of displaying this is a power user curve that illustrates the MAU split by number of active days. If it "smiles," it means that the product has power users, the most engaged players that comprise its core (Figure 14.5).

Additionally, it may make sense to tap into specific stages of user journey through the game. Should we improve retention of 1, 7, 14, 30 days? Retention is essential to understand the product longevity and model its future performance (Figure 14.6). It's especially important at early stages of product lifecycle when key investment decisions should be made. Over time it makes sense to look at retention per time cohorts to understand the quality of the audience coming in as well as the impact of onboarding changes:

- **Day 1–3 Retention:** Assess FTUE, early success, and pacing.
- **Day 7–14 Retention:** Analyze conversion, early progression, and gameplay variety.
- **Day 30+ Retention:** Interactions with game economy, community engagement, and progression mechanics.

The right part under Average Revenue per Daily Active Users is focused on Monetization, which answers questions like "How much my paying players are willing to spend?" or "What share of my players see enough value to spend money?" Usually, these are combinations of ARPU, ARPPU, %Payers, number of transactions in various splits by market, region, player segment, etc. The more complex variations may include reports by items or type of goods, payment methods, storefronts, etc. In the table below you will find the list of the frequent topics and metrics that may need to be reported on as a part of the monetization dashboards (Figures 14.7 and 14.8).

TOPIC	METRIC	PURPOSE
Revenue	Revenue per Active User (daily, weekly, monthly)	Understand overall revenue trends and player spending behavior over time.
Average Revenue per Paying User	Average Revenue per Paying User	Understand spending behavior and preferences of paying users. Identify high-value user groups.
Percentage of Users Making In-App Purchases	Monetization Rate	Calculate the proportion of users who engage with monetization features. Identify factors influencing spending behavior among different player groups.
First Payment per Cohort and Player Age	Timing and Amount of First Payment	Assess the effectiveness of onboarding and monetization strategies.
Monetization Recency and Frequency	Recency and Frequency of Player Spending	Assess engagement with monetization features and identify high-value users.
Monetization by Type	Revenue Breakdown by Monetization Type	Analyze the contribution of different monetization types to overall revenue and assess their popularity among players.
In-Game Currency Flows and Inflation	In-Game Currency Flow Rates	Track the flow of in-game currency within the game economy and monitor for signs of inflation or deflation.
	Currency Inflation/ Deflation	Adjust economic systems to maintain balance in the game economy.
In-Game Currency Deficit and Surplus by Segment	Currency Imbalances	Identify and address currency imbalances to ensure a fair and balanced economic experience for all players.
Player Retention	Daily, Weekly, Monthly Retention Rates	Measure player engagement over time and its correlation with spending behavior.
Conversion Funnel Analysis	Progression through Monetization Funnel	Identify points of friction or drop-off in the conversion process and optimize monetization flows.
Ad Engagement and Revenue	Click-Through Rates, Impressions, Ad Revenue	Maximize revenue from in-game advertisements while maintaining a positive player experience.
Subscription Metrics	Subscriber Numbers, Churn Rates, ARPS	Evaluate subscription offerings and retention strategies to maximize recurring revenue.
Social and Community Metrics	Community Growth, Engagement, Sentiment	Understand the influence of social features and community dynamics on monetization and player satisfaction.
Event Participation and Revenue	Participation Rates, Completion Rates, Event Revenue	Optimize event design and rewards to maximize player engagement and monetization opportunities.

Additionally, it's useful to aggregate all monetization and retention metrics into Lifetime Value. It is important that this view can be adjusted by payback period window, source of acquisition (organic or paid, or channel), relative cost per acquisition, country or region, cohort, etc. (Figure 14.9).

Since the reports are consulted daily, they are most often automated and shared across the organization. The analysts remain available when it comes to additional questions or follow-up research.

Automated and self-service reports are a powerful way to enable decision-makers to use data continuously in decision-making. It is important, however, to ensure that the data is interpreted correctly by educating users on terminology, methodologies, and by establishing a common lexicon.

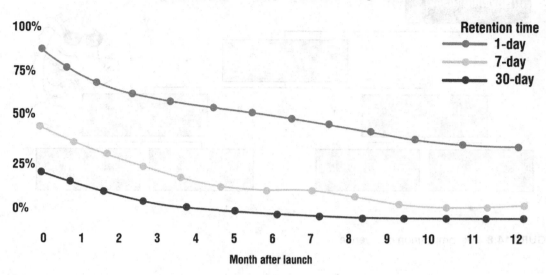

FIGURE 14.6   1, 7, and 30-day retention.

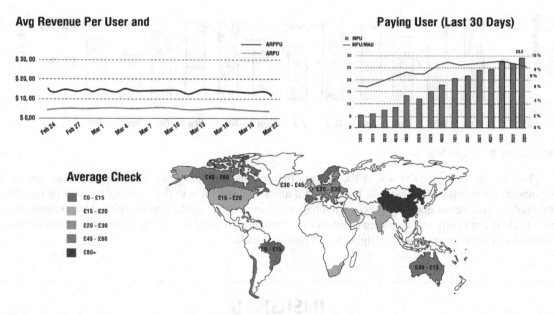

FIGURE 14.7   An example of monetization dashboard.

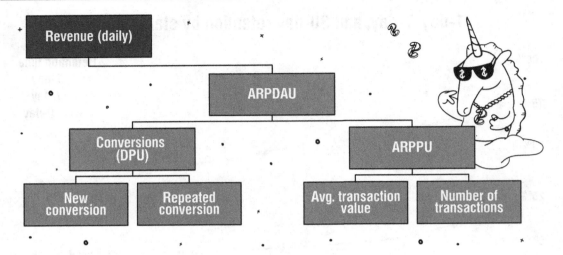

FIGURE 14.8   Decomposition of revenue.

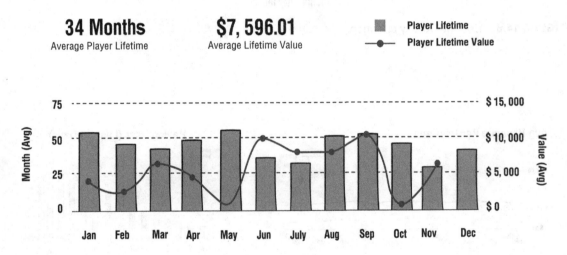

FIGURE 14.9   Player lifetime value.

The beauty of reports is not in the reports themselves, but in all possible business questions and hypothesis these reports may spark. The role of a reporting analyst is to drive clarity by helping business stakeholders ask better questions about what happened in the past, leading to thoughtful hypothesis about what to do in the future and resulting in intentional strategies aligned across the entire team. This is where reports need to be coupled with insights to become actionable.

INSIGHTS

Insights are derivatives of data that may lead to certain shifts in business or product approach. Insights are something new, something that we didn't know before. Insights are rarely generated from dashboards and automated reports—things that we see on a daily basis usually don't spark any novel thinking. Therefore,

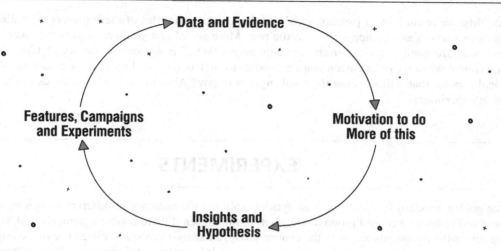

FIGURE 14.10 Turning the flywheel of live operations.

the area of analytics insights in the LiveOps team touches upon almost every piece of information that can be applied to the game.

At a high level the flywheel of LiveOps works by: (1) leveraging data to get insights; (2) building hypothesis and turning insights into actions with intentional outcomes; (3) collective data and evidence from these actions; (4) showing impact and giving motivation to do more of this in the teams. This makes step number 1 akin to the top of the funnel, where everything starts. And the better we are with this, the more potential and opportunities the teams will have (Figure 14.10).

It's valuable to build the reflex for seeking for insights in the analytics team and the LiveOps team in general. Sources of insights may be very different: surveys of players, market research, observations in competitive games, qualitative feedback, and so on.

Out of all the pieces of information that appear like an insight, only a few may actually be so. As with experiments where most of them must fail, if they don't, it means something is wrong. In 2017, 59 out of 78 monthly World of Tanks campaigns went down the drain due to statistically insignificant or negative results. Don't be frightened when only 25% of your ideas will bring you value. Analysts should have a consistency and reflexes in formulating something that can remotely appear as an insight and share it with stakeholders to provoke questions and thinking.

Reports and regular dashboards need to be clear, understandable, stable, and consistent across the organization, because of their goal to create a common language. In contrast, insights need to be impactful. They need to deliver the message in the most visual and inspiring way to attract stakeholders and business decision-makers. Insights are akin to journalism in this regard—they seek to capture the attention and drive the agenda. Some tips to do that:

- Practice within a close circle. Build a habit to create "insights" consistently and regularly and share within a close group of analysts or team members for feedback and peer review. Most won't be seen impactful or useful, but some will and this is a trigger for a broader communication.
- Polish data visualization. A good visual speaks better than a wall of text and this is not an exception here.
- Be contextual, focus on what's important for business or players. Be always on the lookout for insights that confirm or reject ongoing debates within players community, internal company processes, or industry context in general.

The power trick to work on insights is asking open questions about what appears to be common knowledge. For example, what drives certain players to spend on customization with no utility? By diving into this, we could look at psychological and demographic profiles of these players we gathered from previous surveys and compare them to the rest. More social and younger players are likely to be the ones who are more interested in the customization ("Why" is yet another question). Can we build an experiment when we offer customization bundles to such players and focus the messaging on the emotional aspects that will increase their willingness to pay? Absolutely. And it leads us to the next part about experiments.

EXPERIMENTS

The golden standard for experiment analytics is splitting the audience in different groups by each treatment and isolating a control group to see what would happen if there was no treatment at all. By comparing across the treatments and with the control group, an analyst can spot a difference in the target metric (e.g., revenue, conversion, session duration, etc.), check it for statistical significance, and make conclusions (Figure 14.11).

Statistical significance checks provide confidence that the change in the metric that was observed is not a random fluctuation but is actually related to something else (e.g., the treatment) (Figure 14.12).

As simple as it sounds, even this approach is subject to all possible interpretations. For instance, the statistical significance intervals may be set to extremely conservative (or on the contrary) level and will create a certain bias when drawing conclusions. It's important for a business stakeholder to ask themselves a question—are you happy with your results having 70% significance, or do you want to push it to 95% or even 99%? In other words, with 70% confidence you've made a positive impact, are you happy with it? Or with 70% confidence you lost money with this campaign. Are you happy with this confidence interval? Usually, the risk aversion pushes analysts to increase the confidence intervals and they are often right when the risk is considerable (Figure 14.13).

Another tricky part in the game economy is the target KPI. Since the game economy resources are interconnected, it's often possible to improve one but harm something else. For example, if a game team decides to sell experience points, it may make money because this resource is valuable and desirable. At the same time the players may lose in their game activity because they don't need to farm as much of experience anymore, they can just buy it. Our recommendation is to always analyze experiments in 360 degrees—by looking at multiple metrics across target and control groups. If one is up but another is down, it's the business decision to interpret such campaign as a success or not and it should be in accordance with the live game strategy.

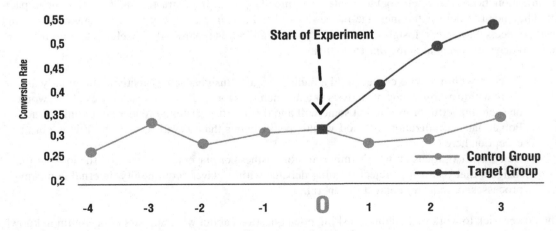

FIGURE 14.11   An example of conversion rate experimental campaign.

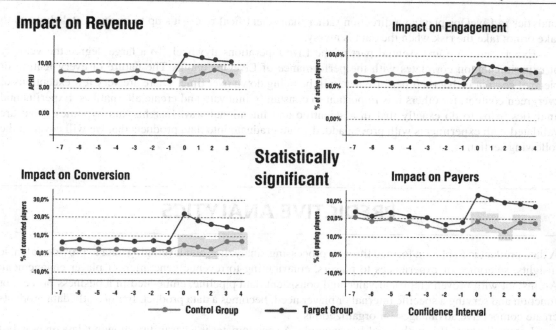

FIGURE 14.12 An example of statistically significant campaign (target group is outside the confidence interval).

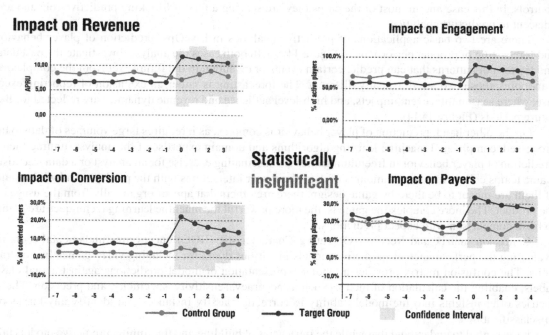

FIGURE 14.13 An example of statistically insignificant campaign (target group is inside the confidence interval).

What to do if it's impossible to isolate a control group? In such cases the analysts may apply all sorts of models, starting from simple regression or time series analysis to more elaborated techniques such as Causal Impact by Google or Facebook's Prophet. They tend to give less precise results, but again—with analytics in LiveOps playing a direction rather than scientifical role—it's up to business stakeholders to take or not take the risk when the data is messy.

Experiments are an essential part of the Live Operations flywheel. To a large degree the velocity of experimentation correlates with the performance of LiveOps teams. The nature of every feature or piece of content is that their performance will be going down over time. There are very few exceptions of evergreen content; for others it is important to constantly innovate and create alternatives. Experimental analytics helps to do exactly that in a scientific and intentional way. Insights and hypothesis that are validated with experiments with proven added value graduate into data products that we will cover in the following section.

PREDICTIVE ANALYTICS

A data product is a solution formed through processing, analyzing, and leveraging data to provide valuable insights, solutions, or experiences to players, contributing to revenue generation or player engagement. An insight with proven empirical value and consistent data pipeline, embedded in a business process or function and serving a specific internal or player need, becomes a data product. Importantly data products create competitive advantages for organizations.

Let us illustrate this with a real-life example. A speedometer is a car utility showing data on how fast the car is moving. An adaptive cruise control adjusts speed based on the requirements, context, surroundings, and other cars. It's directly impacting driving experience. Data products are akin to adaptive cruise controls; in this case and in most of the cases they are serving a forward-looking predictive role and are adjacent to predictive analytics.

There are two basic applications of predictive analytics in LiveOps: prediction of player behavior and forecasting of product performance (Figure 14.15). In both cases the analysts investigate the past data and try to spot patterns that can predict certain events or evolution in the future. Yet from the complexity standpoint, those two are drastically different. The forecasting is rather an extension of reporting exercise, where seasonality, event impacts, and high-level audience and revenue dynamics are reflected for the future periods (Figure 14.14).

On the other hand, prediction of player behavior is complex, as it requires large volumes of data to be processed, complicated machine learning algorithms and domain expertise of the analyst running them. Prediction of player behavior in freemium games is a fascinating exercise for an analyst or a data scientist. Game teams collect incredible amounts of data about user interactions with the product. And while some of them are meant to be there by game design, there are others that appear organically from the usage of the product. The more complex the game is, the more powerful the machine learning techniques are going to be in comparison with expect predictions.

Confusion matrix and Receiver Operating Characteristic (ROC) curves are fundamental tools in evaluating the performance of predictive models in various domains, including video games live operations. The confusion matrix provides a tabular representation of model predictions against actual class labels, enabling the calculation of metrics such as accuracy, sensitivity, specificity, and precision. These metrics offer insights into the model's ability to correctly classify instances and identify any biases or misclassifications.

It's essential to understand that while the intricacies of building and fine-tuning predictive models fall within the realm of data scientists and analysts, as a member of the LiveOps team, your focus should be on the practical application of these models. Our goal here is not to delve into the complexities of model implementation but to empower you with the knowledge of how these models function in a real-world setting. This understanding will enable you to make informed decisions, interpret the data effectively, and utilize the insights generated by these tools to enhance player experience. Let's cover key attributes of confusion matrix that are important for stakeholders operating the models:

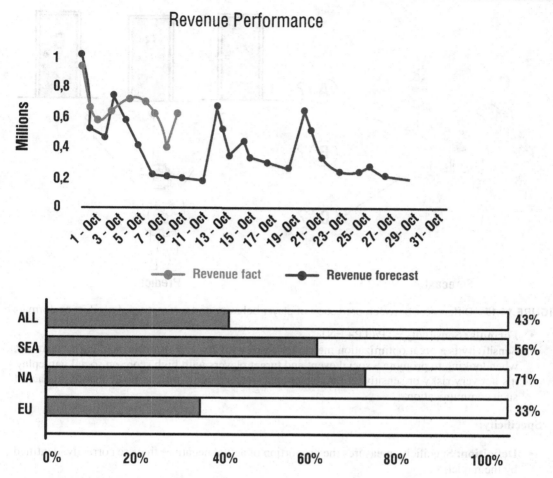

FIGURE 14.14 An example of dashboard that illustrates revenue fact vs. forecast and the percentage of monthly targets completion.

Accuracy:

- **Definition:** Accuracy measures the proportion of correctly classified instances among all instances.
- **Example:** If a churn prediction model correctly identifies 900 out of 1000 players who churned and 800 out of 1000 players who didn't churn, the accuracy would be (900+800)/2000 = 0.85 or 85%.
- **Formula:** $\text{Accuracy} = (TP+TN)/(TP+TN+FP+FN)$
- For cases like churn prediction with churn rate that may be as high as 70% of the cohort or monetization as low as 5%, accuracy alone is not a great indicator of the model quality. For instance, if every player is predicted as non-payer with actual payer share of 5%, the accuracy will be of 95%, while the usefulness of the model is close to zero.

Sensitivity (Recall):

- **Definition:** Sensitivity measures the proportion of actual positives that are correctly identified by the model.
- **Example:** If out of 1000 actual churners, the model correctly identifies 900, the sensitivity would be 900/1000 = 0.90 or 90%.

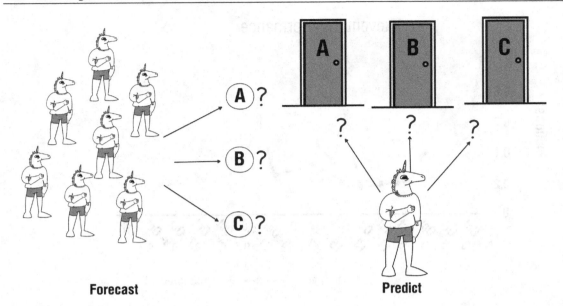

Forecast   **Predict**

FIGURE 14.15   Differences between prediction of player behavior and forecasting of product performance.

- **Formula:** Sensitivity=TP/(TP+FN)
- Sensitivity is a great optimization metric for cases with low risk of mistargeting. For instance, when looking to promote a social event and target players with high score on social gameplay, it's not very risky or sensitive to target solo players as there is little to no economic impact of such communication.

Specificity:

- **Definition:** Specificity measures the proportion of actual negatives that are correctly identified by the model.
- **Example:** If out of 1000 actual non-churners, the model correctly identifies 800, the specificity would be 800/1000=0.80 or 80%.
- **Formula:** Specificity=TN/(TN+FP)
- Specificity may be similar to sensitivity depending on the targeting tactics. For instance, a model predicting payers is also predicting non-payers and for targeting the latter specificity will be a similar role.

Precision:

- **Definition:** Precision measures the proportion of instances predicted as positive that are actually positive.
- **Example:** If out of 1000 instances predicted as churners, 900 are actual churners, the precision would be 900/1000=0.90 or 90%.
- **Formula:** Precision=TP/(TP+FP)
- Precision is important for activities that are distributing valuable rewards or content. For instance, a free premium account could help retain churners, but in many cases would negatively impact non-churners' spending and inflate the economy. It's crucial to optimize for precision in such cases.

ROC curves, on the other hand, illustrate the trade-off between sensitivity and specificity across different decision thresholds. By plotting the true positive rate against the false positive rate, ROC curves visualize

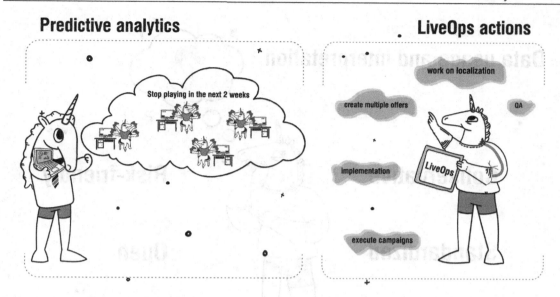

Predictive analytics

LiveOps actions

FIGURE 14.16   The relationship between predictive analytics and LiveOps actions.

the model's discrimination ability and help determine the optimal threshold for classification. The area under the ROC curve (AUC) provides a single metric to quantify the overall performance of the classifier, with higher AUC values indicating better discrimination ability.

Both confusion matrices and ROC curves are indispensable tools for assessing and comparing the performance of classification models, aiding in model selection, optimization, and interpretation.

And yet, however fascinating the predictive analytics may be, it's important to see it in combination with business objectives, offers, and tools. Let's take churn prediction as an example. An analyst did a fantastic job and with a high accuracy you can know which user is expected to play or not play your game within the next 2 weeks. Sadly, it's the simplest part of the churn prevention. In order to make it work, the LiveOps team will have to create multiple offers covering various assumptions or reasons of churn, work on localization, QA, implementation, execute those campaigns, run analysis on those experiments only to find out that you've managed to retain just a proportion of players (in a good case!). If the organization is not ready for such experimentation at scale, the predictive analytics is likely not to reach most of its power (Figure 14.16).

Predictive analytics models have been largely commoditized in recent years with off-the-shelf solutions like Sagemaker from AWS, AI Platform from Google Cloud, IBM Watson, etc. Using predictive analytics has thus become indispensable in running successful and performing live service games. However, to truly leverage this technology it's important to open the black box and understand the parameters and outputs of the model and the business context they need to be operated in.

DATA CULTURE

Finally, it's important to speak about the data culture in the teams. The word "culture" itself means it's something almost ephemeral, subjective. The data culture is not an exception. When thinking of data and analytics we often think that it's determined and unquestionable, but it's not. The culture dictates the conclusions of the analysis, the interpretation, and ultimately usage. It can be conservative or risk-friendly; centralized and standardized or open and liberal; science-focused or scrappy; etc. (Figure 14.17).

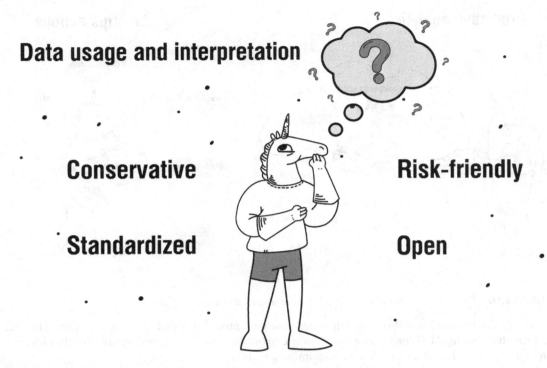

FIGURE 14.17   Types of mindsets while building data culture.

There is no good or bad data culture, but it can be effective and ineffective in certain circumstances. A new product powered by a lot of innovative ideas may benefit from a more balanced data culture that will proactively bring rigor with reports and strict experimental design framework. On the contrary, a mature or stagnating game may benefit from a freer, more liberal approach when data insights can be served for opening more perspective for the stakeholders despite them being not fully precise. This is a trap for many analysts who seek perfection of their analysis, rather than improvement of the business.

Nevertheless, there are certain elements of the data culture that usually enhance live service games.

1. **Bias Awareness:** Data is often manipulated to confirm existing biases of stakeholders and managers. Alternatively, stakeholders misinterpret reports if they are too complex and make false conclusions, because they can't or are reluctant to reach out to analysts. Growing awareness of cognitive biases and establishing process of peer reviews could help the quality of insights interpretation.
2. **Flexibility:** Analysts want to measure things with greatest confidence to minimize the error, as a result many things with high potential are disregarded because they can't be measured at this point. This leads to "analysis paralysis." Coming with a presumption that "If you can't measure it (yet), it doesn't mean it's bad" and pushing for controlled experiments is a great way to gain this flexibility.
3. **Common Lexicon:** Misinterpretation often comes from a lack of common lexicon with the teams when it comes to goals, strategy, assumptions, and drivers. The data function should always push for clarity and objectivity, and it often needs to start with alignment on "what means what." Once established, aligned, and agreed upon, analytics can become this common lens of how we look at our games, players, and businesses. If it fails to do so, it may result in tension, lack of trust, and data being weaponized.

4. **Accountability:** Analysts are often seen as a service function for decision-makers. In the live service environment where data is a lifeblood, analysts are partners and the quality of insights work is a direct influence on the performance.

5. **Learning Culture:** Live teams constantly evolve, but keep track of past experiments and achievements for future references, new team members, next products, etc.

The best scenario, of course, of the data culture is being shaped consciously. There could be certain values proclaimed within the analytics network and procedures that mitigate certain risks. One such risk is a peer review process mentioned above. It's in general a good reflex to develop in analysts to ask for feedback from stakeholders who have read their work. It helps them understand the business question, but also it sometimes explores potential flows in stakeholders' reasoning. There is nothing that is more valuable for data culture than a healthy conversation between analysts and stakeholders on equal terms.

PART V

People's LiveOps

The internet has historically thrived on content produced by "people," with platforms like Wikipedia exemplifying the transformative power of collective contribution. Wikipedia, for example, has eclipsed traditional encyclopedias by harnessing the diverse knowledge of everyday users who contribute content driven by a sheer passion for sharing information. This model of involving people in a platform's content creation not only enriches the variety and quality of the information but also showcases the potential of community-driven development.

Traditionally, video games emerged from the creative fortresses of development studios, crafted without direct input from the players. These games, often premium blockbusters, were finalized before hitting the shelves, their fates sealed as unchangeable physical entities. With the advent of digital distribution, games began to evolve post-release through patches, enhancements, and expansions, but the core vision remained firmly in the hands of the developers.

The rise of live service games has dramatically shifted this dynamic, blending technology with a new cultural trend: community-driven development. As these games flourish and evolve over time, they increasingly reflect the desires and inputs of their player base, moving away from a fixed initial vision. For instance, *World of Warships* started as a historically accurate naval shooter set in the World War II era. Over time, it has integrated diverse elements—ranging from film and music tie-ins to anime collaborations—shaped by what players showed interest in. This transformation hasn't just altered the game; it has shifted "ownership" of its vision toward the players themselves.

Today, titles like *Minecraft*, *Roblox*, and *Fortnite* epitomize this trend, thriving on user-generated content that keeps players engaged and returning. This evolution naturally extends beyond merely adapting to player preferences—it mandates a comprehensive rethinking of how studios operate. More than ever, studios must engage not just with influencers and streamers but also fundamentally embrace revenue-sharing models and substantial structural changes. This shift focuses on external content creation, ensuring that the game environment evolves in concert with its community's creativity and input. Ultimately, it's clear that players are not just consumers but co-creators, wielding substantial influence over the ongoing evolution of live service games.

DOI: 10.1201/9781003427056-20

People's Lives

May I Have Your Attention Please?

15

The reality is that there are only 24 hours in a day (Figure 15.1). Studies show that we spend most of our time sleeping, with work coming in second. In third place is screen time, which includes watching TV, gaming, and using social media, averaging around 3.5 hours per day. For the gaming industry, competing for screen time—or more precisely, playtime—is definitely a red ocean scenario, with tough competition from Netflix, Facebook, and YouTube. Similarly, leisure encompasses a wide range of activities, from cycling and watching movies to playing video games and reading a book.

In this red ocean, platforms like Facebook and YouTube offer their services without a direct monetary cost, which reflects a strategic shift from financial expenditure to time investment. In a world saturated with zero-priced entertainment, people are not constrained by money but by the scarcity of time. Attention thus becomes the critical currency, marking the budget line where people must choose how to allocate their limited hours among various engaging platforms.

The gaming industry fundamentally revolves around capturing attention, regardless of whether the game is free to play or premium, multiplayer or single player, part of live services or available offline. Attention is what any business is hinging on, and without deeply understanding the nuances of you audiences, capturing and keeping player attention becomes a challenging task.

Netflix's decision to enter the gaming industry underscores the intensifying competition for attention in the entertainment sector. Netflix recognized early on that interactive experiences like *Fortnite* represent a significant competitive threat, not just in terms of viewership but in capturing valuable leisure time from a diverse audience. This realization led Netflix to expand its focus from traditional streaming

FIGURE 15.1 How we spend our time. Source: Bureau of Labor Statistics.

DOI: 10.1201/9781003427056-21

to include gaming, a strategic pivot aimed at retaining and engaging its subscriber base in new ways. By incorporating gaming into its offerings, Netflix not only diversifies its entertainment portfolio but also directly competes for the broader attention, vying for time against not just other streaming services but major players in the social and gaming landscapes. This move is indicative of the broader industry trend where companies are no longer just content providers but platforms that offer a range of interactive and immersive experiences to keep users engaged within their ecosystems.

Attention is not only the act of listening to, looking at, or thinking about something/somebody carefully. It's also special care or treatment and things that somebody does to try to please you or to show their interest in you.

In the gaming world, the objective is to captivate players' attention not just during their active "play time" but also throughout their daily "leisure time." These leisure moments—like the minutes before sleep, time spent on commutes, or while doing household chores—present valuable opportunities for LiveOps to show their dedication to enhancing the player experience. By embedding gaming experiences into these everyday activities, developers can deepen engagement and integrate their games more seamlessly into players' lives. This strategy helps transform occasional gaming into a more consistent habit, fostering a stronger bond between the player and the game:

- **Watching:** Provide educational or entertainment content on platforms like Twitch or YouTube, where players can engage with live streams or tutorials related to game strategies or funny moments.
- **Creating:** Allow players to design custom items or environments using in-game tools, which can then be shared within the community for interactive play.
- **Gathering:** Organize offline events such as local community meetups where players can gather in person to discuss strategies, play together, and build stronger connections with fellow gamers.
- **Socializing:** Implement chat functions or collaborative tasks that can be completed with online friends during brief moments, enriching the social aspect of the game.
- **Volunteering:** Establish mentorship programs within the game where experienced players guide newcomers, enhancing community spirit during leisure times.
- **Shopping:** Enhance players' virtual experiences by offering game-themed merchandise, like collectibles and apparel, to extend engagement into real life.

Figure 15.2 outlines how different levels of player engagement—beyond just playing the game—affect playtime and revenue.

- **Circles:** The core of a game's success is engaging players during play sessions. The circles denote players who interact with the game solely during these periods. It's a fundamental truth in gaming that the more games a player is absorbed within a game platform or a publisher's catalogue, the greater the playtime and revenue they generate.
- **Crosses:** Beyond the game, additional layers of engagement can further amplify playtime and revenue. The crosses represent players who have extended their involvement to platforms like Twitch, linking accounts and collecting Twitch drops rewards. This engagement outside the game itself not only nurtures a robust gaming community but also encourages increased playtime and spending within the game.
- **Stars:** Representing an even deeper level of commitment, these players go further by purchasing game-related merchandise and participating in offline community events. This external attention to the game demonstrates potent avenues to enhance player engagement, leading to significant upticks in both playtime and revenue.

The "attention time equation" in gaming underscores a pivotal shift in the industry. While the primary term of the equation, "playtime," remains crucial, supplementary elements such as Watching, Creating, Gathering, Socializing, Volunteering, and Shopping have become essential to sustaining overall attention within the gaming ecosystem. These components not only drive player retention but also contribute to the game's financial success, creating a virtuous cycle of engagement and revenue.

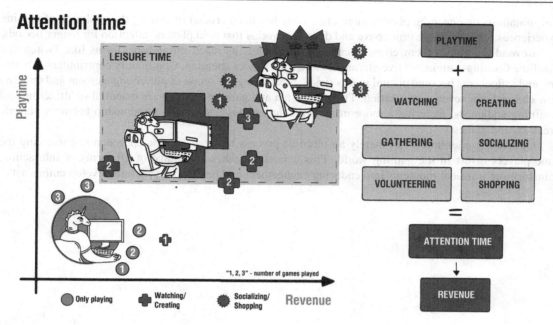

FIGURE 15.2   Attention time equation.

The aim has shifted from solely focusing on a game's core aspects of "play time" to expanding the game's influence on players beyond its primary environment. This paradigm shift from maximizing "play time" to extending "attention time" has led to the implementation of what are known as People's LiveOps (Figure 15.3).

The focus on attention time has redefined game development. With an emphasis on social connectivity, cooperative play, and offline events, the industry has innovated ways to deepen player commitment.

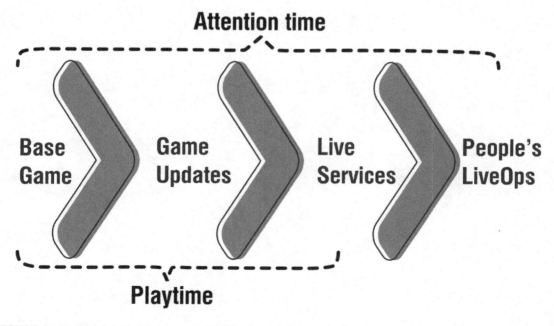

FIGURE 15.3   People's LiveOps paradigm shifts live service game operations from maximizing "play time" to extending "attention time."

This emphasis on engaging players more effectively has been crucial in driving the evolution of gaming experiences, yielding more immersive and dynamic worlds that hold players' attention for longer periods.

Beyond the games themselves, attention time extends its reach through platforms like Twitch and YouTube Gaming—arenas of live-streamed battles for viewer attention. Community contributors, streamers, and influencers become pivotal in this space, broadening the scope of player engagement and opening new channels for revenue generation. Their charisma and gaming acumen are essential in attracting and retaining audiences, fostering a more immersive, interactive, and lasting relationship between players, creators, and games.

Cultivating attention is not merely an intuitive process but a systematic approach to enhancing the time players invest in the gaming world. This ecosystem takes advantage of all forms of interaction, transforming transient moments into enduring engagement and turning players into devoted enthusiasts.

Attention Ecosystem

16

In today's digital age, the concept of the "extended attention time" permeates every facet of our interactions, particularly in the realm of video gaming. Games capture players' attention by seamlessly integrating opportunities for skill improvement, competition, and social interaction into their core experience. This engagement does more than entertain; it harnesses "digital labor," transforming every action—from chatting at the game lobby to blogging about game strategies—into valuable assets.

Even players who never open their wallets inside Free-to-Play games are far from mere participants; they are architects of value within gaming ecosystem. Their daily contributions, be they game commentary, fan interactions, or even the creation of new game mods and virtual spaces, enrich the game environment. This "digital labor," often mistaken for leisure, actually feeds into a complex system of "play labor" where work and play converge, creating surplus value for game developers.

These activities underscore a pivotal transformation in how we perceive labor and leisure, challenging traditional notions of what constitutes work. As players invest their time and creativity, they are not just passing time; they are actively contributing to the game's evolution and vibrancy, reinforcing the foundations of what could be termed an attention economy. This economy thrives on the competitive and cooperative energies of players, turning each session into a microcosm of digital labor.

Creator-driven experiences are oriented around centrally managed platforms such as *Roblox*—where a full suite of integrated tooling, distribution, social networking, and monetization functions has empowered an unprecedented number of people to craft experiences for others. This attention economy operates on foundational economic principles that orchestrate the allocation of resources, orchestration of production, management of distribution, and patterns of consumption. However, it diverges by focusing specifically on amplifying the creative potential of its participants within the digital realm:

- **Resource Allocation:** Games like *Roblox* or *Fortnite* and platforms such as Twitch or YouTube shape the allocation of resources among creators and players, determining who produces content and what type of content is produced.
- **Production:** Creators use software to develop digital content, game mods, and interactive experiences that evolve with plyer feedback and engagement.
- **Distribution:** Creative content is disseminated globally through digital platforms like gaming marketplaces and streaming services to reach a diverse audience.
- **Consumption:** Players actively engage with content, moreover participating in its modification, which deepens their interaction and involvement.

Digital transformation fuels the pace of content consumption growth that pushes gaming studios to find a way to create content in appropriate quantity and quality. We are no longer in the day and age when a game team can hire internal talents and fulfilled players' demands. **The current trend is to engage your best funs and provide them with the ability to earn a living at it.** The future of gaming is to act as a medium for communication between creators and players because it does not have a monopoly anymore on the content or experience creation and on capturing the value of that content.

To extend attention time, games should facilitate interactions between players and creators to effectively utilize the network effect, presenting a great opportunity to create value based on the attention that creators craft for their audience. The main competitive advantage of such an environment is that a game

DOI: 10.1201/9781003427056-22

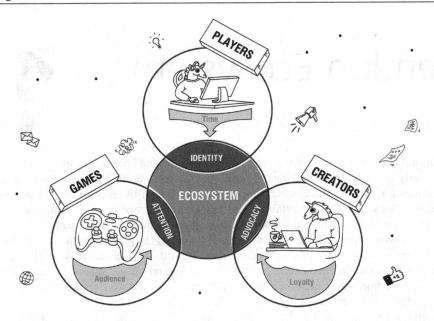

FIGURE 16.1   Attention ecosystem.

creates an ecosystem in which it can communicate with its players via a professional gaming community that includes content creators.

An attention ecosystem (Figure 16.1) is a community of interacting organisms within a system, composed of three main groups: players, games, and creators. These groups are interconnected through technology and mutual benefits, uniting all elements of the attention ecosystem. The fundamental question is, "Why should players, games, and creators coexist in this ecosystem?" This question is at the heart of the core interaction within the network, aimed at continually connecting like-minded individuals who share a passion for games within a trusted environment. With a clear understanding of this core interaction, you can utilize this straightforward framework to guide you.

TIME

Let's put a player in the center of the attention ecosystem. Time is the most valuable thing a player can spend and in return expects the meaning of building his virtual identity by supporting creators and games, contributing to the community, socializing, volunteering, earning, and collecting tangible rewards. Here's how the attention ecosystem can facilitate interactions between a player and a creator to encourage time spending:

Foster Patronage: Since medieval times patrons were far more social and economic power that was considered the primary force behind a work's creation. One creator creates content, and a player watches it, discovering and solving a problem or spending leisure time. Therefore, a patron's virtual identity, reputation, and authenticity could also benefit from the support of a creator by donation or collecting a creator's content.

Encourage Authenticity: Avatar associated with a player's digital persona promotes authenticity, which means that players are allowed to express themselves and contribute from their unique viewpoints and experiences. For example, the progression of the patron's avatar based on the player's contribution to the community, supporting creators or promoting games gives the meaning to exist and stay in the ecosystem.

Urge Volunteering: Facilitating learnings and providing guidance for what players can do to better succeed in the game eases onboarding, increases retention, and simplifies winback. When players form friendships it drives a self-organized playing experience and fosters joint participation in game events. For instance, matching players that are willing to teach newbies or returned players encourages volunteering and underlines the foundation for the future creators.

In the end, all these actions increase overall attention time and incentivize a player to spend time in the ecosystem; a game should propose the meaning and the glue, which combines all desirable actions inside the ecosystem together.

My Nintendo serves as an exemplary model for encouraging players to explore the entire *Nintendo* universe. It provides a relaxed and engaging way for players to delve into their gaming environment. By playing games, using software, and purchasing products, players can earn points to redeem for rewards like digital games or discounts. Moreover, this rewards system adds value not only for players but also for developers within the ecosystem. For example, rather than merely integrating streaming or news feeds, it is more effective to enhance a player's experience by offering opportunities to earn rewards while watching, reading, exploring, and contributing. These are just a few possibilities; the key idea is that the attention ecosystem should be designed to incentivize diverse interactions and use of the ecosystem, thereby enriching it with more value, content, and services through engagement.

LOYALTY

Let's put a creator in the center of the attention ecosystem. Loyalty is the most valuable thing a creator would like to provide and in return expects the growth of his own community, the meaning of sharing his emotions, and the earning allows his talent to pay out his passion. Here's how the attention ecosystem can facilitate interactions between a creator and a player in order to increase the loyalty:

Enable Scale: Audience growth is crucial for success. Both streaming platforms and games aim to expand their audiences, and creators strive to increase their subscriber bases using these platforms and games. Ready-to-use integrations help merge audiences, extend networks, and enhance visibility. For example, a game can give creators an ability to create custom in-game bundles; when players purchase these bundles, they also receive subscriptions to the creator's channel. Ultimately, promoting these bundles helps creators grow their subscriber base, enhances the streaming platform's overall audience, and extends the attention time on games.

Empower Niche: When different player segments have varied preferences, it creates an opportunity for games to encourage creators to tailor their content or services to these niche segments. The ecosystem has the potential to motivate creators and players to explore and develop these niches. In addition to streaming capabilities, specialized player-centric services like "personal game coach" or "private map guide" help creators design experiences that players enjoy.

Facilitate Collabs: Over the last few years (pandemic has boosted the trend even more) brand holders have started to openly experiment with gaming as a way to reach new audiences. Increasingly, the argument goes, games need to be part of a brand's toolkit in communicating with customers. There is a great opportunity to become a mediator or facilitator for companies that want to expand their presence; on the other hand, it's a serious responsibility to cooperate with partners individually to avoid any conflicts of interest. For example, encouraging interactions between local creators and retail brands helps local communities entertain players with appropriate cultural emotions.

In the end, all these capabilities and care nurture creators' loyalty, provide advocacy, and extend players' experience. To incentivize a creator to give loyalty, the ecosystem should offer the greatest variety of experiences, powered by creators who earn a living at it.

Riot Games Southeast Asia embarked on a unique partnership with local artists in Singapore and the Philippines to celebrate the release of Riot's first animated series, *Arcane*. This collaboration involved giving away custom-made *Arcane* toy collectibles, crafted by Southeast Asian artists. These artists brought to life the beloved *League of Legends* champions featured in *Arcane* through various tangible mediums. This example underlines how collaborations between game developers and local creatives can effectively merge gaming with regional artistry, creating a richer, more culturally resonant player experience.

AUDIENCE

Let's put a game in the center of the attention ecosystem. The audience is the most valuable thing a game has and in return expects facilitating attention around game's players via a professional gaming community including content creators. Here's how the attention ecosystem can facilitate interactions between a game and a creator by providing the access to the audience:

Nurture Modding: Mods have become a critical component in enhancing the success of many video games by deepening the original gameplay experience. By establishing a curated environment, games can provide mod creators with access to the game's audience and offer their audience a safe and reliable platform for accessing these mods. This centralized hub ensures a controlled, quality-checked setting. For mod creators, the curated platform not only recognizes their creativity but also opens doors to potential financial rewards, providing a structured avenue for them to share their work with a wider audience.

Cultivate Marketplace: It enables creators to upload a variety of custom content, including maps, skins, models, and other assets, into a shared library. This content is then available for download by the community, facilitating easy access to a diverse range of user-generated content. A key advantage of the Marketplace is its role in connecting players with new creators, broadening their exposure to innovative and creative work. Additionally, the Marketplace fosters collaboration among players, who can join forces to refine and enhance their contributions, leveraging shared interests and complementary skills to enrich the available content.

Facilitate Economy: Establish a revenue share model that allocates a significant percentage of in-game purchase revenues to an engagement pool. This pool distributes funds to eligible creators based on metrics that assess their content's impact on the game's KPI and player engagement. The key is to use engagement metrics such as new player popularity, player retention, and time spend with the creator content, which prioritize content that boosts the game's appeal and longevity. Regular updates and adjustments, informed by creator and player feedback, ensure the economy remains fair, transparent, and adaptive, thereby fostering a thriving environment for creators and enhancing overall player engagement.

To illustrate the benefits of nurturing a modding community, consider *The Sims* franchise by Electronic Arts, which has engaged players since 2001 through user-created mods. Recognizing the potential to enhance gameplay and extend the game's life, EA teamed up with third-party developer Overwolf to launch a formal mod program for *The Sims 4*. This program provides a curated, safe environment for mod creators to share their work and for players to access new mods reliably, enriching the gaming experience and maintaining community engagement. This partnership demonstrates how structured support for modding can amplify a game's appeal and sustain its popularity by integrating community-driven content.

The concept of the Attention Ecosystem is a dynamic framework that enables creators, players, and games to engage deeply with one another. This ecosystem is not just a method for interaction but a thriving environment that facilitates the creation of content and cultivates strong, safe communities where creators can thrive. Through structured systems like curated modding platforms and collaborative marketplaces, creators are empowered to safely share their innovations, thereby strengthening their bonds with a community that values and supports their work. Furthermore, the ecosystem equips creators with a variety of monetization tools, enabling them to earn a living by doing what they love. This economic model ensures that creativity is not only nurtured but also rewarded, making the gaming world a fertile ground for continuous innovation and engagement.

This progression signifies a shift toward viewing games as versatile environments where social interaction, economic transactions, and personalized experiences converge. In this new paradigm, games are not only for play but also serve as platforms for innovation and community engagement, fundamentally altering the landscape of digital interaction. "Game as a Platform" represents the next phase of video game evolution, moving beyond the 'Game-as-a-Service' model to facilitate more than just entertainment. It enables a wide range of activities that leverage gaming IPs as a source of growth for content creators, capturing the value of the content they produce.

Game as a Platform 17

The competition for attention necessitates that gaming studios move toward an adaptive ecosystem. Alone, gaming studios cannot generate the vast amount of content needed to constantly attract players. Moreover, creators from around the world could bring fresh ideas and collaborate with local partners who operate under different business models.

User-generated content (UGC) is typical in live service games, but creators who produce this content often lack the opportunity to act independently and directly monetize their contributions. Encouraging games, brands, creators, and players to combine their diverse resources to create value quickly, flexibly, and at low cost should transform gaming from a "Broker" to an "Integrator," and eventually into an "Orchestrator" that connects multiple partners and encourages them to work directly with each other. This dynamic, where creators and brands complement each other's values and increase players' interactions, leads to the Game-as-a-Platform business model. In this model, content and experience creation, along with the ability to capture the value of that content, are not exclusively controlled by first-party game developers (Figure 17.1).

Fortnite exemplifies the transformation from a game to a platform. Initially launched as a typical *Battle Royale* live service game, it has since evolved by hosting in-game concerts and forming various partnerships, positioning itself as a platform. The addition of a Creative mode was a significant step, enabling players to design their own maps and game modes. Further enhancing this capability, *Fortnite* now allows creators to prototype and test new game ideas efficiently, reducing overhead. This progression

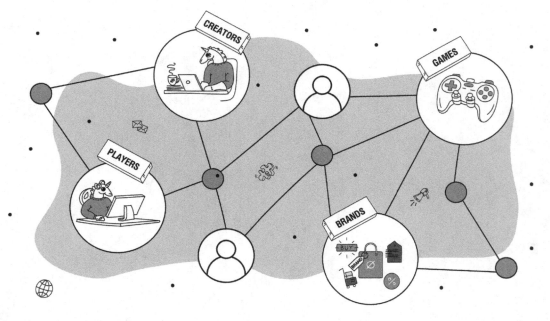

FIGURE 17.1 Game as a Platform encourages games, brands, creators, and players to combine their diverse resources to create value.

DOI: 10.1201/9781003427056-23

culminates in Unreal Editor for Fortnite (UEFN), which empowers creators to directly create and publish their experiences within *Fortnite*, marking its shift toward becoming a full-fledged platform.

The creative economy within the gaming industry, particularly on platforms such as Twitch and YouTube, mirrors the broader global economy, characterized by a few significant success stories amid a vast majority struggling to secure a stable income. The emerging trend of "Game as a Platform" offers a promising avenue for creators, potentially providing them with the means to achieve a stable, middle-class income and enabling sustainable economic growth and career development worldwide.

Historically, the digitalization of content creation has not uniformly democratized success; while it has removed physical barriers like local audiences and enabled niche creators to emerge, it has also led to a stark disparity where top creators thrive significantly more than those in the long tail. This disparity raises the question of whether inequality among creators is inevitable. Although not every creator can achieve celebrity status, there is a viable segment of middle-class creators who are essential as they contribute to a game's diversity and resilience.

For game studios looking to support this trend of external content creation, particularly due to the high costs and limitations of in-house production, there is much to learn from past platforms like Vine. Vine demonstrated that while it pioneered the short-form video format and amassed a large user base, it ultimately failed because it did not provide sufficient opportunities for creators to grow financially and expand their audience, leading to its decline as creators moved to more lucrative platforms.

To cultivate a thriving creator middle class, game studios can transform their games into platforms that enable more creators to succeed. This involves providing robust tools for content creation, fair monetization models, and promoting visibility for new creators to grow their audience. This approach not only supports the creators themselves but also enriches the gaming community as a whole, paving the way for the industry's next evolution into "Game as a Platform," where games serve as foundational environments supporting a wide array of activities beyond entertainment.

Game development and operations teams should embrace the freedom that creators and communities rely on and should drive products and capabilities that create common ground for creators, enabling them to connect with meaningful communities within their own spaces.

CREATOR SPACE

A centralized ecosystem strategy around common creator space works better as the first step. A game acting as a central "Broker" and connecting creators gives an ability to create a critical mass of partners, which share a common vision and culture. The main focus should be on creating an alliance where game LiveOps and creators complement each other's values and increase players' interactions.

Creator Choice: Most streamers or bloggers are creative by their very nature and thereby have various preferences in the same game. It's one thing when LiveOps team creates bundles based on product strategy, operational data, or content demands, and the other when creators endorse a game with mutually aligned packages that reflect their own play style or appearance. Creator choice enables creators to earn money by composing existing game assents; moreover, games can provide customizations that express the creator's authenticity and boost promotion power. The revenue-sharing model implies game shares a predefined percent of either assets price with creators when they manage to sell it through their channels.

Editor Choice: Any game produces guides or tutorials that help its players to get acquainted with gameplay or help them overcome a problem during progression. Moreover, LiveOps team has all the necessary data at its disposal to clearly understand players' pitfalls and tailor their experience to address those problems. On the other hand, creators constantly craft new content, which also explains gameplay and teaches how to use certain mechanics. Editor choice is a curated content of Twitch streams or YouTube videos that feature some of the videos inside game universe (website, launchers, or emails) from creators' channels. Internal game editors choose these videos for quality and long-term popularity, but most importantly for originally showing the game in action, which helps players to master their skills. In return, creators benefit from receiving a decent amount of traffic, which increases their visibility inside a game community and boosts channel growth.

Creator Challenges: A mission, or quest, is a task that helps LiveOps teams to keep the focus of players on the game goals, objectives, or beats. To some extent, creators—with all their gaming experience—are game LiveOps or at least have objective expectations on how a player-controlled vehicle, party, or platoon of characters may finish in-game challenges in order to get a reward. Creators convey their personal stories and share intimate emotions by playing their favorite games; nevertheless, even the most talented creators can't always stream extemporaneously and without a plot. Creator challenges give an ability to combine conditions, adjust difficulty level, and select rewards, which in turn leads to a more tailored stream, provides extra meaning for content creation, and builds a storyline.

Creator Subscription: The subscription business model has changed consumption habits by placing the player at the center who can now choose what, when, and where to consume. The biggest challenge in the demanding subscription content model is to maintain the development supply chain, and creators could be a component that extends the variety of game content. It could be any type of relatively cheap creators' related customizations that do not impact the gameplay, like skins or voiceovers, but allow players to stand out and show their support. Players donate to streamers to express their gratitude for the content and to provide them with a financial incentive to produce more. Creator subscription can combine a player's intangible emotion of supporting a creator and the tangible emotion of ownership in the game. Moreover, by utilizing the functionality of third-party platforms like Twitch Drops, a game can extend the creator's subscription with extra benefits while creating a natural connection between the game and the creators' content.

Creator Events: With that being said, the LiveOps event is the quintessence of players' engagement with the visual design, gaming mechanics, and business techniques concentrated around regional, cultural, or content beats. Creators also have their emotional beats connected with birthdays, streaming anniversaries, or charity events. Creator events could leverage on the storyline where the personal aspect is put at the center and design is based on the creator's audience progression, special missions, or external collaborations.

While most players use social platforms to communicate with their friends, creators consider streaming channels to share their voices. They position themselves as influencers within the game they are interested in, or as champions of the social causes they are passionate about. Players enjoy the authenticity of creators' content; moreover, the freedom of storytelling attracts their audience and makes content so charming.

CREATORS-FOR-CREATORS

Keeping the audience's attention and entertainment at a decent level is not an easy task, even for the most creative people. That is why extended capabilities in the creator space are of paramount importance. There are always tasks that a creator is not good at, and it refers to the area of incompetence. Area of competence refers to the tasks that a creator is suitably good at doing; however, sometimes it takes a lot of the creator's time away from value-added activities. Acting as an "Integrator" for a game creates an open architecture that supports the ease of collaborations and operations. The main focus should be on a highly configurable environment for every creator's needs and less expensive operational processes for a game.

Game Enthusiasts: The most powerful and motivated workforce is the one that is totally in the fine and exceptional culture of the game. In addition to buying all the goods related to their favorite game and spending long hours playing, many of those enthusiasts are working as designers, video editors, marketing specialists, developers, etc. Let's pretend that when a streamer wants to have a highlight of replays which stands out from the others in quality, camera angles, or visual effects, he can easily ask game mates who are willing to do it.

Mentorship: Effective mentorship begins with a mutual connection where experienced mentors choose protégés who share common values and show potential, establishing a foundation for a sustainable creative network. Leveraging referral program features or providing special grants for newcomers who aspire to join well-established creator squads of a game can significantly enhance these relationships. Such initiatives not only foster a supportive environment but also encourage self-scaling through co-op content creation, social advocacy, or events.

Internship: Envision a program where internships are not just a transition into the corporate world but a vibrant, hands-on experience that involves direct interaction with novice creators under the guidance of well-established professionals. By arranging bootcamps styled on corporate internships, with experienced creators acting as trainers, the industry can effectively cultivate the next generation of content creators—true embodiments of "play labor." These bootcamps would enable interns to develop professional skills actively, assist with game-related tasks, and contribute to expanding the audience base for creators.

Shared Facilities: Sharing usage isn't a new business model in which resources are shared by individuals in a collaborative way. Gaming studios heavily invest in development infrastructure including streaming facilities, audio equipment, and video rooms for their in-house creations. Inviting creators into sanctuary of their favorite game raises not only morale but provides unique opportunity to increase the quality of creator's content by utilizing studio facilities.

Growing number of creators enable establishing alliances of compliments that make their own audience mutually more valuable. By fostering an environment where creators can collaborate, learn, and thrive, games transcend traditional entertainment roles and become dynamic platforms for innovation and community building.

PLAYERS-FOR-PLAYERS

One of the most important advantages of being a member of a meaningful community is an opportunity for this network to help members from diverse backgrounds and viewpoints communicate on common values. Access to tutorial alone is not a silver bullet to help players address a larger set of gameplay issues. Players often refine their gaming skills and look for new causes as a result of personal relationships, which could be a valuable addition to the game's capabilities as a "Integrator."

Adopt-a-Tomato: "Free Walking Tours" has taken the world by storm. Guests are invited to join the tour without paying in advance and without a reservation and when the tour is over, guests are welcome to pay whatever they think the visit was worth, but payment is always optional. Players are happy to do things occasionally and by providing appropriate services or products to facilitate players' skills, gaming studios are encouraging to connect with players on a social level to gain trust.

Support-by-You: Mobile virtual network operator (MVNO) business model exists thanks to its community: members help each other with any questions (and earn points if they do), are motivated to recruit new members (for a modest check), and share ideas and strategies that help growth. Such an approach allows for creating a community that no other company has, and speaks to game-savvy players that would like to engage in more advanced relationships. It's not just game services that create a social component, it is also committed to its players with their best interests in mind: for instance, each month, a game could get back to players with some recommendations about how to earn money by helping other players with their issues.

In order for players to productively collaborate and cope with challenges, first, they need to acknowledge their shared interests or beliefs. Games can help players connect to other players before exposing themselves to hard battles that are truly important to be in an enjoyable way.

DEVS-FOR-CREATORS

Game development has evolved dramatically from the early arcade era to today's sophisticated digital landscapes. The advent of accessible game engines has significantly lowered the barriers to entry for aspiring game developers. Unity has been pivotal in democratizing game development by simplifying the workflow for 3D graphics. Games like *Minecraft*, *Roblox*, and *Fortnite* have further expanded development capabilities for a broader range of creators by incorporating these features into the nature of the games. To capitalize on this trend, gaming studios can enhance their games with features that allow creators to customize player experiences.

Mods: Developers can integrate mod tools directly into their games, allowing creators to modify or create new game elements. These mods can range from custom skins and textures to entirely new gameplay mechanics. By providing a robust set of modding tools, developers enable creators to tailor game experiences to their audiences, fostering a vibrant modding community that continually breathes new life into the game.

Extensions or Widgets: Developers can create extensions or widgets specifically designed for third-party platforms like Twitch and YouTube. These tools can enhance the streaming experience by adding layers of interactivity. For instance, extensions that allow viewers to influence game decisions in real time, such as choosing character actions or directing gameplay strategies, can make streams more engaging and interactive.

APIs: By offering open APIs that allow creators to access and use game data, developers can help creators build custom applications or tools that enhance the gaming experience. These APIs can enable everything from statistical analysis tools that help players improve their gameplay to external applications that track in-game events and updates in real time, providing creators with the data they need to produce informed and compelling content.

PEOPLE'S LIVEOPS: TRANSFORMING GAMES INTO PLATFORMS

The business model of People's LiveOps, led by innovations from Epic Games' *Fortnite* and *Roblox*, is shaped by market factors that present both challenges and opportunities in the industry. From a commercial and P&L perspective, there are general indications of how People's LiveOps can generate value for both game makers and players.

The first angle is on the supply side and can be nicknamed as **People's Product**. R&D and content creation remain the largest costs in the video game business. Content production margins have been on a race to the bottom recently, with inflation hitting the cost side and saturation lowering the demand. Many live service game teams have found themselves on the "content treadmill," churning out more and more content to support the business while losing focus and priorities on gameplay innovations.

Investing in technology that allows players to co-create content and experiences could help developers focus more on what truly matters to players. Many companies have successfully improved their profit margins by outsourcing content creation. The move toward a People's Product model builds on this evolution, supported by two significant trends: the increasing creativity of players and advancements in tools and AI that make content creation more accessible. These developments are set to enhance both the appeal and quality of user-generated content in games.

Roblox and *Unreal Engine* for *Fortnite* are leading the charge by enabling side developers and players to create their own experiences within their games, illustrating a shift toward a People's Product model. With the emergence of artificial intelligence solutions that make coding, gameplay programming, and asset creation more accessible, we can expect both the quality and quantity of player-generated content to increase within the game ecosystems. While some games, particularly those with protected IPs, may not adopt user-generated content, others will find economic and financial reasons to incorporate features and assets created by non-core game teams into their ecosystems. Just as digital distribution evolved games from products to services, user-generated content is transforming services into platforms, enabling various services to coexist within a shared technological, legal, and financial framework.

The next commercial factor, codenamed as **People's Promotion**, delves into the demand side of the equation. Historically, the gaming industry heavily relied on marketing to fuel sales, acquisitions, and revenue. This battle for attention began on the shelves of video game stores and the covers of gaming magazines, then shifted to distribution platforms like Steam and PlayStation Store. More recently, it expanded to include targeted performance-driven marketing and engagement through communities of interest and influencers.

However, a new challenge is emerging: the competition for people's attention spans. With the rise of apps and platforms like TikTok and YouTube, consumers are increasingly dedicating their time to these services, which diverts attention from gaming. This shift is leading to a potential decrease in spending on video games as other media apps become more popular.

Escaping this trend doesn't mean trying to outshine other forms of entertainment in the battle for attention. Instead, it's about finding synergies that allow gaming to coexist and thrive within this shifting landscape. This involves adapting promotional strategies to meet audiences where they are, engaging with them authentically, and leveraging the power of content creators and influencers to capture and retain attention in a crowded digital space.

This aligns with two key enablers of People's Promotion: equipping content creators with advanced tools and establishing business incentives. By providing creators with sophisticated streaming software, editing suites, and exclusive assets, they're better equipped to produce engaging content. At the same time, implementing revenue-sharing agreements, offering exclusive content access, and performance-based bonuses ensure that the interests of creators and game companies are aligned, which drives sales and supports a mutually beneficial ecosystem.

We spoke at length about Influencer Marketing for Acquisition in Chapter 7. Here are some of the examples how People's Promotion enhances traditional live service game marketing techniques by adding value in several key areas:

Awareness about Content:

- Traditional techniques often rely on articles, newsletters, and developer digests to spread awareness.
- People's Promotion, on the other hand, leverages user-generated content shared through streams and videos, accompanied by statistics showcasing fandom engagement.
- **Impact:** This approach leads to improved conversion rates, particularly for premium items, as it provides authentic insights and experiences shared by content creators.

Conversion:

- Traditional techniques typically utilize discounts and pop-ups to encourage conversion.
- People's Promotion employs strategies such as providing gameplay tips and revenue-sharing arrangements with content creators.
- **Impact:** These tactics result in higher conversion rates, as users are more likely to engage with and trust recommendations from their favorite content creators, leading to increased MPU numbers.

Spending Level:

- Traditional techniques often focus on upselling and bundling to encourage higher spending.
- People's Promotion introduces initiatives like Creator's Choice and Creator Challenges, empowering content creators to drive spending among their communities.
- **Impact:** This approach leads to higher ARPPU by providing personalized incentives and challenges tailored to the preferences of the audience, thereby encouraging increased spending.

Marketplaces introduce another factor that influences both the supply and demand sides, which can be termed **"People's Pricing."** This occurs when players themselves determine the value and cost of content. According to various estimates, the gaming industry reached $200 billion in annual revenue in the first half of the 2020s. Despite all the bumps and challenges, the game industry business trajectory has been incredible. In recent years it has been largely powered by Live Service games; 50% of our industry revenue is coming from mobile, where close to 99% of revenue is coming from Live Service games (and free to play). The other half of our video games business is spread across PC, console, and smaller platforms like VR and Web. And while the share of pure premium "boxes" games is higher in this segment, the biggest chunk is still in Live Service (and, to a lesser extent, free to play). All in all, free-to-play live services generate around 80% of our industry revenue. And as we discussed previously in this book, the free-to-play audience is asymmetric with 1% of players often generating over 70% of the revenue.

And this is both incredibly dangerous and inefficient. It is dangerous because as game makers we are increasingly incentivized to target and satisfy this 1% of high spenders. This pushes developers to use design patterns that prioritize so-called *Whales* and, often, ignore the needs of other players. There is always a chance of gaming taking elements or full path of pay-to-win, pay-for-power, distorted gambling, or other pretty grim choices. Needless to say, doing this is a negative reinforcement loop that usually leads to audience decline.

It is inefficient, because in this pursuit for the *Whales* revenue game teams are often put on the "content treadmill," having to produce more and more to keep up with the demand. With appetites growing, content inflation pushes for either high quality (and higher production costs) or lower prices, with both leading to lower margins for game makers.

Marketplaces offer a promising solution to the challenges facing the gaming economy for several compelling reasons.

Firstly, pricing dynamics within marketplaces are influenced by the interplay of supply and demand, leading to greater accessibility for players across various budgetary constraints. Market-driven pricing reflects the elasticity of demand, ensuring that games are priced in a manner that resonates with their respective player segments. In traditional live service games, the pricing is set arbitrarily by the game team in accordance to (a) cost of production; (b) game economy value in broad strokes. People's pricing changes these dynamics and aims at the ecosystem turnover maximization. Speaking in LiveOps terms, People's Pricing can theoretically improve conversion of low spending players by leveraging elasticity on old and less valuable content.

Secondly, the ability for players to purchase in-game content introduces a lower risk factor, as they retain the option to resell items if they find them unsatisfactory. This flexibility mitigates potential buyer's remorse and encourages experimentation with different in-game offerings. This is expected to improve conversions by creating more psychological safety when purchasing items.

Moreover, marketplaces leverage the psychological principle of the endowment effect, wherein individuals place a higher value on items they perceive as their own. By fostering a sense of ownership over in-game assets, marketplaces elevate the perceived value of the gaming ecosystem, enriching the overall player experience.

Furthermore, the introduction of marketplaces introduces a framework that caters to the needs of collectors, providing avenues for potentially limitless spending on coveted items. This appeals to a niche segment of players who derive satisfaction from acquiring rare or exclusive in-game content.

Lastly, marketplaces facilitate more efficient content recycling, enabling developers to repurpose existing assets and reduce the need for constant content creation. This streamlining of development efforts contributes to a more sustainable and cost-effective approach to game design and production (Figure 17.2).

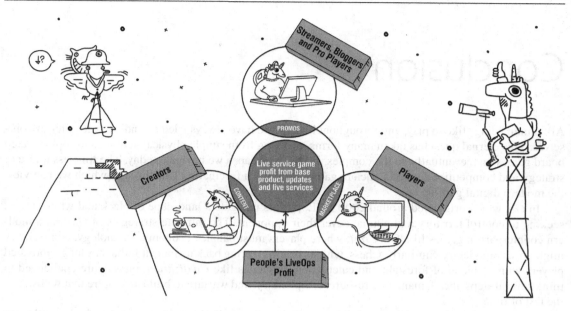

FIGURE 17.2 How People's LiveOps generates profit for players, creators, streamers, bloggers, and pro players.

In essence, the Game-as-a-Platform model revolves around **People's Profit**, which encompasses both financial gains and experiential benefits derived from the collaborative dynamics within the gaming ecosystem. It underscores the mutual enrichment of players, content creators, and game developers through their engagement with one another.

Embracing the People's LiveOps philosophy holds promise for achieving higher margins in content creation, sales, and marketing, while also expanding the scope of monetization through marketplaces. However, it's crucial to recognize that this enhanced profitability may be unsustainable if not balanced with equitable distribution and reinvestment into creators and players. As our industry undergoes a transformative phase, striking this new equilibrium is essential for fostering more inclusive economies and inviting broader participation from a more engaged player base.

Gaming companies often adopt either a centralized or decentralized operational structure to implement management protocols and facilitate clear communication. While both approaches have their pros and cons, there is no definitive right or wrong system. The concept of "Game as a Platform" transcends this binary choice by acting as an "Orchestrator," extending content production beyond the game itself. It provides creators with tools, frameworks, and guidance previously reserved for in-house development and LiveOps teams. The focus is on adding an extra level of value to the game and enhancing the overall value creation chain.

This approach disrupts the traditional game-as-a-service model by positioning the game as a central hub where creators converge to build a network, provide content, and govern development. This new "Game-as-a-Platform" model fundamentally alters all aspects of the gaming experience, including how we spend our leisure time. It fosters a vibrant creator economy that not only generates employment but also enriches the gaming landscape.

People's LiveOps networks, along with professional game development and operations teams, are poised to increase demand for games that function as platforms. This model benefits creators, players, and gaming companies alike through aligned incentives and network transparency. Imagine a scenario where players have diversified roles within the same ecosystem: a player could coach in the morning, create and sell a mod in the afternoon, and stream content in the evening. This expansion of the creator economy, amplified by games, would create new kinds of employment opportunities, transforming how creators engage with gaming platforms.

Conclusion

All human beings like to play, and throughout history, we have always tried to find ways to entertain ourselves. This eternal quest has taken many forms, evolving from simple physical activities to sophisticated board games and, eventually, to the complex digital landscapes we navigate today. The timeless allure of strategy and competition found in ancient games provides a fascinating lens through which we can view the modern digital gaming era.

In *Go*, which originated around 2000 BCE, players navigate a landscape of black and white stones, seeking to control territory and outmaneuver their opponent. The intricate strategies of *Go* find a modern counterpart in games like *StarCraft*, where players must balance economy, technology, and military might to secure victory. Similarly, Chess, with its origins tracing back to ancient India, has long captivated players with its blend of foresight and calculation. In games like *Civilization*, players are challenged to think several steps ahead, managing resources, diplomacy, and warfare to build an empire that withstands the test of time.

As we stand at the precipice of the future, the trajectory of video games extends far beyond mere entertainment. Arguably bold predictions offer glimpses into a world where gaming transcends its current boundaries, shaping not only how we play but also how we live, work, and connect.

Imagine a future where remote meetings at work unfold not in sterile virtual conference rooms but in vibrant digital landscapes where colleagues strategize, collaborate, and innovate in ways previously unimaginable. In this brave new world, adults may find themselves embarking on romantic journeys that begin not with awkward coffee dates but with virtual encounters in the realms of gaming. Aspiring fashion designers could achieve fame by presenting innovative designs to a worldwide audience, even without prior experience in physical fashion.

While the future scenarios can certainly provoke debate, there are some projections we can approach with a higher degree of confidence. For instance, global population trends indicate a rise to 8.5 billion by 2030 and an anticipated growth to 9.7 billion by 2050. Crucially, this demographic expansion includes Generation Z (born mid-1990s to 2009) and Generation Alpha (born after 2010), cohorts that have been raised with video games as a staple of their cultural and recreational landscape. As these generations mature, they are set to become the main economic force, with a predisposition for digital and interactive forms of entertainment deeply embedded in their consumer behavior. This transformation suggests that the gamers of today will inevitably evolve into key economic agents of tomorrow. Today's gamers are poised to become tomorrow's business partners, valued customers, and innovative employees.

Building on the certainty of demographic growth and the ingrained gaming habits of emerging generations, if we assume that half of the global population will engage in gaming within the next decade, this presents an extraordinarily positive outlook for the gaming industry, particularly from a market size perspective. This potential surge in gamer numbers not only indicates a massive expansion in market reach but also underscores a significant shift in entertainment consumption patterns across the globe.

This shift isn't just about higher sales of games themselves; it encompasses a broader ecosystem including game development tools, digital and physical merchandise, and interactive media. The growing acceptance and normalization of gaming as a mainstream leisure activity will catalyze significant opportunities for professionals skilled in marketing, sales, legal, or operations to transfer their expertise and align their careers with the evolving landscape of live service game operations. This shift underscores the expanding career prospects within the gaming industry, opening new avenues for professional growth and development in an industry increasingly recognized as a central component of the digital entertainment economy.

DOI: 10.1201/9781003427056-24

This book lays out the essential areas you need to understand if you're looking to join the gaming industry, especially if you're interested in studios that focus on live service games. While hands-on experience will eventually deepen your understanding, the guidelines provided here will help you start your career with more confidence.

Start by getting to know games from a player's perspective. Play the games extensively to really feel what players experience, see what excites them, and what could be improved. This first-hand knowledge is invaluable; it helps you see the game's strengths and weaknesses, and identify opportunities to add new features or content that could enhance the gaming experience.

Next, learn to see the game from the studio's perspective. Dive into the game's design documents, study its economic model, and get familiar with its content and the plans for future updates. This comprehensive understanding will allow you to contribute to the game's development meaningfully and help push the game to new heights.

Begin your practical training in Live Game Operations by taking apart existing events in the game. Analyze these events and use what you know about different types of LiveOps events to ensure there's a good mix that keeps players engaged. Getting a handle on the schedule for planning these events will make it easier to organize regular and special events that enhance the overall game experience.

Use the 3LAPs framework to manage the flow of events in the game. This helps ensure that players aren't overwhelmed by too many activities at once. Consider four key questions to help guide players through the game, making their experience unique and enjoyable. This thoughtful approach will help keep players happy and make the game a success.

As you move forward, fine-tune every part of the game. Pay attention to how players make purchases within the game and tailor the virtual storefronts accordingly, using the basic principles of the 4Ps framework. When planning new events with the LiveOps Event Canvas, think about including exciting game mechanics and features that not only entertain players but also help achieve specific goals set for the product.

Developing personalized plans to improve LiveOps events and the overall player experience is crucial. Focus on strategies that enhance player onboarding, engagement, winback, and monetization. These efforts will boost player retention and ensure your game remains competitive in the bustling gaming market.

As you gain more experience with live operations, you will begin to see ways to add value for players and work effectively with different teams. You'll move into advanced operational management, optimizing how game content is designed, produced, and delivered to meet and exceed player expectations.

Understanding game analytics is vital. Become proficient in using data to generate reports, gain insights, run experiments, and predict trends. These skills will help you improve game performance and make the playing experience better for everyone.

Finally, think about how to engage with players outside the game itself. Shift your focus from increasing playtime to extending attention time, you can foster deeper connections with your most dedicated fans.

To further enrich the reader's journey, we approach this book much like a live service game, where the moment of publishing mirrors the release day. On the website VASI.UK, we will continually enhance the book's value by adding "DLC" that includes additional chapters and short instructional videos. Readers can also access exclusive "skins" featuring infographics and schematics, adding a visual dimension to the learning experience. Moreover, we'll introduce "partnership" content, collaborating with developers of live service toolsets to bring you the latest tools and techniques. Diverse selection of related "merchandise" such as posters and stickers ensures that the book extends beyond its pages. These tangible items bring the content into the real world, offering more interactive and enjoyable ways to consume and interact with the material. This commitment to ongoing content updates and community engagement makes the book not just a static resource but a vibrant, ever-evolving guide that equips you with the necessary knowledge and tools to successfully manage a live service game that captivates thousands of players.

Index

Note: *Italic* page numbers refer to figures.

Printed in the United States
by Baker & Taylor Publisher Services